D0348178

9 9002 10660375 7

TAPAS

TAPAS

The Little Dishes of Spain

PENELOPE CASAS

PHOTOGRAPHS BY TOM HOPKINS

PAVILION

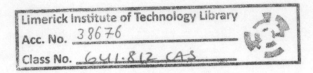

Limerick Institute of Technology Library
Acc. No. 38676
Class No. 641.812 CAS

This edition published in Great Britain in 1991 by
PAVILION BOOKS LIMITED
196 Shaftesbury Avenue, London WC2H 8JL

First published in hardback in 1985

Text copyright © Penelope Casas 1985
Photographs copyright © Tom Hopkins 1985

All rights reserved. No part of this publication
may be reproduced, stored in a retrieval system,
or transmitted, in any form or by any means,
electronic, mechanical, photocopying, recording or
otherwise, without the prior permission of the
copyright holders.

A CIP catalogue record for this book is available
from the British Library

ISBN 1 85145 1676 (hbk)
ISBN 1 85145 7976 (pbk)

10 9 8 7 6 5 4 3 2

CONVERTING AMERICAN CUPS

Quantities for all fluids and some solids in this book are given in American cups. The cup is a measure of volume and represents a container which holds 8 fluid ounces. If you don't have an American measuring cup, put 8 fluid ounces of water in a measuring jug and pour the exact quantity into one of your own cups. Experiment until you find a cup which holds 8 fluid ounces of water when it is full and use this as your measuring cup. (If you don't have a measuring jug, 8 fluid ounces is just under half a pint.)

OVEN TEMPERATURE CHART

°F	°C	Gas mark
225	110	¼
250	130	½
275	140	1
300	150	2
325	170	3
350	180	4
375	190	5
400	200	6
425	220	7
450	230	8
475	240	9

CONTENTS

ACKNOWLEDGMENTS

Tapas, a centuries-old tradition in Spain, are part of the fiber of Spanish life, but have only recently attracted attention in this country. A few years ago, when tapas were still unknown here, Craig Claiborne expressed interest in my tapas recipes and suggested a book on the subject. Thanks to him, the idea became firmly implanted in my mind and eventually led to the writing of *Tapas: The Little Dishes of Spain.*

Many thanks to all our friends in Spain who took so much interest in this book, in particular José Sanz Tobes and Chalo Peláez, who tirelessly accompanied us to dozens of tapas bars until all hours of the morning; Paqui and Pepe Delfín, who spared no time or effort showing us the best of their beloved city, Cádiz; food writer and friend Enrique Torán, who directed us to his favorite tapas bars; and Carmen and Pepe González, tapas companions for more than twenty years. In my search for tapas I have found wonderful new friends at tapas bars all over Spain: especially helpful were Ruperto Blanco of Bar Casa Ruperto in Sevilla; Alfonso Merlo of O'Merlo in Pontevedra; Gonzalo Córdoba Gutiérrez of El Faro in Cádiz; and Salvador Lucero of Bar Bahía, who always brightens our visits to Cádiz with his quick wit and creative cooking.

Here in New York support was equally generous. My daughter, Elisa, who has spent a good part of her twenty years eating tapas, could always be counted upon to judge my tapas in her forthright and good-humored style; and my husband, Luis, joined into my projects with the same zest he has always shown for all things Spanish and made what could have become a chore a most exciting and memorable experience.

Ramón San Martín of the Café San Martín in New York City was, as always, quick to offer his assistance and advice whenever called upon, and the following establishments, which have been most supportive over the course of this book's development, graciously provided some of the foods for photography: De Choix Specialty Foods Company, Woodside, New York; Edig Roosevelt Market, Flushing, New York; and D & B Delicatessen, Whitestone, New York.

I am so pleased to have had as my editor once again Judith Jones, who successfully guided me through my first book, *The Foods and Wines of Spain.* Her unfailing attention to detail and remarkable literary and culinary insight surely make her the finest editor a cookbook author could ever hope to have.

INTRODUCTION

Tapas: the delicious little dishes of Spain, consumed with great gusto at bars and taverns before lunch and again before dinner, have been a tradition in Spain for as long as anyone can remember. While Spaniards have been enjoying hundreds of varieties of exquisite tapas, here in America we have, for the most part, been enduring endless cocktail hours of salty pretzels, peanuts, potato chips, and soggy canapés.

A glance at almost any cookbook will give you an idea of the sorry state of "predinner" foods before tapas arrived on the scene. Chances are you will find little more than the tiresome aforementioned canapés, a few cheese balls, and several cracker spreads—all bready, much too filling, and of minimal nutritional value. Americans are obviously just as fond of "little bites" as Spaniards, and tapas take appetizers into a whole new world, placing them squarely at center stage and creating an entirely new style of eating and entertaining.

The tapas spirit is spreading throughout America, from New York north to Connecticut, Boston, and Toronto, south to Houston, and west to California, as more and more people discover the wonderful variety of foods that can be served as tapas and realize as well the benefits of the tapas eating style. Let's face it: traditional cocktail parties are generally dull affairs, attended more often than not as social obligations. I always feel vaguely cheated at the end of a cocktail party; the time was too short and personal interaction too superficial to be stimulating or meaningful, and I am neither hungry enough to move on to dinner nor convinced that my food needs have been satisfied. I never quite know what to do with the evening that still lies ahead.

On the other hand, sit-down dinner parties, which have clearly defined beginnings and ends, can be stodgy events, where your conversations are limited, for better or for worse, to dinner companions on your left and on your right. Now, thanks to tapas, the yawning gap between cocktail and dinner parties has been bridged, creating a relaxed, free-flowing atmosphere in which the desire for a tidbit to accompany a drink merges successfully with the need for a well-balanced meal.

Spain's tapas and its tapas tradition have fascinated me ever since my very first visit to Spain some twenty years ago. As a student in Madrid I found the casual tapas style of eating and its low prices ideal for my limited budget. My evenings were spent in one tapas bar after another, looking for the best each had to offer. I particularly remember a bar near the Plaza Mayor that served nothing but chicken wings, another in the Rastro where great cauldrons of snails simmered in a *chorizo* and spicy paprika sauce, and two on Victoria Street, one serving garlicky grilled mushrooms and another batter-fried pimientos. Yet another offered nothing but shrimp, which everyone shelled himself, tossing the shells on the floor to accumulate in veritable mounds. (Since those days wastebaskets have come into fashion.) As the years passed, I grew more and more interested in the study of Spanish food and in what the fine and elegant restaurants of Spain had to offer. Yet I still indulged my passion for tapas, because the more I explored, the more I realized the infinite variety of dishes to be found.

Finally the time seemed ripe to introduce tapas in this country on a grand scale. (In my first book, *The Foods and Wines of Spain*, I collected almost sixty tapas recipes, but that just skimmed the surface.) In the past few years my husband, Luis, and I have dedicated our trips to Spain to the pursuit of tapas. We traveled everywhere, to big cities and tiny villages, where friends told us the tapas were unusually good. And we returned to other places where we had fond memories of good times and exceptional tapas. But mostly we relied on logic and instinct to unearth the best each city or town had to offer. Even though restaurant handbooks have proliferated in Spain in recent years, there is still no guide to eating tapas, and finding the best is still based largely on chance.

I asked everyone I knew to define tapas. (This often led to some interesting historical and etymological discussions.) I asked chefs, who over the years have become good friends, for their best tapas recipes. At tapas bars all over Spain, owners and waiters, while considering my interest in their "humble" fare rather surprising, unreservedly shared their recipes with me.

In my search for tapas I found that despite the modernization and industrialization that have overwhelmed Spain in the past twenty years—not to mention a parallel burgeoning of fine new restaurants, often dedicated to nouvelle cuisine—the tapas tradition remains as strong and immutable as ever.

WHAT ARE TAPAS?

It is difficult to say exactly what tapas are, for tapas are not necessarily a particular kind of food; rather, they represent a style of eating and a way of life that are so very Spanish and yet so adaptable to America. Tapas are as varied as the cooks who create them and in Spain range from the simplest fare, like grilled *chorizo* sausage, flavorful *jamón serrano* (cured ham), tangy Manchego cheese, and simple canapés (almost anything atop a piece of bread becomes an instant canapé in Spain) to surprisingly sophisticated dishes using quail, frogs' legs, fresh snails, caviar, and *angulas* (baby eels). They can be foods we traditionally eat as appetizers, but more often than not cross the line into what we might think of as first course or main course dishes.

All tapas do, however, have several things in common. They are generally served in small portions (there are actually two sizes: the tapa and the *ración*, which is about double the size), and they are meant for immediate gratification. In Spanish bars and taverns, tapas are served quickly and consumed just as quickly; any delay in service diminishes the tapa's raison d'être. I have devised many other definitions, but all were quashed as I investigated tapas more thoroughly and found tapas in Spain to contradict every rule. I once thought it was safe to say that a tapa was something eaten without the aid of a knife, until I was served a fillet of lemon-marinated meat with a miniature knife and fork set. I had never seen dried beans or soups as tapas, but sure enough, in Santiago de Compostela I ate lentils as a tapa; in Cádiz, chickpeas; in Galicia, Caldo Gallego soup; and in Sevilla, gazpacho. Steak and fried eggs are the only things that come to mind that I have never been served as a tapa. Of course, some things lend themselves better to tapas than others. Sauced dishes, for example, are fine if the food is cut in small pieces; shellfish and firm-fleshed fish are more appropriate than those that fall apart easily, and I think soups are generally too filling and too difficult to eat in casual settings. Aside from these reservations, the possibilities are limitless.

Tapas in Spain are, of course, closely related to Spanish cuisine. For those of you still unfamiliar with the joys of Spanish cooking, let me say that the cooking of Spain is not the hot and spicy cooking of Mexico and South America. It is as fine and exciting as the other great cuisines of Europe and has tremendous variety, partly a result of centuries of Moorish occupation, which lent Arab overtones to some Spanish cooking, and partly because Spain is a country of such great cultural and geographical diversity. Certainly the foods brought back from the New World (potatoes, peppers, and tomatoes, for example) enriched the cuisine of Spain, but Spain utilized these products in its own distinctive style—quite different from the way they were used in America. The tapas in this book are representative of Spanish cuisine. You will find the great green and garlic sauces, the almond sauces, the wonderful seafood marinades, and the exceptional Galician savory pies, to name a few of Spain's contributions to world cuisine—and I hope these tastes will stimulate you to investigate further the glories of the food of Spain.

time and be much better disposed to confront the less pleasurable aspects of daily life. Even business meetings may be combined with tapas (Spaniards have great difficulty separating work from pleasure), and although it can be argued that business that functions thusly cannot be very efficient, so be it. It is only what might be expected from a country that lives by the tapas tradition!

Tapas, besides serving an important social function in Spain, are also a means to fill the long hungry hours between meals. In a country where lunch is rarely eaten before 2:00 or 3:00 P.M. and dinner is typically served at 10:00 P.M., tapas are almost a necessity. Whether the tapas tradition developed because of the eating hours or the eating hours merely evolved around the wonderfully pleasurable tapas hours is beside the point. For a Spaniard a tapa is just an appetite teaser—as light or as hearty as it may be—to be followed by a three-course lunch and in the evening by a complete dinner.

THE TAPAS LIFE-STYLE

The tapas way of life is completely in tune with the Spanish character. To eat tapas-style is to eat by whim, free from rules and schedules. It is meant for those who wish to enjoy life to the fullest and who love to while away the time with friends. Since home entertaining is not common in Spain, the thousands of bars and taverns in the country become logical meeting places.

A Spaniard will rarely visit a tapas bar with the express purpose of eating; he is there to parley with the owner, jockey with the waiters, strike up conversations with other patrons, and invariably come upon friends who frequent the same bar. Jokes will fly, arguments will rage, and everyone will have a grand

BRINGING TAPAS TO YOUR HOME

Although in Spain tapas traditionally belong to the streets, and depend on Spain's widely spaced meal hours and the freedom of its midday siesta, they lend themselves splendidly to our American life-style and to American food tastes. Tapas bars are catching on as fun places to spend an entire evening, and tapas have brought new life to home entertaining. Ever since my husband and I returned from Spain to live in the United States, we have been inviting friends to our home for tapas, and although they are often unfamiliar with the tapas traditions and life-style that we had left behind in Spain, they fall into the spirit easily, finding great pleasure in the tasting and experimenting that are a part of eating tapas. I find there is nothing that does more to promote a lively evening at home than an exciting food experience.

Tapas cover a wide range of possibilities for home entertaining, from small parties, limited to perhaps three or four tapas for a handful of guests, to gala affairs, such as the one I always give during the Christmas holidays for seventy guests, where I serve more than twenty different tapas. I am always amazed to see how people who don't know one another mix and mingle and become friends over the course of the evening, and I attribute this to the good feelings that tapas seem to generate.

For an intimate gathering you can serve tapas at a leisurely pace (you might even try to "orchestrate" the tapas, beginning with the lighter ones and progressing to more filling tapas), but for larger parties you will want to bring out most of the tapas at the start so that guests can help themselves. Arrange the cold and room-temperature tapas attractively on serving dishes and saucy tapas in casseroles (Spanish earthenware *cazuelas* are ideal for this) kept warm on hot plates. Tapas with last-minute preparation, meant to be eaten as soon as they are ready, should be spaced over the course of the evening and passed around the room. Plates may be provided or not for tapas, depending on the type of tapa served and the size of the party. In general, what can be picked up with fingers or with toothpicks is usually more appropriate for large tapas parties, while other tapas that may require forks and dishes can more comfortably be handled at smaller affairs.

Just like any well-considered meal, tapas must present a variety of tastes and textures that are complementary to one another. Too many marinades or bread-based tapas will quickly tire the palate and diminish your appetite. Choose, therefore, at least one tapa from each of this book's four categories: something cold or marinated; a tapa in a sauce; another with bread or pastry; and one that is fried, baked, or grilled at the last minute. Select from vegetables, seafood, and meat to create a nourishing

and well-balanced "meal." (Incidentally, there are many recipes in this book that are wonderful as dinner dishes.) Fortunately, most tapas can be prepared completely or partially in advance, and the logistics of a tapas party are really much simpler than they might at first seem.

What to drink with tapas? Just about anything you would ordinarily serve at a party or with dinner, like red and/or white wine, mixed drinks, or beer. If you are not already familiar with Spain's exceptional yet quite inexpensive wines, now is the right time to learn about them. (For a more complete look at Spanish wines, consult *The Foods and Wines of Spain*.) Another possibility is a good home-prepared sangría. And Champagne or sparkling wines made by the Champagne method (Spain produces some of the best) would certainly give added spirit to any tapas party. But for a truly elegant Spanish flair, try the quintessentially Spanish drink, chilled dry *fino* sherry, which accompanies tapas as no other drink can.

THE ORIGIN OF TAPAS

Sherry, in fact, is probably responsible for the development of the tapas tradition in Spain. Tapas as a way of life, most generally agree, go back to the nineteenth century and began in Andalucía, where all Spanish sherry is made. Sherry is not considered appropriate as a dinner accompaniment because of its strength (over 18 percent alcohol). It is therefore usually sipped as an aperitif (I am of course talking about the very dry *fino* sherry and the moderately dry *amontillado*—sweet sherries are meant as dessert wines) and as such cries out for a tapa of some kind.

There is another reason that tapas originated in Andalucía: nowhere in Spain is there more joie de vivre than in southern Spain. I have never known an *andaluz* to be at a loss for words, and he positively thrives on endless hours of conversation. Tapas and the conviviality they embrace are an essential part of his social world.

Andalucía is also historically the region of noble fighting bulls (some of Spain's most popular tapas, like *banderillas*, take their name from the bullfighting vocabulary of southern Spain) and landed aristocrats, who had the luxury of keeping late hours and arising at their leisure. Their lunches and dinners would inevitably be late ones, delayed further still by time spent with friends over a drink. In Spain there is an expression that reflects this relaxed life-style: when a meal is served unusually late, Spaniards say they are eating *a la hora de los señoritos*—"at the young masters' hours." The aristocratic spirit of leisure and the good life are an integral part of Andalucian life, as important to the blue-collar worker as to the wealthy. While the gap between rich and poor is still wide in Andalucía, life is curiously more "democratic," in the true sense of the word, than anywhere else in Spain.

Originally the tapa was a slice of cured ham or *chorizo* sausage placed over the mouth of a wineglass (some say this was to keep flies out of the drinks) and served compliments of the house. The verb *tapar* means "to cover"; thus the origin of the word *tapa*. Since these meats were salty, they produced thirst, and smart tavern owners embraced the tapa as a means to increase their wine sales. As the custom grew, so did the selection of tapas; today they come in hundreds of varieties—and are rarely complimentary.

EATING TAPAS IN SPAIN

When I am in Spain there is nothing I love quite so much as joining friends for tapas, and I am sure you too will wish to adopt the tapas spirit when you visit Spain. Although a Spaniard will rarely eat tapas in place of lunch or dinner, Americans, less accustomed to heavy meals, find tapas a more than adequate substitute for a meal. And because tapas hours (about 12:00 P.M. to 3:00 P.M. and again from 7:00 P.M. to 10:00 P.M.) are close to American lunch and dinner hours, there is yet another reason to try tapas.

And then there is the most compelling reason of all. Participating in the *tapeo* provides an opportunity to feel the pulse of the nation and to be charged by its electricity. Tapas bars are, like Spain itself, far from orderly; as many as possible squeeze along the bar, while the rest stand two and three deep and place their orders by yelling across the room. In really crowded bars the clientele spill over into the street, taking with them glasses of wine or beer and dishes of tapas. Sometimes the flow of traffic is disrupted, yet Spanish motorists, usually so volatile, don't seem to mind at all. In a tapas bar there are no bills and no written count taken of what you consume; when the time comes to pay, a combination of the incredible ability of the barman to keep tabs on everyone, coupled with the client's honesty (he may remind the barman of a tapa or drink that has been overlooked), brings a more or less accurate accounting.

Discovering what food a tapas bar offers is just as chaotic a proposition. You may ask, and the barman will rattle off a seemingly endless litany of tapas, never pausing between items or stopping to catch his breath. Some bars will paint a list of tapas on the outside display window, others will write them on a chalkboard, and a more serious tapas bar might even have a typewritten tapas menu. Of course, platters and earthenware casseroles of tapas are always lined up along the bar to stimulate your appetite. In some cities it is the custom to take what you please from those dishes and give your own count to the waiter when it is time to pay. In other bars, where tapas come speared on toothpicks, a toothpick count is taken at the end. And there are still some bars where a tapa is automatically brought to you as part of the price of a drink. In any case, eating tapas is a communal experience. Forks, if needed, are provided for all, but everyone in your party will share from the same plate.

Tapas bars in Spain go by different names and are subtly different one from another. There is the *bodegón*, which concentrates mainly on drinks and keeps tapas to the minimum (some shellfish, marinades, olives); the *tasca*, which is the most typical tapas bar; the *mesón*, an establishment of rustic décor that will have a tapas bar, but a restaurant as well; the *cervecería*, which, as its name indicates, specializes in beers and only tapas, like shellfish, that are appropriate for that drink; and the *xampanyeries* or champagne bars of Barcelona, highly stylized versions of tapas bars, which concentrate on tapas (cured ham and strongly flavored cheeses, for example) to complement the region's outstanding *cavas* (sparkling wines), served by the glass.

If you're going to Spain and wonder how to find the best tapas bars in any city or village, there are several rules to follow. In general the best tapas bars with the most variety of tapas are in large and moderately large cities, where there is enough population to create a need for diversification and a demand for top quality. Cities that are university centers also tend to have good tapas, since students find tapas affordable and in step with their casual style of living. And then there are towns that have become tapas centers because they happen to be at a point along a main road where people are likely to arrive at tapas time.

Once within a city or town, head for downtown (this will usually be near the Plaza Mayor—the old central plaza), where tapas bars tend to be concentrated, and look for the bars that are most crowded. Spaniards know good food, and this is a sure sign that the bar has something special to offer. Ask around—everyone is an expert in tapas and will have a favorite place to recommend. And if you are still unsure where to have tapas, go to any bar that looks appetizing and just order a drink. While you sip it examine the tapas on display, try one, then either stay for more or move on to another.

In my years of travel in Spain I have enjoyed tapas all over the country, from the lush green northern lands of Galicia, Asturias, and the Basque country to the arid plains of Castilla and Extremadura, the coasts of Cataluña and Valencia, and south to light-hearted Andalucía. Each region and each city has its tapas specialties and its own style of serving tapas. In Gijón grilled fresh sardines join with the regional drink, *sidra* (hard cider), as the most popular tapa; in Bilbao huge triple-decker sandwiches predominate; in San Sebastián almost all tapas are speared on toothpicks, beautifully presented, and taken on the honor system; in Pamplona batter-fried shrimp excel; in Oviedo, where tapas bars are called *chigres*, small crusty rolls come with just about every conceivable filling; while in Valencia those diminutive rolls become huge hero sandwiches. Just about everywhere, but most particularly along the coast, fresh glistening fish and shellfish are exceedingly popular tapas, while in the interior grilled meats, *chorizo* sausage, cured ham, and cheese are more commonly found. The region of Galicia has its succulent savory pies, which will be found nowhere else in Spain, and in Madrid and Barcelona you will find just about everything imaginable.

Although most of Spain's great tapas are found in its important cities, I can recall memorable tapas in the most unlikely places: an incredible 100 varieties of exceptional tapas at Nuestro Bar in the central plains of Albacete; wonderfully creative tapas at O'Merlo in the Galician town of Pontevedra; a basket of freshly fried eggplant, compliments of the house in the out-of-the-way northern village of Cabezón de la Sal at Mesón Picu-La-Torre; deliciously fresh kidneys in paprika sauce on a Sunday morning on the village square of Posada de Valdeón, overlooking the majestic peaks of Picos de Europa; succulent baby squid grilled with garlic at Bellamar in Foz, Galicia; and the first-class tapas from Salvador, at the lively Bar Bahía in Cádiz, to name but a few. (See p. 207 for more tapas bar recommendations.)

Overall, the best tapas in Spain are still found where the tapa originated—in Andalucía. Tapas are prepared there with love and tremendous pride, and they are fresh, exquisitely presented, and highly creative. Sevilla in particular is tapas heaven, and just about every tapas bar there is cheery and gaily decorated; the service is always warm, and there is an enormous variety of inviting, inventive tapas.

Tapas are uniquely Spanish and one of the most delightful aspects of Spanish cuisine. They are also a cherished and time-honored tradition in Spain, and I hope that as tapas are adopted in this country, the camaraderie, spontaneity, and good times that are so much a part of tapas in Spain will also accompany the food as it makes the transition to a new cultural setting across the Atlantic.

TAPAS

1

TAPAS

IN

SAUCE

Spain is not generally known for its sauces, yet it has some of the world's finest: green sauces, garlic sauces, paprika sauces, saffron sauces, sherry sauces, and sauces of ground almonds and pine nuts, to name but a few of the most outstanding. Savor all of these sauces in the tapas of this chapter. At least one tapa in sauce should be a part of any tapas selection. Your choices are wide, ranging from vegetables to fish, poultry, and meats and from slow-simmering dishes to rapid stir-fry preparations. Most of the dishes can be begun or completed in advance.

When cooking tapas in sauce ahead, keep in mind that reheating will take a few minutes. Undercook slightly initially so that the tapa will be at its proper point when ready to serve. A sauce may thicken slightly when left to stand, in which case thin with a little water or other liquid appropriate to the recipe.

Stewed Zucchini, Peppers, and Tomatoes

(PISTO MANCHEGO)

Pisto Manchego is a classic vegetable dish from La Mancha—land of Don Quijote—in the central plains of Spain. It can be served in a variety of ways—hot, cold, or enclosed in potato nests (see p. 149)—and can be made up to a day in advance. SERVES 6

3 tablespoons fruity olive oil
1 green pepper, cut into
  3/4-inch squares
1 medium onion, chopped
1 medium zucchini (about 6 ounces),
  cut into 1/2-inch slices, then cubed
5 cloves garlic, minced
3/4 pound tomatoes, skinned and diced
1 tablespoon minced parsley
Salt
Freshly ground pepper

Heat the oil in a large saucepan and sauté the pepper, onion, zucchini, and garlic until the onion is wilted. Add the tomato, parsley, salt, and pepper and cook over medium heat, uncovered, for 30 minutes. At the end of the cooking time, turn up the heat to reduce the liquid—the stew should be thick, not soupy.

Chickpeas in Onion Sauce

(GARBANZOS CON CEBOLLA)

A large quantity of slowly stewed onions lends a touch of sweetness to this chickpea recipe. It's one of my mother-in-law's favorites. SERVES 4

START PREPARATION ONE DAY IN ADVANCE

1/4 pound dried chickpeas
1 clove garlic, peeled
1 slice onion
1 bay leaf
Salt
2 tablespoons olive oil
1 medium onion, chopped
1 tablespoon skinned
  and chopped tomato

Soak the chickpeas overnight in cold water to cover. Drain and place in a deep casserole with the garlic, onion slice, bay leaf, salt, and water to cover. Bring to a boil, then simmer, covered, for about 1 1/2–2 hours, or until the chickpeas are tender. Drain, discarding the garlic and bay leaf.

In a skillet heat the oil and sauté the onion for a minute. Add the tomato, cover, and cook very slowly until the onion is cooked but not colored, about 15 minutes. Combine with the chickpeas. [May be prepared ahead]

Chickpeas and Spinach

(GARBANZOS CON ESPINACAS)

This is a dish that I never expected to find as a tapa, but sure enough, it appeared on the extensive tapas menu at Bodegón Torre de Oro, a huge, very pleasant "mesón"-style bar of whitewashed walls and arches, wine barrels, and hanging strings of garlic. Chickpeas with spinach most often appears in Spanish cuisine as a Lenten soup, but this version has less liquid and is suitable as a tapa. SERVES 4

START PREPARATION ONE DAY IN ADVANCE

¼ pound dried chickpeas
2 cloves garlic, peeled
1 slice onion
4 tablespoons skinned, seeded, and
  chopped tomato
1 bay leaf
Coarse salt
¼ pound spinach leaves
  (weight after stems removed),
  coarsely chopped
Few strands saffron
2 tablespoons olive oil
2 tablespoons finely chopped onion
½ teaspoon grated
  semisweet chocolate

Soak the chickpeas overnight in cold water to cover. Drain and place the chickpeas in a deep casserole with 1 clove of the garlic, the onion slice, 2 tablespoons of the tomato, the bay leaf, salt, and water to cover. Bring to a boil, then simmer, covered, about 1½–2 hours, or until the chickpeas are just tender. Drain, reserving several tablespoons of the cooking liquid and discarding the garlic and bay leaf.

Leave the spinach damp after washing, and place in a covered pot with salt to cook slowly for about 5 minutes, or until just tender.

In a mortar, crush the remaining clove of garlic with the saffron and a little salt. In a skillet heat 1 tablespoon of the oil and sauté the chopped onion until it is wilted. Add the remaining 2 tablespoons of tomato and cook until the tomato has softened. Stir in the spinach, the remaining tablespoon of oil, and the saffron mixture.

Combine the spinach mixture with the chickpeas and stir well to distribute the spinach evenly. Mix in about 1 tablespoon of the reserved cooking liquid—or a little more if you wish the mixture thinner—and the grated chocolate. [May be prepared ahead]

Mushrooms in Garlic Sauce

(CHAMPIÑONES AL AJILLO)

SERVES 6

3 tablespoons fruity olive oil
½ pound mushrooms, stems trimmed,
    brushed clean, whole if very small,
    or cut in ¼-inch-thick slices
4 cloves garlic, peeled and
    thinly sliced
2 teaspoons fresh lemon juice
2 tablespoons dry (fino) Spanish sherry
¼ cup veal broth, or a mixture of
    chicken and beef broth
½ teaspoon paprika,
    preferably Spanish style
½ dried red chili pepper, seeded and
    crumbled, or ¼ teaspoon crushed
    red pepper
Salt
Freshly ground pepper
1 tablespoon minced parsley

Heat the oil in a skillet until very hot and stir fry the mushrooms and garlic over high heat for about 2 minutes. Lower the heat and stir in the lemon juice, sherry, broth, paprika, chili pepper, salt, and pepper. Simmer a minute or two [May be prepared ahead], sprinkle with parsley, and serve.

Spicy Pimientos

(PIMIENTOS PICANTES)

Slow cooking makes these red peppers delicate and unusually delicious. I prefer them at room temperature, and they complement any tapa that is not saucy. SERVES 6

4 medium sweet red peppers
2-3 tablespoons chicken broth
    or water
2 tablespoons olive oil
4 cloves garlic, lightly
    crushed and peeled
¼ teaspoon cayenne pepper
Salt

Place the peppers in an ungreased roasting pan in a 375°F oven for 17 minutes. Turn the peppers and continue roasting for another 17 minutes. Remove from the oven, cover the pan tightly with foil, and let cool.

Remove the peppers and deglaze the pan with the chicken broth. Reserve. Peel the peppers, remove the core and seeds, and cut each into 8 strips. In a skillet heat the oil till warm but not sizzling hot. Add the peppers, garlic, cayenne, and salt and sauté slowly over low heat for 3 minutes. Add the reserved pan juices, cover, and cook slowly 5 minutes more. [May be prepared ahead] Serve at room temperature.

Red Peppers Stuffed with Hake

(PIMIENTOS RELLENOS DE MERLUZA)

Red peppers filled lightly with fish (the peppers are precooked and have only 2 tablespoons of filling, so they lie flat) are extremely popular in Spain, and this version of the dish is the best of the many I have sampled. Small red peppers work best as a tapa because they can be served one to a person; otherwise, they will have to be cut in half. You can use crab meat instead of the fish (eliminating the fish cooking time if the crab is precooked). SERVES 6

7 **very small, or 4 medium, red peppers**
2 **tablespoons olive oil**
1 **small carrot, scraped and chopped**
1 **medium onion, finely chopped**
1/2 **cup plus 3 tablespoons dry white wine**
1/2 **pound hake or fresh cod steaks**
1 **small bay leaf**
1 **sprig parsley**
Salt
1 **tablespoon minced shallots**
1 1/2 **tablespoons brandy,
    preferably Spanish brandy or Cognac**
2 **tablespoons lightly beaten egg**

WHITE SAUCE
1 **tablespoon butter**
1 **tablespoon flour**
1/2 **cup milk**
Salt
White pepper, preferably freshly ground

Roast and skin the peppers according to the instructions for pimiento on page 204. Heat 1 tablespoon of the oil in a shallow, medium casserole and sauté the carrot and half of the chopped onion until the onion is wilted. Add 1/2 cup of the white wine and cook over high heat until the liquid is reduced by half. Add the fish and water to barely cover, the bay leaf, parsley, and salt. Bring to a boil, cover, and simmer for 20 minutes. Remove the fish from the liquid, cool and shred, removing any bone and skin. Reserve 6 tablespoons of the cooking liquid and the pieces of onion, carrot, and parsley. Discard the bay leaf. Wipe out the casserole.

To make the white sauce, melt the butter in a small saucepan, stir in the flour, and cook for a minute. Add the milk gradually and stir constantly until thickened and smooth. Season with salt and pepper.

In a small skillet heat the remaining tablespoon of oil and sauté the remaining onion and the shallots until the onion is wilted. Add the shredded fish and the brandy. Standing well away, ignite. When the flames die, stir in the remaining 3 tablespoons of wine and cook over high heat until most of the liquid has evaporated. Remove from the heat and stir in the egg and 1/4 cup of the white sauce.

In a processor or blender place the reserved onion, carrot, and parsley with one of the cooked red peppers (use only half a pepper if the peppers are large and save the other half for some other use). Beat until as finely minced as possible. With the motor running, add the reserved cooking liquid and the remaining white sauce and beat until smooth. Strain into the shallow casserole.

Stuff each pepper with about 2 tablespoons of the fish filling (4 tablespoons for the larger peppers). Place the filled peppers on top of the red pepper sauce (do not pour the sauce over the peppers), cover, and cook at 350°F for 30 minutes. [May be prepared ahead]

Vegetable Crêpes

(CANELONES DE LEGUMBRES)

The fascinating city of Segovia, famed for its 2,000-year-old Roman aqueduct—still in use today—its ship-shaped Alcázar castle, and its baby roast suckling pig, now has its own *parador*, a sweepingly modern structure on a hilltop right outside Segovia that takes advantage of the spectacular panoramic vistas of the city. The *parador*'s stunning restaurant, where we were served these delicious and subtly flavored crêpes as a tapa to start our meal, is popular with townsfolk and tourists alike.

SERVES 6 (MAKES 12)

Crêpes (p. 191)
1/2 pound collard greens
  or Swiss chard
4 thin carrots (about 1/2 pound),
  scraped and cut into 2-inch lengths
1 cup chicken broth
3 tablespoons olive oil
Salt
2 medium onions, minced
1 clove garlic, minced
1 tablespoon minced parsley
1/4 teaspoon thyme

SAUCE
2 tablespoons butter
1/2 cup dry white wine
1/2 teaspoon Dijon-style mustard
Salt
Freshly ground pepper,
  preferably white
1 1/2 cups heavy cream

Make the crêpes and set aside.

Bring a large pot of water to a boil, add the collard greens and carrots, and cook for 5 minutes. Drain. Return the vegetables to the pot, barely cover with water and the chicken broth, then stir in 1 tablespoon of the oil and the salt. Bring to a boil, cover, and cook over medium heat for about 10 minutes, or until the greens and carrots are tender. Drain the vegetables and reserve the cooking liquid. Return the liquid to the pot and boil down to about 1 1/2 cups. Chop the vegetables finely.

Heat the remaining 2 tablespoons of oil in a skillet, sauté the onion and garlic for a minute, then cover and cook slowly until the onion is tender, about 20 minutes. Add the chopped greens and carrots, the parsley and thyme, sauté for a minute, and turn off the heat.

To make the sauce, melt the butter in a medium skillet, then add the 1 1/2 cups reserved vegetable broth, the white wine, mustard, salt, and pepper. Boil the liquid down to half. Stir in the cream and simmer, uncovered, until the sauce is thickened.

Mix 1/2 cup of the sauce with the vegetables. Place about 1 tablespoon of the vegetable mixture in the center of each crêpe and roll up. Grease a baking dish and spread with a thin layer of the sauce. Arrange the crêpes seam side down [May be prepared ahead] and cover with the remaining sauce. Bake at 350°F for about 5 minutes, just to heat.

Shrimp in Spicy Tomato Sauce

(GAMBAS PACO ALCALDE)

Around the bend from Barcelona's harbor is the city's beach, which is backed by a small triangle of land that is one of the most charming sections of the city. Known as La Barceloneta—Little Barcelona —it is isolated from the bustle of downtown and looks like a tiny Mediterranean fishing village. Although the beach is lined with a succession of excellent seafood restaurants, my favorite is not along the waterfront but a few blocks inland at Paco Alcalde, where the tapas number over fifty and are displayed most artistically over a bed of tree branches. The *pà amb tomaquet*—Catalán garlic bread (see p. 119)—is great here, as is all the seafood, including these spicy shrimp, which are also sometimes called "Andalucian-style" shrimp. SERVES 4

2 tablespoons olive oil
3 tablespoons finely chopped onion
1 clove garlic, minced
1 teaspoon flour
1 teaspoon paprika,
   preferably Spanish style
¼ cup tomato sauce,
   preferably homemade (p. 66)
¼ cup dry white wine
¼ cup fish broth (p. 27)
   or clam juice
½ dried red chili pepper,
   seeded
¼ teaspoon thyme
½ bay leaf
1 tablespoon minced parsley
Salt
Freshly ground pepper
Pinch sugar
½ pound small-medium
   shrimp, shelled

Heat 1 tablespoon of the oil in a skillet or earthenware casserole large enough to hold the shrimp and sauté the onion and garlic until the onion is wilted. Stir in the flour and paprika. Add the tomato sauce, wine, fish broth, chili pepper, thyme, bay leaf, parsley, salt, pepper, and sugar. Cover and cook slowly for 20 minutes. [May be prepared ahead]

In a separate skillet heat the remaining tablespoon of oil until it is very hot. Add the shrimp and stir fry quickly over high heat, about 1 minute. Add the shrimp to the tomato sauce and continue cooking for 4–5 minutes.

Shrimp and Mushrooms in Almond Sauce

(FRICANDÓ DE LANGOSTINOS)

This Catalán recipe is perhaps one of the most delicious ways to prepare shrimp that I have ever encountered. SERVES 4

START PREPARATION ONE DAY IN ADVANCE

2 slices onion
1 small carrot, sliced
1 clove garlic, lightly crushed
  and peeled
¼ cup dry white wine
1 bay leaf
¼ teaspoon thyme
Dash of cinnamon
Salt
Freshly ground pepper
½ pound jumbo shrimp, shelled
  except for the last tail segment
Flour for dusting
2 tablespoons olive oil
1 small tomato, chopped
½ cup fish broth (p. 27)
  or clam juice
2 medium mushrooms, preferably
  wild, halved or diced
1 tablespoon ground
  blanched almonds

In a bowl mix together the onion slices, carrot, garlic, wine, bay leaf, thyme, cinnamon, salt, and pepper. Add the shrimp and stir. Cover and refrigerate overnight, stirring occasionally. Strain, reserving the liquid and the contents of the strainer (except the bay leaf).

Drain the shrimp well on paper towels, then dust with flour. In a skillet, heat the oil. Sauté the shrimp lightly over medium heat for a minute or so, turning once, and remove to a warm platter. Add to the skillet the reserved onion, carrot, and garlic and sauté until the onion is wilted (add more oil if necessary). Stir in the tomato and cook for a minute, then add the reserved marinade and the fish broth. Simmer, uncovered, for 10 minutes. Strain the sauce, pressing with the back of a wooden spoon to extract as much liquid as possible, and return the strained sauce to the skillet. Stir in the mushrooms, almonds, salt if necessary [May be prepared ahead], and the shrimp. Cover and cook slowly for about 3 minutes, or until the shrimp are done.

Stuffed Eggs with Shrimp

(GAMBAS CON HUEVOS RELLENOS)

This may seem like a complicated way to make "stuffed eggs," but they are really much more than that—the eggs are coated with crumbs and fried, then served in a sauce that includes garlic, saffron, crushed pine nuts, and shrimp. A good part of the work can be done in advance. SERVES 6-8

¼ pound monkfish (p. 86),
    halibut, or fresh cod
Cooking Liquid (p. 157)
4 hard-boiled eggs, cut in halves
    lengthwise, yolks separated
Coarse salt
2 cloves garlic, peeled
2 tablespoons minced parsley
Few strands saffron
2 teaspoons pine nuts
2 tablespoons olive oil
1 teaspoon flour
1 small onion, finely chopped
1 small tomato, skinned
    and finely chopped
Freshly ground pepper
Flour for dusting
1 egg, lightly beaten
    with 1 teaspoon water
Bread crumbs
Oil for frying
8 large shrimp, shelled or unshelled
2 tablespoons fresh or frozen peas

Barely cover the monkfish with the cooking liquid. Bring to a boil, cover, and simmer for 10 minutes. Remove the fish and reserve ¾ cup liquid. Flake the fish with your fingers and mix with 2 mashed egg yolks and salt.

In a mortar mash to a paste 1 clove of the garlic, 1 tablespoon of the parsley, salt, saffron, and pine nuts. Reserve.

Heat 1 tablespoon of the olive oil in a medium skillet, add the flour, and cook until the flour becomes a light brown. Remove and reserve. Wipe out the skillet. Mince the remaining clove of garlic. Heat the remaining tablespoon of oil in the skillet and sauté the minced garlic, the remaining tablespoon of parsley, and the onion until the onion is wilted. Stir in the reserved flour and cook for a minute. Add the tomato, salt, and pepper and continue cooking for 2 minutes. Transfer to a processor or blender and beat until very finely chopped.

Fill the egg whites one-third full with the tomato mixture (reserve the rest), then fill with the fish mixture. Dust with flour, dip in the beaten egg, then coat with bread crumbs. [May be prepared ahead] Heat the oil at least ½ inch deep in a skillet and fry the coated eggs carefully until golden.

In a shallow serving casserole mix the ¾ cup reserved cooking liquid and the remaining tomato mixture. Add the pine nut mixture, the shrimp, peas, and stuffed eggs. Cook, uncovered, for 5 minutes. Turn the shrimp and cook 5 minutes more. Serve in the same dish.

Shrimp in Garlic Sauce

(GAMBAS AL AJILLO)

This is the classic Spanish tapa, found in every region of Spain. Fresh shrimp—not frozen—are very important in this tapa, but I have discovered that if the previously frozen shrimp are well salted, they regain some of the briny taste of the sea that has been lost. This recipe is a slight variation on the traditional shrimp~garlic~oil~hot pepper recipe. I feel it works best when cooked in smaller quantities (in Spain it is usually an individual portion); therefore I prefer, although it is not essential, to prepare the following recipe in at least two separate casseroles. SERVES 4

1/2–3/4 pound shrimp,
   preferably very small, shelled
Coarse salt
8 tablespoons olive oil
3 large cloves garlic, peeled and
   very coarsely chopped
1 dried red chili pepper, stem and
   seeds removed, in 2 pieces
1/2 teaspoon paprika,
   preferably Spanish style
1 tablespoon minced parsley

Dry the shrimp well and sprinkle salt on both sides. Let sit at room temperature for 10 minutes.

Heat the oil in four ramekins or one shallow 8-inch casserole, preferably earthenware. Add the garlic and chili pepper, and when the garlic starts to turn golden (be careful not to overcook) add the shrimp. Cook over medium-high heat, stirring, for about 2 minutes, or until the shrimp are just done. Sprinkle in the paprika, parsley, and salt. Serve immediately, right in the cooking dish if possible. Provide lots of good bread for dunking.

Clams in Sherry Sauce

(ALMEJAS EL FARO)

This excellent clam tapa comes from El Faro restaurant (see p. 56) in Cádiz, not far from Jerez, where Spanish sherry is made. Not surprisingly, in this area of Andalucía sherry—dry and sweet—is a common cooking ingredient. SERVES 3-4

2 tablespoons olive oil
1/4 pound onion, finely chopped
1/2 cup (about 2 ounces) cubed
   cured ham, cut from
   a 1/8-inch-thick slice
2 tablespoons semisweet (oloroso)
   Spanish sherry
1 dozen very small clams (see p. 203)

Heat the oil in a skillet, sauté the onion for a minute, then cover and cook very slowly until the onion is tender but not colored, about 15 minutes. Stir in the ham, then add the sherry and the clams. Turn the heat up to medium, cover, and cook, removing the clams as they open. Return them to the sauce, making sure the clam meat is covered by the sauce. [May be prepared ahead]

Clams in Green Sauce
(ALMEJAS LAS POCHOLAS)

Las Pocholas is a longtime Pamplona restaurant, frequented by Hemingway when he visited the city for the famed "Running of the Bulls." Green sauce is commonly served in Spain over fish (as in Merluza a la Vasca) but rarely found with clams, even though it is a great combination. SERVES 3-4

1 dozen very small clams (see p. 203)

GREEN SAUCE
2 tablespoons olive oil
2 tablespoons finely chopped onion
4 cloves garlic, minced
4 teaspoons flour
1/4 cup dry white wine
1/2 cup plus 2 tablespoons
   fish broth (p. 27) or clam juice
2 tablespoons milk
1/2 cup minced parsley
Salt
Freshly ground pepper

To make the green sauce, heat the oil in a shallow casserole and sauté the onion until it is wilted. Stir in the garlic. Add the flour and cook for a minute, then pour in gradually the wine, broth, and milk and stir in the parsley, salt, and pepper. Cook, stirring constantly, until thickened and smooth. [May be prepared ahead] Add the clams, cover, and cook over low heat, removing the clams as they open. Return the clams to the sauce, making sure the clam meat is covered by the sauce. Serve in the cooking casserole.

VARIATION
You can also make this tapa with mussels, increasing the quantity to 1 1/2 dozen and reducing the fish broth to 6 tablespoons (the mussels give off more liquid).

Clams in Pine Nut and Almond Sauce
(SUQUET DE ALMEJAS)

Almonds, pine nuts, garlic, and a whiff of saffron flavor this typically Catalán sauce. If you wish to serve these clams as a first course, or lunch or supper main course instead of tapa, you may do as the highly regarded and most charming Hispania restaurant just north of Barcelona in Arenys de Mar does —add some peas, even a few cubes of potatoes, and decorate with quartered hard-boiled egg. SERVES 4-6

2 tablespoons olive oil
A 1/4-inch slice long crusty
   loaf bread
2 cloves garlic, peeled
6 blanched almonds
1 tablespoon pine nuts
1 small onion, finely chopped
1 small tomato, skinned and
   finely chopped
1 tablespoon minced parsley
1/4 cup dry white wine
3/4 cup fish broth (p. 27)
   or clam juice
Few strands saffron
2 dozen small clams (see p. 203)
1 tablespoon minced cured ham,
   cut from a 1/4-inch-thick slice
Salt
Freshly ground pepper

Heat the oil in a shallow casserole in which the clams will fit. Fry the slice of bread until golden on both sides, then transfer to a processor or blender. Add to the casserole the garlic, almonds, and pine nuts and sauté until golden. Transfer to the processor. In the remaining oil sauté the onion until it is wilted, add the tomato and parsley, and cook until the tomato is softened. Stir in the wine, broth, and saffron. Cover and simmer for 20 minutes.

Grind the contents of the processor as finely as possible. When the sauce in the casserole has finished cooking, add it very gradually (including the pieces of onion, tomato, and parsley) to the processor and blend until quite smooth. Return to the casserole (you may strain first, if you wish). [May be prepared ahead] Add the clams and the ham, cover, and cook until the clams open. (To prevent toughening, remove the clams as they open, then when all have opened, return them to the sauce.) Taste for salt and pepper.

Clams with Mushrooms and Cured Ham

(ALMEJAS A LA MARINERA)

Clams were once called "a la marinera" because they were prepared by fishermen, combining the day's catch with the most basic ingredients on hand. Today the term can refer to clams in almost any kind of sauce, be it simple or more sophisticated, as is this version that adds mushrooms and cured ham. SERVES 3-4

3 tablespoons olive oil
1/4 pound mushrooms,
   halved or quartered
2 cloves garlic, sliced
6 tablespoons veal broth, or a mixture
   of chicken and beef broth
2 tablespoons diced cured ham,
   cut from a 1/8-inch-thick slice
1 teaspoon fresh lemon juice
1/2 dried red chili pepper, seeded,
   or 1/4 teaspoon crushed red pepper
1 bay leaf
1 dozen clams (see p. 203)
1 tablespoon minced parsley

Heat the oil in a shallow casserole and sauté the mushrooms and garlic for about 2 minutes. Remove to a warm platter. Add the broth, ham, lemon juice, chili pepper, bay leaf, and clams. Cover and cook, removing the clams as they open. Return the clams to the casserole, making sure the clam meat is covered by the sauce. [May be prepared ahead] Sprinkle with the parsley and serve in the same dish.

Sautéed Mussels
(MEJILLONES SALTEADOS)

These mussels, served without their shells, are a specialty at Bar Suso in Santiago de Compostela. If you engage the bar's affable owner, Señor Suso, in conversation, he will most likely whip out his huge collection of postcards, some mounted and most in an unwieldy pile, sent to him by fans from all points of the globe. And with a little encouragement he will proudly show you a dog-eared copy of Dante's *Divine Comedy*, in which, to my surprise, the city of Santiago de Compostela is mentioned.

SERVES 4

1½ dozen medium mussels (see p. 204)
½ cup water
1 slice lemon
6 tablespoons olive oil
1 small onion, minced
1 clove garlic, minced
1 tablespoon minced parsley
½ teaspoon paprika,
    preferably Spanish style
½ dried red chili pepper,
    seeded and crumbled, or ¼ teaspoon
    crushed red pepper

Place the mussels in a skillet with the water and the lemon slice. Bring to a boil and remove the mussels as they open. Do not overcook. Discard the shells and drain the mussel meat on paper towels.

Heat the oil in a medium skillet. Stir fry the mussels for a minute and remove. Add the onion and garlic and sauté slowly, covered, for about 5 minutes. Remove from the heat. Stir in the parsley, paprika, and chili pepper. [May be prepared ahead]

Return the skillet to the heat and add the mussels (with their accumulated juices). Give the mussels a turn in the sauce just to heat them, remove from the heat, cover, and let sit for a minute or two before serving. The mussels are also good at room temperature.

Mussels in White Wine Sauce
(MEJILLONES A LA MARINERA)

SERVES 4

2 tablespoons olive oil
1 small onion, finely chopped
2 cloves garlic, minced
1 teaspoon flour
½ cup dry white wine
1 bay leaf
2 tablespoons fresh lemon juice
Freshly ground pepper
Salt
2 dozen medium mussels (see p. 204)
1 tablespoon minced parsley

Heat the oil in a shallow casserole, preferably Spanish earthenware. Sauté the onion and garlic until the onion is wilted. Stir in the flour and cook for a minute. Add the wine, bay leaf, lemon juice, pepper, and a little salt. Simmer, covered, for 5 minutes. [May be prepared ahead]

Add the mussels to the sauce, cover, and cook until the mussels have opened. Sprinkle with the parsley and serve.

Mussels in Chervil Sauce

(MEJILLONES CANTABRIA)

A wonderfully fragrant sauce of scallions and chervil, an herb in the parsley family that has been used since Roman times, makes these mussels excitingly different and bread-dunking good. SERVES 4-6

2 tablespoons olive oil
2 scallions or 1 small leek, chopped
1½ teaspoons flour
½ cup white wine
1 teaspoon Dijon-style mustard
½ teaspoon dried chervil or
   1 tablespoon fresh
White pepper, preferably freshly ground
Salt
2 dozen medium mussels (see p. 204)
Fresh lemon juice

Heat the oil in a shallow casserole, preferably Spanish earthenware, and sauté the scallions until they are wilted. Stir in the flour, cook for a minute, then add gradually the wine, mustard, chervil, pepper, and a little salt. Cover and simmer for 5 minutes. [May be prepared ahead]

Add the mussels to the sauce, cover, and cook until they have opened. Sprinkle with lemon juice and serve.

Scallops Poached in White Wine

(VIEIRAS AL VINO BLANCO)

A delicate and altogether delicious quick way to prepare scallops. The dish is best presented divided into four scallop shells. SERVES 4

¼ cup dry white wine
½ teaspoon wine vinegar,
   preferably white
½ medium carrot,
   in julienne strips
2 thin slices onion, cut in halves
½ stalk celery,
   in julienne strips
1 small bay leaf
¼ teaspoon thyme
1 clove
Salt
Freshly ground pepper, preferably white
½ pound bay scallops,
   or sea scallops cut in halves
2 teaspoons butter
2 teaspoons minced parsley

In a small saucepan combine the wine, vinegar, carrot, onion, celery, bay leaf, thyme, clove, salt, and pepper. Bring to a boil, cover, and simmer for 10 minutes. [May be prepared ahead]

Add the scallops and simmer for 6 minutes. Remove the scallops, cover, and keep warm. Combine the cooking liquid with the butter, parsley, and salt (if needed). Return the scallops to the sauce to warm them, transfer to scallop shells and serve.

Scallops with Cured Ham and Saffron

(VIEIRAS ESTOFADAS)

Casa Simón, just outside the city of Vigo on the Vigo estuary, is one of Galicia's finest restaurants, famed for its extraordinary Galician shellfish. Scallops, of course, are native to this area of Spain (see p. 167) and found on almost every menu in the region. This scallop recipe, so simple to prepare, makes a distinctive tapa. SERVES 6

> 3 tablespoons olive oil
> 2/3 cup finely chopped onion
> 2 tablespoons minced parsley
> Several strands saffron
> 1 pound bay scallops, or sea scallops cut in halves
> 1/4 cup (about 2 ounces) diced cured ham, cut from a 1/8-inch-thick slice
> 2 tablespoons dry white wine

Heat the oil in a skillet and sauté the onion and parsley very slowly, about 10 minutes, until the onion just begins to color. Add the saffron, cook for a minute or two, then add the scallops and continue cooking over medium heat until the scallops are done, about 5 minutes. Stir in the ham and wine, lower the heat, and cook for a minute or so until the sauce is slightly thickened. Serve right away.

Small Squid in Beer Sauce

(CHIPIRONES EN CERVEZA)

A wonderful recipe for squid, from an excellent restaurant in Murcia, Rincón de Pepe, which also offers tapas at its bar. If very small squid are not available, cut the squid into rings instead of leaving whole. SERVES 4

> 4 tablespoons fruity olive oil
> 3 cloves garlic, lightly crushed and peeled
> 1 medium onion, chopped
> 1 medium tomato, skinned, seeded, and chopped
> 1 bay leaf
> 1/4 teaspoon sugar
> Salt
> Freshly ground pepper
> 1 pound very small squid (the body should not be more than 4 inches long), cleaned (see p. 204), with tentacles
> 1/3 cup beer

In a skillet heat 2 tablespoons of the oil with the garlic. When the garlic starts to color, add the onion, lower the heat, cover, and cook slowly for 10–15 minutes, or until the onion is tender but not brown. Stir in the tomato, bay leaf, sugar, salt, and pepper and cook uncovered, over medium heat, 5 minutes.

In a shallow casserole heat the remaining 2 tablespoons of oil. Add the squid bodies and tentacles and sauté over high heat for 2 minutes. Stir in the beer, lower the heat, cover, and cook for 10 minutes. Add the tomato mixture and cook 25 minutes more. Remove the squid to a warm platter and boil down the sauce until it is thickened. Return the squid and cook about 10 minutes more, or until the squid is tender. [May be prepared ahead]

Octopus with Red Peppers and Potatoes

(PULPO CON PATATAS)

This tasty octopus dish is a specialty at Casa Vilas in Santiago de Compostela. It can be made in advance and reheated. SERVES 4

1 pound octopus, preferably small
½ pound potatoes,
    in ½-inch cubes
3 tablespoons olive oil
1 red pepper, skinned
    and chopped
1 medium onion, chopped
8 cloves garlic, minced
1 teaspoon paprika,
    preferably Spanish style
1 bay leaf
Salt

Cook the octopus according to the instructions on page 170, reserving the cooking liquid. Bring the potatoes to a boil in 1 cup of the reserved cooking liquid, cover, and cook until tender.

Remove the loose skin from the octopus and cut the tentacles with scissors into 1-inch pieces. In an ovenproof casserole heat the oil, add the red pepper, onion, and garlic, and cook slowly until the onion is tender. Add the octopus and sauté for a minute or two. Stir in the paprika, bay leaf, and potatoes. Add ¾ cup of the liquid in which the potatoes have cooked, taste for salt [May be prepared ahead], bring to a boil, then bake, uncovered, at 350°F for 15 minutes.

Octopus Stewed in Onions

(PULPO A LA LEONESA)

I tasted this wonderful dish in a bar right off the Ramblas in Barcelona on Escudellers Street, where it was prepared with octopus so tiny that one octopus hardly made a mouthful. SERVES 4

1½ pounds octopus,
    preferably small
2 tablespoons olive oil
2 medium onions, sliced thin,
    each slice cut in half
Salt
1 teaspoon red wine vinegar
2 teaspoons dry white wine

Prepare the octopus according to the instructions on page 170. Cut the tentacles with scissors into 1-inch pieces. Heat the oil in a skillet, add the onions, and sauté until they are wilted. Cover and cook very slowly until tender, about 20 minutes. Add the octopus pieces, salt, vinegar, and wine, cover, and cook slowly for 15 minutes. [May be prepared ahead]

Octopus in Spicy Paprika Sauce

(PULPO EN SALSA PICANTE)

This is a very simple and tasty preparation for octopus that, despite its name, has very little sauce. SERVES 6

2 pounds octopus, preferably small
4 tablespoons olive oil
4 cloves garlic, minced
Coarse salt
2 teaspoons paprika,
   preferably Spanish style
1/2 dried red chili pepper,
   seeded and crumbled,
   or 1/4 teaspoon
   crushed red pepper

Cook the octopus according to the instructions on page 170. Reserve 1/4 cup of the cooking liquid.

With scissors, cut the octopus tentacles into 1-inch pieces. Heat the oil in a skillet, then add the octopus, garlic, and salt. Cook for a minute, sprinkle with the paprika and chili pepper (you may add more if you like it hotter), and stir in the reserved cooking liquid. Reduce the liquid a little. [May be prepared ahead]

Smelts Stuffed with Cured Ham and Spinach

(BOQUERONES RELLENOS DE JAMÓN Y ESPINACA)

Chef Gregorio Camarero (see p. 140) from the elegant Los Monteros hotel in Marbella is the creator of this wonderful recipe. SERVES 4-5

10 small smelts or other similar fish,
   not more than 5 inches long
   with heads
1/4 pound spinach leaves,
   finely chopped
Salt
Freshly ground pepper, preferably white
1 tablespoon olive oil
1 small clove garlic, minced
2 ounces cured ham, in very thin slices

WHITE SAUCE
1 tablespoon butter
1 1/2 tablespoons flour
1/2 cup fish broth (p. 27),
   clam juice, or chicken broth
1/2 cup milk
Salt
Freshly ground pepper, preferably white
A grating of nutmeg

Clean the fish, removing the head and the spinal fin and pulling out the spinal bone with your fingers. Wash the spinach and leave it damp. Place it in a pot with salt and pepper (no water needed) and cook slowly until just tender, about 5 minutes. In a skillet heat the oil, sauté the garlic lightly, then add the spinach and sauté for another minute.

To make the white sauce, melt the butter in a saucepan. Add the flour and cook, stirring constantly, for a minute or two. Gradually pour in the fish broth and milk, stirring constantly until thickened and smooth. Season with salt, pepper, and nutmeg.

Combine 2 tablespoons of the white sauce with the spinach. Fit the ham slices in the cavities of the fish and spread about 1 teaspoon of the spinach mixture in each. Coat the bottom of an ovenproof dish with a little of the sauce. Arrange the fish on top and pour on the remaining sauce. [May be prepared ahead] Bake at 350°F for 10 minutes and serve in the same dish.

Salmon Trout in Saffron Sauce

(REO EN SALSA DE AZAFRÁN)

The saffron in this delicate "nouvelle"-style fish dish from the outstanding Cabo Mayor restaurant in Madrid turns the sauce a bright orangy color. For a beautiful presentation, serve the fish with a lively green garnish on a patterned dish. SERVES 4–5

½ cup dry white wine
¼ cup well-flavored fish broth (p. 27)
   or clam juice
⅛ teaspoon saffron
1 pound fillets of salmon trout
   or salmon, skin on
½ cup heavy cream
1 egg yolk
Saffron strands for garnish
Parsley sprigs or watercress
   for garnish

In a small skillet bring to a boil the wine, fish broth, and saffron. Cover and simmer slowly for 15 minutes. Strain and return the liquid to the skillet. [May be prepared ahead]

Steam the fish skin side down until just done, about 4–6 minutes. To improvise a steamer, bring to a boil a large pot of water and rest something flat and perforated, such as a mesh cooling rack, on top. The water should reach to within 1 inch of the rack. Place the fish skin side down, cover, and steam over simmering water.

While the fish is steaming, add the cream to the liquid in the skillet and boil down to a sauce consistency, stirring frequently. In a small bowl combine the egg yolk with a few tablespoons of the hot sauce. Return to the skillet, cook slowly for a minute, then remove from the heat.

Skin the fish, cut into tapas-size portions, and arrange on a platter. Pour on the sauce and garnish with the saffron and parsley or watercress.

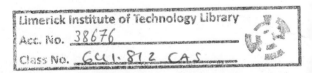
Limerick Institute of Technology Library
Acc. No. 38676
Class No. 6(1.812 CAS

Swordfish in Saffron Sauce

(PESCADO EN AMARILLO)

One of the simple and delicious dishes that has made Salvador and his Bar Bahía (see p. 37) so popular in Cádiz. SERVES 4

1 tablespoon olive oil
2 tablespoons finely chopped onion
1 clove garlic, minced
1 tablespoon finely chopped
   Italian style green pepper
2 tablespoons skinned and finely
   chopped tomato
1 bay leaf
2 tablespoons brandy, preferably
   Spanish brandy or Cognac
$1/4$ cup strong chicken broth
Salt
Freshly ground pepper
$1/8$ teaspoon nutmeg
Several strands saffron
$3/4$ pound swordfish or shark,
   in $1^{1}/2$-inch cubes

Heat the oil in a shallow casserole and sauté the onion, garlic, and green pepper until softened. Add the tomato and bay leaf and cook for a minute. Stir in the brandy, chicken broth, salt, pepper, nutmeg, and saffron. [May be prepared ahead] Add the fish, cover, and cook for 10 minutes.

Fish in Orange Sauce

(MERO A LA NARANJA)

Mero, a kind of grouper, which in turn is related to the sea bass, is considered a great delicacy in Spain and lends itself particularly well to quick cooking methods. For this recipe you can substitute any kind of white, firm-fleshed, and mildly flavored thick fish steak or fillet.

This dish comes from the magnificent Moorish-style Hotel Alfonso XIII in Sevilla, where it is served for dinner, although its preparation works equally well for tapas. It is a dish of last-minute preparation, but if all preliminary jobs are done in advance (flouring fish, cutting and separating the orange, measuring liquids), the final cooking is very rapid. SERVES 6-8

2 oranges
1 pound thick boneless fish steak or fillet,
   such as grouper, halibut, or fresh cod,
   cut into tapas-size portions
Flour for dusting
10 tablespoons butter
4 tablespoons orange liqueur, such as
   Torres, Cointreau, or Grand Marnier
4 tablespoons fresh orange juice
$1/2$ cup veal broth, or a mixture of
   chicken and beef broth
2 tablespoons minced parsley

Cut the orange rinds (orange part only) in julienne strips. Clean the oranges of all white skin and divide them into sections.

Dust the fish pieces well with flour. Heat 6 tablespoons of the butter in a skillet, add the fish, and sauté until golden on both sides and cooked through (be careful not to burn the butter). Remove to a warm platter.

Add the orange sections and the rind to the skillet and toss to coat with the butter. Add the remaining 4 tablespoons of butter and cook for another minute. Pour in the orange liqueur, stand well away, and ignite. Stir until the flames die, then add the orange juice and veal broth and stir until the sauce is smooth and syrupy.

Arrange the orange sections and the julienne rind over the fish. Pour on the sauce, sprinkle with parsley, and serve.

Monkfish Baked in Foil

(RAPE ESTOFADO)

This is an exquisite tapa, delicately flavored with cream and vegetables. And its individual foil packets make it easy to serve and fun to eat. SERVES 4

½ carrot, scraped and
   in julienne strips
4 green beans, in julienne strips
2 tablespoons butter
1 scallion, in julienne strips
½ cup heavy cream
½ pound boneless monkfish
   (see p. 86) or a firm-textured fish
   like halibut, about 1 inch thick
Salt
Freshly ground pepper,
   preferably white

VEGETABLE BROTH
¾ cup water
2 carrots, scraped and sliced

4 scallions, cut in pieces
1 stalk celery, cut in pieces
½ teaspoon thyme
2 sprigs parsley
1 bay leaf
Salt
Freshly ground pepper

Combine the vegetable broth ingredients in a pot, bring to a boil, cover, and simmer slowly for 40 minutes. Strain, pressing with the back of a wooden spoon to extract as much liquid as possible. There should be about ½ cup.

Arrange the carrot and green beans in a skillet and add vegetable broth just barely to cover. Bring to a boil, cover, and simmer briefly until the vegetables are cooked but still crisp. Drain, reserving the vegetable broth.

Melt the butter in a small skillet and sauté the scallion until it is just barely tender. Remove, leaving the butter in the skillet. To the skillet add ¼ cup of the vegetable broth and the cream. Boil until the sauce is reduced and thickened.

Cut the fish into 4 thick pieces and place each on a piece of foil. Sprinkle with salt and pepper and arrange the julienne of carrots, green beans, and scallions on top. Cover with the sauce, seal the foil packets [May be prepared ahead], and bake at 350°F for 10 minutes.

Tuna Balls in Wine Sauce

(FIAMBRE DE BONITO)

We climbed the steep narrow streets of the old fishing town of Laredo on the Cantabrian coast to its highest point, where we discovered Bar Miguelón, a good seafood tapas bar that serves these exceptional "meatballs" of fresh albacore tuna. Unable to find fresh white meat tuna here, I substituted canned, and the difference in taste was ever so slight. This is an excellent and extremely inexpensive tapa and, strangely enough, you and your guests will be hard pressed to identify the main ingredient as tuna. SERVES 4-6 (MAKES 12)

> 5 tablespoons bread crumbs
> 10 tablespoons chicken broth
> 6 tablespoons dry white wine
> A 6½-ounce can white meat tuna
>   packed in water, drained and flaked
> 1 hard-boiled egg, finely chopped
> 1 egg, lightly beaten
> 3 tablespoons minced parsley
> 2 large cloves garlic, minced
> Salt
> Freshly ground pepper
> Flour for dusting
> 2 tablespoons olive oil

In a bowl moisten the bread crumbs with 3 tablespoons of the chicken broth and 1 tablespoon of the wine. Mix in the flaked tuna, hard-boiled egg, beaten egg, parsley, garlic, salt, and pepper.

Form the tuna mixture into 1½-inch balls and dust with flour. Heat the oil in a skillet and brown the tuna balls on all sides. Add the remaining 5 tablespoons wine, the remaining 7 tablespoons of chicken broth, and salt. Cover and simmer for 30 minutes. (The tuna balls seem to absorb a lot of liquid during cooking, so add more chicken broth if necessary.) [May be prepared ahead]

Fresh Salmon in Puréed Red Pepper Sauce

(SALMÓN AL ESTILO DE ZALACAÍN)

Zalacaín is nothing less than the finest restaurant in Madrid, the best restaurant in Spain, and, according to many, one of the world's great restaurants. Dining here is, indeed, a memorable experience in every way — table settings are sumptuous, service is impeccable, and every dish is a gustatory and visual work of art.

A tasting menu, *menú de degustación* (which, you might say, brings the tapas concept of eating to restaurants), is perhaps the best way to narrow down an overabundance of tempting possibilities. This rich and subtle salmon dish was one "tapa" at a recent tasting. SERVES 6

> 3 tablespoons plus 1 teaspoon sweet butter
> 1 pimiento, home prepared (see p. 204),
>   cut in several pieces
> ¾ cup plus 1 tablespoon heavy cream
> 1½ teaspoons minced shallot
> ¼ cup dry white wine
> 2 tablespoons dry vermouth
> ¼ cup fish broth (p. 27) or clam juice
> Fresh lemon juice
> Salt

White pepper, preferably freshly ground
1 pound fresh salmon fillets,
    skin removed, cut in 6 pieces

In a small skillet melt 2 teaspoons of the butter. Sauté the pimiento for a couple of minutes and transfer to a processor or blender. Beat, adding 1 tablespoon of the cream, until as smooth as possible. Strain; there should be about 2 tablespoons of purée.

Wipe out the skillet and heat another 2 teaspoons of butter. Sauté the shallot until it is soft but not colored. Add the wine, vermouth, and fish broth and cook down for a few minutes until thickened and syrupy. Stir in the remaining ¾ cup of cream and cook down for another minute or two until thickened. Add 2 tablespoons of the pimiento purée, season with a few drops of lemon juice, salt, and pepper. [May be prepared ahead]

In a larger skillet melt another 2 tablespoons of butter. Sauté the salmon briefly on each side, until just done (about 2–3 minutes to a side, depending on the thickness). Transfer to a warm serving platter. Spoon on the sauce and serve.

Seafood Medley with Brandy and Sherry

(MERLUZA COMBARRO)

This excellent dish comes from Combarro, a fine Galician restaurant in Madrid. SERVES 5-6

¾ pound hake or fresh cod steak,
    in 1¾-inch chunks
Salt

Flour for dusting
2 tablespoons olive oil
1 small onion, finely chopped
1 clove garlic, minced
1 small bay leaf
Dash of crushed red pepper
1 tablespoon brandy, preferably Spanish
    brandy or Cognac
1 tablespoon dry (fino) Spanish sherry
2 teaspoons butter
2 teaspoons heavy cream
1 medium tomato, skinned and puréed
    in a blender or processor
12 medium shrimp, shelled
    or unshelled
¼ pound large sea scallops,
    in ¼-inch "fillets"
6 very small clams (see p. 203)
1 tablespoon minced parsley

Sprinkle the fish pieces with salt and dust with flour. Heat the oil in a skillet and brown the fish quickly (it will cook more later). Remove the fish to a platter.

To the skillet add the onion and garlic and sauté for a minute. Add the bay leaf and crushed red pepper, cover, and simmer slowly for 5 minutes. Add the brandy and, standing well away, ignite. When the flame dies, stir in the sherry, cook for a minute, then add the butter and cream and simmer for 5 minutes. Add the puréed tomato and cook 5 minutes more. [May be prepared ahead]

Spread the tomato mixture over the bottom of an ovenproof casserole in which the seafood will fit snugly. Add the fish, shrimp, and sliced scallops, and turn to coat them lightly with the sauce. Bake at 350°F, uncovered, for 15 minutes. While the seafood is baking, place the clams in a dry skillet. Cover and cook slowly until the clams have opened. Add the clams in their shells and any juices to the casserole, sprinkle with parsley, and serve.

Hake in Brandy Sauce

(MERLUZA AL COÑAC)

This dish, using two ingredients produced in southern Spain—sherry and brandy—comes from the city of Cádiz. SERVES 4

1 pound hake or fresh cod steak,
  about 1 inch thick
Coarse salt
2 tablespoons olive oil
Flour for dusting
1 medium onion, chopped
6 cloves garlic, minced
½ pound tomatoes,
  skinned and finely chopped
¼ cup dry (fino) Spanish sherry
Freshly ground pepper
1 tablespoon brandy, preferably
  Spanish brandy or Cognac

Sprinkle the hake well on both sides with salt. Let sit for 15 minutes.

Heat 1 tablespoon of the oil in a shallow casserole. Dust the fish lightly with flour and sauté quickly for a couple of minutes. Remove to a warm platter. Wipe out the casserole and heat the remaining oil. Sauté the onion and garlic very slowly, covered, until the onion is tender but not brown. Add the tomato and cook slowly for another 10 minutes.

Stir in the sherry, salt, and pepper. [May be prepared ahead] Add the fish, cover, and cook slowly for about 10 minutes, or until almost done. Add the brandy and cook 4 minutes more over low heat. (This dish is not saucy and will dry out if the heat is too high.) Remove the skin and bone from the fish and divide into tapas-size portions.

Galician-Style Fish Steaks

(MERLUZA A LA GALLEGA)

The wonderfully fresh fish in the northwestern region of Galicia makes this a favorite preparation for hake, because it adds character to the fish without masking its freshness. SERVES 4

¾ pound potatoes, preferably red,
  in ¼-inch slices
4 thin slices onion
6 cloves garlic, minced
2 sprigs parsley
Salt
¼ teaspoon thyme
1 bay leaf
7 tablespoons olive oil
1 teaspoon red wine vinegar
2 hake or fresh cod steaks,
  about 1 inch thick
½ teaspoon paprika,
  preferably Spanish style

In a shallow casserole large enough to hold the fish in one layer, place the potatoes, onion, 2 cloves of the minced garlic, parsley, salt, thyme, bay leaf, 1 tablespoon of the oil, ½ teaspoon of the vinegar, and water to barely cover. Bring to a boil, cover, and simmer for 10 minutes, or until the potatoes are about half cooked.

Place the fish steaks over the potato mixture and add some more water to barely cover the fish. Sprinkle the fish with salt, cover, and cook for another 10 minutes, or until the potatoes and fish are done. Pour off all the liquid from the casserole. Remove the skin and bones from the fish carefully, leaving 4 fillets.

In a small skillet heat the remaining 6 tablespoons of oil, then add the remaining 4 cloves of minced garlic and sauté for a minute. Turn off the heat; add the remaining vinegar and the paprika. Pour over the casserole and serve right away.

Fish Steaks with Shrimp Sauce
(MERLUZA CON SALSA DE GAMBAS)

Although *merluza* (hake) is Spain's most popular and plentiful fish, found along the northern shores as well as in the south, it is uncommon in America. Fresh cod, a close cousin, makes an admirable substitute. In this recipe the fish is topped with a sauce of ground shrimp and baked, preferably in an earthenware casserole. SERVES 8

½ pound small shrimp, unshelled
2 fresh cod steaks (about 1 pound each)
Salt
Freshly ground pepper, preferably white
Flour for dusting
4 tablespoons olive oil
2 onions, sliced, each slice cut in half
2 cloves garlic, minced
1 tablespoon flour
½ cup milk
½ cup heavy cream
4 teaspoons dry (fino) Spanish sherry
Minced parsley

COOKING LIQUID (FISH BROTH)
NOTE: To use this recipe for fish broth, add 1 small cleaned fish such as whiting, head on.
1 cup dry white wine
2½ cups water

Salt
6 peppercorns
1 bay leaf
¼ teaspoon thyme
1 sprig parsley
2 slices onion

Shell the shrimp and place the shells in a saucepan with the cooking liquid. Bring to a boil, cover, and simmer slowly for 40 minutes. Strain, reserving 1 cup (boil down if necessary).

Meanwhile, skin and bone the cod, leaving 4 fillets (add the bones to the simmering broth). Cut each fillet in half crosswise to make 8 tapas-size portions. Sprinkle the cod steaks with salt and pepper and dust with flour. Heat 2 tablespoons of the oil in a skillet and sauté the fish briefly, about 1 minute to a side, until golden. Transfer the fish to a shallow ovenproof casserole. Wipe out the skillet.

Heat the remaining 2 tablespoons of oil in the skillet and sauté the onion and garlic until the onion is wilted. Add the shrimp and sauté until they turn pink. Transfer the shrimp to a processor, reserving 8 whole shrimp. (Leave the onion in the skillet.) Blend the shrimp in the processor until as finely chopped as possible. With the motor running, add the reserved shrimp broth gradually. Process until smooth.

Heat the onion that remains in the skillet, stir in the tablespoon of flour, and cook a minute. Gradually pour in the shrimp sauce, then stir in the milk, cream, sherry, salt, and pepper. Boil down for a minute or so to thicken to sauce consistency. [May be prepared ahead]

Pour the shrimp sauce over the fish. Bake at 350°F for 15 minutes. Place the reserved shrimp on top of the fish, spoon on some sauce, and continue to bake 5 minutes more. Sprinkle with minced parsley and serve in the baking dish.

Mixed Seafood in Almond and Wine Sauce

(ZARZUELA DE PESCADO)

In Cataluña they love to flavor their sauces with ground almonds, as in this extraordinarily tasty seafood medley. SERVES 8

4 cups fish broth (p. 27) or
    diluted clam juice
4 cups water
16 jumbo shrimp, unshelled
Coarse salt
Freshly ground pepper
1 carrot, scraped and coarsely chopped
1 onion, coarsely chopped
½ pound monkfish (see p. 86)
    or halibut steak
12 very small squid, cleaned (see p. 204),
    with or without tentacles
4 tablespoons butter
4 tablespoons olive oil
⅔ cup very finely chopped onion
2 medium-large tomatoes, skinned,
    seeded, and chopped
1 cup dry white wine
4 cloves garlic, minced
12 blanched almonds, lightly toasted
2 tablespoons minced parsley
Minced parsley for garnish

In a large saucepan combine the fish broth and water. Shell the shrimp and add the shells to the pot, along with salt, pepper, carrot, and the coarsely chopped onion. Bring to a boil and cook, uncovered, over medium heat for about 30 minutes. The liquid should be reduced to about half. Strain and reserve 4 cups.

Sprinkle the fish steak well on both sides with salt (this helps to firm the flesh) and let sit for 10 minutes. Sprinkle the shrimp and the squid lightly with salt and pepper. Melt the butter in a large, shallow casserole. Sauté the fish steak, shrimp, and squid over high heat, turning once, until the shrimp turn pink (this will take only a minute or two). Remove all the seafood to a warm platter (it will cook more later). Divide the fish steak into tapas-size portions, discarding any skin and bones.

Heat 2 tablespoons of the oil in the same casserole and sauté the finely chopped onion slowly, covered, until tender. Add the tomato and cook over medium heat, uncovered, for about 5 minutes, or until the liquid from the tomato evaporates. Add the white wine and boil down to half, then add the reserved fish broth. Return to a boil and keep simmering.

In a blender or processor beat salt, pepper, garlic, almonds, and the 2 tablespoons minced parsley until as finely chopped as possible. With the motor running, add gradually the remaining 2 tablespoons of oil and 10 tablespoons of the simmering liquid and blend until smooth. Add the contents of the processor to the casserole where the broth is simmering.

Thicken the sauce by reducing to about 1½ cups. Strain and return to the casserole. [May be prepared ahead] Add the seafood and cook for about 3 minutes, or until just done. Garnish with parsley and serve in the same casserole.

Dried Cod in Garlic Mayonnaise
(BACALAO PIL PIL)

This dish is one of the most famous from the Basque country, where cooks pride themselves on the quality of their cod. In *pil pil* recipes the cod is cooked slowly in oil, giving off a good amount of gelatin that thickens the oil into a kind of mayonnaise. Although I have watched chefs prepare this dish many times, the cod I buy here seems to be less gelatinous; consequently, the mayonnaise never forms. I therefore supplement the gelatin by adding egg, and I must say the result is just as delicious.
SERVES 4

START PREPARATION ONE DAY IN ADVANCE

½ pound dried salt cod (see p. 203),
    in thin pieces with the skin on and as
    much of the bone removed as possible
½ cup olive oil
4 cloves garlic, peeled and thinly
    sliced lengthwise
½ dried red chili pepper, seeded,
    or ¼ teaspoon crushed red pepper
2 tablespoons lightly beaten egg

Soak the cod in cold water to cover for 24–36 hours at room temperature, changing the water occasionally. Drain well.

Pour the oil into a shallow casserole, preferably Spanish earthenware. Add the garlic and chili pepper and heat slowly until the garlic just begins to turn golden. Remove the garlic and reserve. Add the cod skin side down and cook, shaking the pan constantly, for 3 minutes. Turn the fish and cook slowly for another 3 minutes. Add 1 tablespoon water, cover, and cook slowly for 15 minutes.

Remove the cod and chili pepper to a warm platter. Cut the cod into 4 tapas-size portions. [May be made in advance up to this point, reheating the oil before continuing] Beat the egg in a processor or blender and, with the motor running, pour in the oil from the casserole gradually—a mayonnaise will form. Pour over the cod. Decorate with the garlic and chili pepper.

Frogs' Legs in Green Sauce
(ANCAS DE RANA EN SALSA VERDE)

Green sauce, great for clams (see p. 14) and snails (see p. 32), is also admirable with frogs' legs.

Green Sauce (p. 14)
¾ pound small frogs' legs
Salt
Flour for dusting
2 tablespoons olive oil

Prepare the green sauce and set aside.

Separate the frogs' legs if they are joined. Dry well on paper towels. Sprinkle with salt and dust with flour.

Heat the oil in a skillet and sauté the frogs' legs quickly until lightly browned. Transfer them to the green sauce and simmer, covered, for about 10 minutes. [May be prepared ahead]

Dried Salt Cod with Apples

(BACALAO CON MANZANA)

As unlikely as the combination of cod and apples (along with raisins, almonds, and pine nuts) may sound, it is one of the greatest sauces I have ever tasted for cod. SERVES 4

START PREPARATION ONE DAY IN ADVANCE

½ pound skinned and boned
  dried salt cod (see p. 203),
  preferably the thick end
1 tablespoon raisins
Flour for dusting
3 tablespoons olive oil
A ¼-inch-thick slice long crusty
  loaf bread
3 tablespoons finely chopped onion
1 small tomato, skinned, seeded, and
  finely chopped
1 tablespoon pine nuts
½ cup chicken broth
White pepper, preferably freshly ground
4 blanched almonds, lightly toasted
¼ apple, peeled, cored, and
  chopped (about 3 tablespoons)
Salt
1 clove garlic, minced

Soak the cod for 24–36 hours in cold water at room temperature, changing the water occasionally.

Soak the raisins in warm water to cover for 2 hours.

Dry the cod on paper towels and cut into tapas-size portions. Dust with flour. Heat 2 tablespoons of the oil in a shallow casserole. Fry the slice of bread on both sides until it is golden. Remove to a proces-

sor or blender. Fry the cod in the same oil quickly, about 1 minute to a side (add more oil if necessary). Remove to a warm dish. Wipe out the pan.

Heat the remaining tablespoon of oil and sauté the onion until it is wilted. Add the tomato and cook for about 3 minutes. Drain the raisins and stir them in, along with the pine nuts, broth, and pepper. Cover and cook for 10 minutes.

While the sauce is cooking, in the processor grind the bread with the almonds. With the motor running, add a few tablespoons of sauce from the casserole and process until the mixture is as smooth as possible. Add to the casserole and continue cooking for another 5 minutes. Add the cod and apple and cook 10 minutes more, adding a little water if the sauce thickens too much. Taste for salt, sprinkle with the garlic, and serve. [May be prepared ahead]

Chicken in Garlic Sauce

(POLLO EN SALSA DE AJO)

This is a slightly more sophisticated version of Pollo al Ajillo, a dish that finds its way to just about every menu in Spain and is a favorite of visitors and Spaniards alike. For easy serving use chicken wings, although a whole chicken cut in tapas-size portions will also work. SERVES 4-6

8 chicken wings or half a 3-pound
  chicken, cut in tapas-size portions
4 tablespoons olive oil
8 large cloves garlic, peeled
1 tablespoon brandy, preferably
  Spanish brandy or Cognac
½ teaspoon flour
2 tablespoons dry white wine

2 tablespoons chicken broth
Salt
1 tablespoon minced parsley
Few strands saffron
3 peppercorns

Discard the wing tips and split the rest of the wing into two parts. Heat the oil in a skillet, add the wings and garlic cloves, and sauté until the garlic is golden (remove the garlic as it is done and reserve in a mortar) and the chicken brown on all sides. Add the brandy and, standing well away, ignite, then sprinkle in the flour and stir in the wine, broth, and salt. Cover and simmer for 15 minutes.

In the mortar, make a paste of the garlic with the parsley, saffron, peppercorns, and salt. Stir this mixture into the chicken, cover, and continue cooking for another 15 minutes. [May be prepared ahead]

Quail with Pearl Onions and Pine Nuts

(CODORNICES CON CEBOLLETAS Y PIÑONES)

Besides making an excellent tapa, these quail also could be the center of a very elegant dinner party (double the number of quail). SERVES 4

2 quail, split in halves
Salt
2 tablespoons olive oil
8 small pearl onions, peeled and cut
   in halves lengthwise
2 medium carrots, scraped and
   thinly sliced
1 clove garlic, minced

2 tablespoons chopped pimiento,
   preferably home prepared (see p. 204)
   or imported
1/2 cup dry white wine
1/4 cup chicken broth
2 tablespoons pine nuts
1 tablespoon minced parsley
1/2 teaspoon thyme
1 bay leaf
Freshly ground pepper

Sprinkle the quail with salt. Heat the oil in a shallow casserole and brown the quail. Remove to a warm platter. Add to the casserole the onions, carrots, and garlic and cook, covered, over low heat until the onions are tender. [May be prepared ahead] Return the quail to the casserole, along with any juices, and add the pimiento, wine, chicken broth, pine nuts, parsley, thyme, bay leaf, salt, and pepper. Cover and cook for 15–20 minutes, or until the quail are just tender.

Remove the quail to a warm serving dish (or to individual serving casseroles) and boil down the sauce for a minute or two. Pour over the quail and serve.

Snails
in Green Sauce
(CARACOLES EN SALSA VERDE)

Snails in garlicky green sauce are a wonderful and delicious change from the all-too-common garlic and butter sauce. These snails are baked in their shells and served on a bed of coarse salt, just as they are at a top Catalán restaurant, Hispania, in Arenys de Mar (see p. 14). The purpose of the salt is to keep the snail shells from tipping over and to create a very attractive presentation. SERVES 6 (MAKES 24)

Green Sauce (p. 14), omitting the milk
 and adding another 2 tablespoons
 fish broth
24 large canned snails, drained, with
 their shells
Coarse salt

Make the green sauce according to instructions. Add the snails, cover, and simmer for 5 minutes. In a shallow casserole large enough to fit the snails, pour coarse salt to within about ¾ inch of the rim. Push the snails well into their shells and spoon in the sauce. Arrange on the bed of salt [May be prepared ahead] and bake at 475°F for 5 minutes.

Meatballs
in Almond Sauce
(ALBÓNDIGAS EN SALSA DE ALMENDRA)

In Spain cooks often flavor and thicken sauces with ground almonds. These meatballs come from Santa María del Paular, a hotel (which, besides having an excellent restaurant, serves tapas at its bar) on the grounds of a Benedictine monastery. Guests are told to "respect the silence of these grounds," and the utter serenity of the enclave is indeed a welcome respite from the hectic world of Madrid, some forty miles away. SERVES 6-8

¾ cup bread crumbs
1¼ cups dry white wine
13 cloves garlic, peeled
½ pound ground beef
¾ pound ground pork
¾ pound ground veal
2 eggs
5 tablespoons minced parsley
2½ teaspoons salt
Freshly ground pepper
2 tablespoons olive oil
1 onion, finely chopped
1 carrot, scraped and finely chopped
20 blanched almonds
1¾ cups beef broth
½ cup fresh or frozen peas
1 bay leaf
2 scallions

Soak the bread crumbs in ¼ cup of the white wine. Mash 3 cloves of the garlic and combine with the ground meats, softened crumbs, eggs, 3 tablespoons of the parsley, salt, and pepper. Form into cocktail-size meatballs.

Heat the oil in a large, shallow casserole. Sauté the meatballs until well browned on all sides. Remove to a warm platter. Add the onion and carrot to the casserole and sauté until the onion is wilted (add more oil if necessary). Stir in the remaining cup of white wine and the remaining 10 cloves of garlic and boil until most of the liquid has evaporated.

Meanwhile, in a processor or blender grind the almonds as finely as possible. Pour in the beef broth very gradually. Transfer this mixture to the casserole and add the meatballs, peas, the remaining 2 tablespoons of parsley, the bay leaf, scallions, and salt and pepper if needed. Cover and cook slowly for 45 minutes. [May be prepared ahead]

Home-Style Meatballs

(ALBÓNDIGAS CASERAS)

Here is another tasty meatball recipe, with plenty of garlic and nutmeg, that comes by way of the excellent Tritón bar/restaurant in Barcelona, which, except for these meatballs, serves seafood almost exclusively. SERVES 6-8

1/2 pound ground beef
1 pound ground veal
1/2 pound ground pork
3/4 cup bread crumbs
5 cloves garlic, minced
2 eggs
1/2 teaspoon ground nutmeg
2 teaspoons salt
3/4 teaspoon freshly ground pepper
Flour for dusting

3 tablespoons olive oil
1 medium onion, coarsely chopped
1 green pepper, cut in strips
1 small tomato, skinned and
  coarsely chopped
1/2 cup dry white wine
3/4 cup chicken broth
Salt
Freshly ground pepper

In a bowl combine the ground beef, veal, and pork with the bread crumbs, 4 cloves of the garlic, the eggs, nutmeg, salt, and pepper. Form into cocktail-size meatballs. Dust with flour.

Heat the oil in a large casserole. Sauté the meatballs until well browned on all sides. Add the onion, the remaining clove of garlic, and the green pepper and cook until the onion is wilted. Add the tomato, wine, broth, salt, and pepper. Cover and simmer for 45 minutes. [May be prepared ahead]

Veal Meatballs in Spicy Chorizo Sauce

(ALBÓNDIGAS EN SALSA DE CABRILLAS)

Bar Casa Ruperto, in the Triana section of Sevilla across the Guadalquivir River, is an unprepossessing bar, yet its tapas are quite extraordinary. Owner Ruperto Blanco has devised an intriguing sauce ("All our cooking here is pure artisanship!") that includes *chorizo*, blood sausage, coriander, and cumin. He serves it with snails, but also uses similar ingredients as a marinade for pork (see p. 135) and quail (see p. 184). I have used the sauce here to flavor meatballs, and it also works exceptionally well with scallops (see variation below). SERVES 6

1 tablespoon olive oil
1 small chorizo sausage (2 ounces),
   skinned and minced
2 ounces morcilla (blood sausage) (see
   p. 204), skinned and minced
2 cloves garlic, minced
1 small tomato (4 ounces), skinned
   and chopped
1 pimiento, home prepared (see p. 204)
   or imported, chopped
1 teaspoon crushed coriander seed
1/2 teaspoon freshly
   crushed cumin seed
1/4 teaspoon paprika,
   preferably Spanish style
1/2 dried red chili pepper, crumbled,
   or 1/4 teaspoon crushed red pepper

MEATBALLS
1 pound ground veal
4 tablespoons dry white wine
1 egg, lightly beaten
3 tablespoons bread crumbs

1 clove garlic, minced
1 tablespoon minced parsley
Salt
Freshly ground pepper
2 tablespoons olive oil
4 tablespoons chicken broth

To make the sauce, heat the oil and sauté the *chorizo* and *morcilla* slowly for a minute or two. Stir in the garlic, then add the tomato, pimiento, coriander, cumin, paprika, and chili pepper. Cover and simmer for 5 minutes. Transfer to a processor and blend until as smooth as possible. With the motor running, thin gradually with 2 tablespoons or more water to a sauce consistency.

To make the meatballs, combine the veal with 1 tablespoon of the white wine, the egg, bread crumbs, garlic, parsley, salt, and pepper. Form into small balls (about 1¼ inches). Heat the oil in a skillet and brown the meatballs well on all sides. Add the prepared sauce, the remaining 3 tablespoons of wine, and the chicken broth. Cover and simmer for 45 minutes, thinning with more chicken broth or water if necessary. [May be prepared ahead]

VARIATION
In a saucepan combine ½ cup of the prepared sauce with ½ pound scallops. Simmer for a few minutes until the scallops are done.

Tiny Meatballs in Saffron Sauce

(ALBONDIGUITAS AL AZAFRÁN)

These tiny meatballs in a wonderful sauce of saffron with a last-minute punch of garlic will surely enhance a tapas party. SERVES 5-6

½ pound ground veal
½ pound ground pork
1 slice bacon, ground or very
   finely chopped
2 cloves garlic, minced
2 tablespoons minced parsley
3 tablespoons minced lettuce
   (white rib portion only)
1 egg, lightly beaten
1 slice bread, crusts removed, soaked
   in milk or water and squeezed dry
About 1½ teaspoons coarse salt
Freshly ground pepper
Flour for dusting
2 tablespoons olive oil
2 tablespoons minced onion
1 teaspoon flour
¼ teaspoon paprika,
   preferably Spanish style
½ cup veal broth, or a mixture
   of chicken and beef broth
2 tablespoons white wine
Several strands saffron
Minced parsley for garnish

In a bowl mix together lightly the veal, pork, bacon, half of the garlic, 1 tablespoon of the parsley, the lettuce, egg, bread, salt, and pepper. Form into very small balls, not larger than 1 inch. Dust with flour.

Heat the oil in a shallow casserole large enough for all the meatballs. Brown the meatballs well on all sides. Add the onion and sauté until it is wilted. Sprinkle in the teaspoon of flour and the paprika and cook for a minute. Stir in the broth and wine, bring to a boil, cover, and simmer for 40 minutes.

Meanwhile, mash together in a mortar the remaining minced garlic, the remaining tablespoon of parsley, the saffron, and a little salt. Stir this mixture into the meatballs, sprinkle with parsley, and serve.

These meatballs can be made several hours or a day in advance and reheated. I suggest, however, adding the saffron mixture just before serving.

Lamb Meatballs in Brandy Sauce

(ALBÓNDIGAS "SANT CLIMENT")

I discovered these delicious meatballs some years ago in Tahull, a charming village high in the Pyrenees, and have yet to find another meatball quite so unusual, so I am repeating them in this book. SERVES 8–10

> 1 pound ground lamb (see Note)
> 1 egg
> 2 cloves garlic, mashed to a paste
>   or put through a garlic press
> 2 tablespoons chopped parsley
> Salt
> 1 tablespoon coarsely ground pepper
> 1/2 cup bread crumbs
> 2 tablespoons dry red wine
> 1 tablespoon olive oil
> 1 small onion, chopped
> 2 tablespoons brandy, preferably
>   Spanish brandy or Cognac
> 4 1/2 teaspoons tomato sauce
> 1/2 cup beef or lamb broth (see Note)

Combine the ground lamb, egg, garlic, parsley, salt, and pepper. In a separate bowl, soften the bread crumbs in the wine, then add the crumbs to the meat mixture. Mix well. Form into about 30 bite-size meatballs. Heat the oil in a large casserole and brown the meatballs on all sides. Add the onion and continue cooking until it is wilted. Pour in the brandy. Staying well away from the pan, ignite the liquid and stir until the flames subside. Add the tomato sauce and the broth. Salt to taste. Cover and cook slowly for 45 minutes. [May be prepared ahead]

NOTE: If you have the lamb ground, or grind it yourself, keep the bones and use them to make the broth (seasoned with salt and pepper).

Pork Ribs in Garlic Sauce

(COSTILLAS AL AJILLO)

A typical Spanish garlic sauce is great for tapas-size ribs. SERVES 4

> 3 tablespoons olive oil
> 1 3/4 pounds pork spare ribs,
>   smallest available, cut into individual
>   ribs and each rib cut crosswise into
>   1 1/2–2-inch pieces
> 1/2 cup chicken broth
> 1 bay leaf
> 1 large clove garlic, peeled
> 1 tablespoon minced parsley
> Salt
> Freshly ground pepper

Heat the oil in a deep casserole and brown the ribs well. Add the broth and bay leaf, cover, and simmer for 45 minutes. Uncover and boil away most of the broth. Skim off part of the fat, leaving about 2 tablespoons in the sauce.

In a mortar mash together the garlic, parsley, salt, and pepper. Stir into the ribs, cover, and let sit for a minute before serving. You can prepare the ribs in advance, but do not add the mortar mixture until the last minute.

Pork Ribs in Paprika Sauce

(COSTILLAS BAR BAHÍA)

There is a small, unprepossessing bar, Bar Bahía, on Cádiz's waterfront, where the city's residents know they can find excellent tapas and fine company. Salvador, the bar's lively owner, seems to spend as much time in front of the counter, joking with his customers, as behind the counter, tending to his simmering pots. But when a guest comes from New York, his enthusiasm knows no bounds, and drinks and tapas are often on the house ("We don't have a cent in Cádiz, but what the hell!"). Here is Salvador's recipe for tasty ribs, Cádiz style. SERVES 4

1 tablespoon olive oil
1³/4 pounds lean pork spare ribs,
    smallest available, cut into individual
    ribs and each rib cut crosswise into
    1¹/2–2-inch pieces
Freshly ground pepper
2 teaspoons oregano
2 teaspoons paprika,
    preferably Spanish style
1 bay leaf
1 cup dry white wine
8 cloves garlic, peeled and crushed
Salt
1 cup water

Combine all ingredients except salt and water in a deep cooking casserole. Marinate 1 hour. Add the salt and water, bring to a boil, then lower the heat and cook slowly, covered, for 1 hour or until the ribs are tender. Uncover and boil down the liquid until just a small amount remains to coat the ribs.

Oxtail Stew, Cádiz Style

(RABO DE TORO ESTILO GADITANO)

Here is another dish that I certainly never imagined as a tapa, but it was served as such at El Callejón, a bar in Cádiz where scenes of bullfighting dominate the decor. The owner's wife, Isabel Cantos, is in charge of the kitchen, and she is one of those brilliant, unheralded cooks whom one sometimes finds in the most unexpected places. Her version of oxtail stew, light and exquisitely flavored, is the best I've ever eaten, and very simple to prepare. Don't be put off by the large amount of garlic—the long cooking gives it a very mellow flavor. SERVES 6-8

2 pounds small oxtail
1 head garlic, separated and peeled
1 small onion, peeled
1 bay leaf
1 clove
Salt
Freshly ground pepper
¹/2 cup dry white wine
¹/4 cup olive oil
1 cup water
1 cup chicken broth

Combine all ingredients in a stew pot, bring to a boil, cover, and simmer until the meat is extremely tender, about 3¹/2–4 hours.

Pour the stew into a strainer, returning the broth and meat to the cooking pot. Discard the bay leaf and clove. In a processor or blender purée the garlic and onion. Beat in about ³/4 cup of the broth gradually, then stir this mixture into the pot. Cover and cook 20 minutes more. [May be prepared ahead]

Stuffed Pork Loin

(CARNE MECHADA)

Isabel Cantos in Cádiz (see p. 37) insisted that we taste her outstanding stewed pork loin, stuffed with egg, carrot, pimiento, and *chorizo*. As she cut slices, revealing the appetizing filling, and spooned on the sauce, her husband remarked, "Serve this in New York and people will certainly die of pleasure!"

SERVES 4–6

START PREPARATION ONE DAY IN ADVANCE

¾ pound pork loin
3 thin slices chorizo sausage
1 hard-boiled egg, cut in half lengthwise
A long, thin, cooked carrot, the length
    of the meat
2 strips pimiento, home prepared
    (see p. 204) or imported
3 cloves garlic, peeled
1 slice onion
1 small bay leaf
1 clove
¼ cup dry white wine
1 tablespoon olive oil
½ cup water
½ cup chicken broth
Salt

MARINADE
3 tablespoons olive oil
1 large clove garlic, minced
½ teaspoon crushed
    coriander seed
½ teaspoon freshly crushed
    cumin seed
½ teaspoon paprika,
    preferably Spanish style
½ dried red chili pepper,
    seeded and crumbled, or ¼ teaspoon
    crushed red pepper

Butterfly the pork loin, splitting lengthwise just far enough so that the meat opens up into one flat piece. Pound lightly to flatten a little more. In a small, shallow bowl just big enough to hold the meat, mix together the marinade ingredients. Add the meat and turn to coat on both sides with the marinade. Cover and refrigerate overnight, turning the meat occasionally.

Place the meat cut side up on a work surface. Arrange the *chorizo* slices in a row down the center of the meat. Place the egg halves over the *chorizo*, trimming the ends if the egg extends beyond the meat. Split the carrot lengthwise and put a piece on each side of the egg, then arrange the pimiento strips on top. Close the meat and sew together with a large needle and heavy thread or string, sewing up the ends as well.

In a deep casserole combine the garlic, onion, bay leaf, clove, wine, oil, water, broth, and salt. Add the meat, bring to a boil, cover, and simmer for 1¾ hours. Remove the meat to a warm platter, boil the sauce down to half, and return the meat to the casserole. [May be prepared ahead] To serve, cut in ⅜–½-inch slices and pour on some sauce. This is also good at room temperature.

Sausages with Sweet-Sour Figs

(SALCHICHAS CON HIGOS AGRI-DULCES)

It is rare to find a sweet-sour sauce in Spain today, even though centuries ago these sauces were fairly common. I tasted this sausage and fig combination at a former convent, now the beautiful *parador* Vía de la Plata in the city of Mérida. Mérida was once a Roman capital and still boasts an impressive aqueduct and one of the best-preserved Roman theaters in the world.

My guests at tapas parties praise this dish perhaps more than any other and always remember it as a highlight of a tapas evening. Fresh figs, when in season, work best for this tapa, but at other times of year I use bottled figs with excellent results. SERVES 8

PREPARE THE FIGS ONE DAY IN ADVANCE

1½ pounds sausage,
   preferably homemade (see
   pages 311–12 of THE FOODS AND WINES
   OF SPAIN), otherwise lean breakfast
   sausage or sweet Italian sausage
1 tablespoon olive oil
4 tablespoons white wine
2 teaspoons tomato sauce
Salt
Freshly ground pepper

SWEET-SOUR FIGS
1 cup sugar
1 cup red wine vinegar
1 stick cinnamon
4 cloves
1 slice lemon

1 pound fresh small figs,
   or 1 pound bottled figs
   in syrup, drained

To make the figs, combine the sugar, vinegar, cinnamon, cloves, and lemon slice in a saucepan. Bring to a boil, then simmer for 5 minutes. Add the figs, cover, and simmer for 20 minutes (for bottled figs, simmer for 5 minutes only). Cool the figs in the syrup and let them sit, covered, at room temperature overnight.

Cook the sausages in the oil and 2 tablespoons of the wine until the wine evaporates and the sausages are cooked and brown. Remove the sausages to a warm platter. Pour most of the fat from the pan. Deglaze the pan with 4 tablespoons water and the remaining 2 tablespoons of wine. Add the tomato sauce, salt, and pepper and simmer, uncovered, for 2 minutes.

Drain the figs (the syrup will not be used). Add them to the pan, along with the sausages. Cover and cook briefly until the figs are heated. To serve, cut each sausage into 3 or 4 slices. Cut the figs in halves or quarters, depending on their size. Spear pieces of sausage and fig on toothpicks and transfer them with the sauce to a serving casserole, preferably Spanish earthenware. The tapa can be assembled in advance and reheated, covered, when ready to serve.

Beef Tenderloin Tips in Garlic Sauce

(PUNTITAS DE SOLOMILLO AL AJILLO
"SOL Y SOMBRA")

A delightfully congenial Sevilla taxi driver, Miguel Ruz Abad, took us on a tapas tour of his city one steamy summer Sunday afternoon. It led us to his favorite tapas bars in the Triana section of Sevilla across the Guadalquivir River and to Sol y Sombra.

Sol y Sombra has an ambience so typically *andaluz* that the scene seemed more like a set from a theatrical production than the locale for a real bar. There was sawdust on the floor, flamenco music playing, bullfight memorabilia everywhere, cured hams and dried red peppers hanging from the ceiling, and even a client wearing an elegant Cordoban hat and sipping a glass of chilled *fino* sherry. We were treated like old friends and immediately presented with the house specialty: tender beef in garlic sauce with lots of good bread for dunking. This tapa can be prepared in about 5 minutes. SERVES 4

3 tablespoons fruity olive oil
8 cloves garlic, lightly crushed and peeled
3/4 pound beef tenderloin tips,
   in 1-inch cubes, or other cuts
   of beef used for steaks
Coarse salt
1 tablespoon dry (fino) Spanish sherry

Heat the oil in a skillet until very hot. Add the garlic and the meat cubes and stir fry over high heat until brown and done as desired. Sprinkle with salt, stir in the sherry, and transfer to a serving dish, preferably a large or individual Spanish earthenware *cazuelas*. Further deglaze the pan with several tablespoons of water, loosening the brown particles. Add this to the sauce and serve right away.

Veal Kidneys in Paprika Sauce

(RIÑONES EN SALSA DE PIMENTÓN)

It was late on a summer Sunday morning, and we were just wrapping up an exciting few days in the Picos de Europa, one of Spain's most majestic and awe-inspiring mountain ranges, only thirty miles from the Cantabrian Sea. Our last stop was at Posada de Valdeón, a tiny village dwarfed by a backdrop of soaring snowcapped peaks. The bar on the village square was noisy, bursting with villagers dressed in their Sunday best who were relaxing with friends and family over the first tapas and drinks of the day. Everyone was eating the same, compliments of the house: small oval dishes of the freshest kidneys I had ever tasted in a simple, spicy paprika sauce. SERVES 6

2 very fresh veal kidneys
   (about 1 1/2 pounds)
Juice of 1 lemon
Coarse salt
Freshly ground pepper
2 tablespoons olive oil
2 tablespoons chopped onion
2 tablespoons minced parsley
2 teaspoons flour (see Note)
1/4 cup chicken broth
2 tablespoons dry white wine
1 small bay leaf
1/2 teaspoon paprika,
   preferably Spanish style
1/2 dried red chili pepper,
   seeded, or 1/4 teaspoon
   crushed red pepper

Let the whole kidneys sit in the lemon juice for 10 minutes, then cut the kidneys into ¾-inch cubes, removing all fat and membrane. Run them under hot water and drain on paper towels. Sprinkle with salt and pepper.

Heat the oil in a shallow casserole. Quickly stir fry the kidneys to brown (they will cook more later) and remove to a warm platter. Add the onion and parsley to the pan and sauté slowly until the onion is softened. Stir in the flour, then pour in the broth and wine gradually and season with the bay leaf, paprika, chili pepper, salt, and pepper. Cook, stirring constantly, until thickened and smooth. [May be prepared ahead] Return the kidneys to the sauce, cover, and cook for about 5 minutes. The kidneys should be slightly pink within—do not overcook or they will toughen. Serve in the cooking dish, preferably Spanish earthenware.

NOTE: If you prefer a thin sauce, the flour can be eliminated.

Chicken Livers in Sherry Sauce
(HIGADILLOS AL JEREZ)

The addition of truffle, mushrooms, and green olives gives a special flavor and a touch of elegance to these chicken livers. SERVES 6

1 pound chicken livers
3 tablespoons butter
Salt
3 scallions, chopped
4½ teaspoons flour
¾ cup plus 3 tablespoons chicken broth
3 tablespoons dry (fino) Spanish sherry
Freshly ground pepper
1 tablespoon chopped truffle (optional)
6 medium mushrooms, halved or quartered
1 tablespoon minced green Spanish olives
1 tablespoon minced hard-boiled egg yolk
1 tablespoon minced parsley

Pick over the livers and cut in halves. Heat the butter in a shallow casserole and brown the livers quickly (they will cook a little more later). Remove to a warm platter and sprinkle with salt.

Sauté the scallions in the butter remaining in the casserole (add more if necessary) until they are softened. Stir in the flour, then add the chicken broth and sherry gradually, stirring constantly, until thickened and smooth. Add salt, pepper, the optional truffle, and mushrooms. Cover and simmer for 4 minutes. [May be prepared ahead]

Return the livers to the sauce and cook for a couple of minutes. Sprinkle with the olives, egg yolk, and parsley and serve right away.

Calves' Liver in Almond Sauce

(HÍGADO DE TERNERA EN SALSA DE ALMENDRA)

Almonds, saffron, and garlic are the ideal complement to the rich taste of liver, and this is one of my favorite preparations. The recipe is simple—the trick is to take special care not to overcook the liver.
SERVES 4

9 blanched almonds
2 cloves garlic, minced
Few strands saffron
½ pound calves' liver fillets,
    cut in 1½-inch pieces
Salt
Freshly ground pepper
Flour for dusting
2 tablespoons olive oil
1 teaspoon flour
½ cup veal broth, or a
    mixture of chicken and beef broth
1 tablespoon minced parsley

In a processor or blender grind the almonds, 1 clove of the garlic, and the saffron. With the motor running, add 1 tablespoon water and continue blending until as smooth as possible. Reserve. [May be prepared ahead]

Sprinkle the liver with salt and pepper. Dust with flour. Heat the oil in a skillet. Brown the liver quickly over very high heat (the liver should not be completely cooked). Remove to a warm casserole, preferably earthenware. To the oil remaining in the skillet (add a little more if necessary) add the remaining clove of garlic, then the flour. Cook for a minute, then stir in the broth. Season with salt and pepper to taste and cook until thickened and smooth. [May be prepared ahead]

Add the mixture from the processor, cover, and cook for 5 minutes. Pour this sauce over the liver, heat very briefly on top of the stove, sprinkle with parsley, and serve.

Chickpeas and Tripe, Cádiz Style

(MENUDO GADITANO)

Yes, this *is* a tapa, served to me as such in Cádiz, even though in larger portions it becomes a hearty cold-weather meal. Tripe and chickpeas are a great combination, and although the cooking time is long, the dish can be made days in advance. SERVES 12

START PREPARATION ONE DAY IN ADVANCE

½ pound dried chickpeas
2 pounds beef tripe, preferably a
   combination of the smooth and
   honeycombed kinds
1 pig's foot, split in half
1 ham or beef bone
1 onion, peeled and halved
Salt
Freshly ground pepper
2 tablespoons olive oil
1 medium onion, chopped
8 cloves garlic, minced
1 chorizo sausage (about 2 ounces),
   skinned and chopped
¼ pound cured ham, chopped
2 teaspoons paprika, preferably
   Spanish style
2 bay leaves
2 tablespoons minced parsley
1 teaspoon chopped fresh mint leaves,
   or ¼ teaspoon dried
¼ teaspoon freshly ground nutmeg
1 dried red chili pepper, seeded, or
   ½ teaspoon crushed red pepper

Soak the chickpeas overnight in cold water to cover.

Place the tripe in a large pot and cover with water. Bring to a boil and drain the tripe right away. Cut into 1-inch pieces and return to the pot with the pig's foot (preferably enclosed in a net bag or cheesecloth so the small bones will not mix into the stew), the ham or beef bone, an onion half, salt, pepper, and water to cover. Bring to a boil, cover, and simmer for 3 hours.

Drain the chickpeas and place in another pot with water to cover, the other onion half, and salt. Bring to a boil, cover, and simmer for 2 hours, cooking the tripe for another 2 hours as well. Meanwhile, in a skillet heat the oil and sauté the chopped onion and garlic until the onion is wilted. Add the *chorizo* and ham and sauté for a minute until the *chorizo* begins to give off its oil. Stir in the paprika and turn off the heat.

Uncover the tripe and boil down until the liquid is slightly thickened. Discard the onion and bone. Bone the pig's foot and chop its meat, returning the meat to the pot. Drain the chickpeas, discarding the onion. Combine the chickpeas with the tripe, stir in the onion-meat mixture from the skillet, and add the bay leaves, parsley, mint, nutmeg, and chili pepper. Taste for salt and pepper. Cover and cook 2 hours more, or until the tripe is extremely tender. Uncover and cook down the sauce some more if it is still too soupy. [May be prepared ahead]

2

MARINADES, PÂTÉS, SALADS, AND OTHER COLD TAPAS

By the very nature of this chapter, the tapas are almost all made in advance, often days before they will be needed. A cold tapa—or I would prefer to say room-temperature tapa, for most are best when not chilled—is a necessary and refreshing contrast to tapas in sauce, or tapas that are baked, grilled, or fried. Do be careful, however, not to serve too many marinades, for although they are exceptionally appealing, especially in warm weather, an excess of them will quickly dull the appetite. Vegetables and seafood (especially shellfish) lend themselves particularly well to dressings like vinaigrette and mayonnaise and are therefore an important part of this chapter. The pâtés, of course, fall into a separate grouping, and although usually made with meat, can be based on vegetables or seafood as well.

When serving cold tapas be sure your seafood is tender and succulent (if overcooked it will be tasteless and unpleasantly dry) and your vegetables lightly cooked (or uncooked), crisp, and brightly colored.

Mayonnaise

(MAYONESA)

So simple, yet so superior to anything you can buy in a jar. MAKES ABOUT 1¼ CUPS

    1 egg plus 1 yolk
    ¼ teaspoon Dijon-style mustard
    1 teaspoon salt
    2 tablespoons fresh lemon juice
    1 cup olive oil, or a mixture of olive
        and another vegetable oil

Place in the bowl of a blender or processor the whole egg, egg yolk, mustard, salt, and lemon juice. Blend for a few seconds. With the motor running, pour in the oil very gradually and continue beating until thickened and silky.

Green Olives, Sevilla Style

(ACEITUNAS A LA SEVILLANA)

One Spanish writer calls this marinade "ingenious and Baroque," and, I might add, typically Andalucian. One whiff of these spicy olives leaves little doubt of their Arab origins.

PREPARE SEVERAL DAYS IN ADVANCE

    A 7-ounce jar large green Spanish
        olives, lightly crushed
    ½ teaspoon ground cumin
    ½ teaspoon oregano
    ¼ teaspoon crushed rosemary
    ½ teaspoon thyme
    2 bay leaves
    ½ teaspoon fennel seed
    4 cloves garlic, lightly crushed
        and peeled
    4 tablespoons vinegar
    4 anchovy fillets (optional)

Place the olives in a glass jar in which they just fit. Add all other ingredients, then fill the jar with water. Shake well and marinate at room temperature for several days. They will keep for weeks in the refrigerator, but do bring them to room temperature before serving.

Thyme-Scented Green Olives
(ACEITUNAS AL TOMILLO)

These olives, found in a small bar in the town of the "hanging houses"—Cuenca (see p. 129)—are characterized by the large amount of thyme that seasons them.

PREPARE SEVERAL DAYS IN ADVANCE

A 7-ounce jar large green
    Spanish olives
1/4 cup olive oil
2 cloves garlic, lightly crushed
    and peeled
1 tablespoon thyme

Crush the olives lightly—this can be done by hitting them with the flat side of a broad knife.

Combine all ingredients in a glass jar. Cover tightly and shake to mix. Keep at room temperature for 24 hours, then refrigerate for at least a few days. The olives will keep for many weeks. Bring to room temperature to serve.

Pickled Cucumbers
(PEPINILLOS EN VINAGRE)

Spicy pickled cucumbers are exactly what is needed to complement cheese puffs (see p. 151), or they can be used to accompany a variety of other tapas.

PREPARE SEVERAL HOURS IN ADVANCE

2 kirby cucumbers or
    1 medium cucumber, peeled
    and quartered lengthwise
Coarse salt
Tarragon vinegar
Water
4 peppercorns, crushed
1/2 teaspoon fennel seed
1 clove
1 small bay leaf
1/2 small onion, slivered
1 clove garlic, peeled and halved

Sprinkle the cucumber quarters with coarse salt and leave in a colander to drain for 1 hour. Cut each quarter into 1-inch chunks. Place in a glass jar and cover with vinegar and water, in the proportion of 1 part vinegar to 2 parts water. Season with salt, peppercorns, fennel seed, clove, and bay leaf. Add the onion and garlic, cover, and refrigerate for at least several hours or better still several days. (The cucumbers will keep for months in the refrigerator.)

Onion Marmalade

(MERMELADA DE CEBOLLA)

The flavor of sweet fruit preserves combined with the tartness of onion and the piquancy of crushed peppercorns makes this sauce an exceptional accompaniment for meat pâtés. Try it with Pâté with Turkey Breast (p. 95), Duck and Cured Ham Pâté (p. 96), or Partridge and Liver Pâté (p. 97). MAKES ABOUT 1¼ CUPS

1 small onion, peeled
1 small orange
2 tablespoons raisins
2 large pitted prunes
1 teaspoon minced shallots
3 tablespoons medium-dry (amontillado) Spanish sherry
½ teaspoon grated lemon rind
1 teaspoon fresh lemon juice
1 cup good-quality red currant preserves or jelly
1 teaspoon crushed white peppercorns
3 tablespoons finely chopped pine nuts
¼ teaspoon Dijon-style mustard

Cut the onion in quarters lengthwise and soak in salted water for 1 hour. Cut half the orange rind in julienne strips. Squeeze and reserve 2 tablespoons orange juice.

In a small saucepan combine the raisins, prunes, shallots, sherry, the julienne strips of orange rind, the reserved orange juice, the lemon rind, and lemon juice. Bring to a boil, then simmer slowly, uncovered, for 20 minutes. Cool and coarsely chop the raisins, prunes, and julienne strips of orange rind. Reserve the cooking liquid.

Rinse and drain the onion, then mince. In a bowl combine the red currant preserves, minced onion, crushed peppercorns, pine nuts, and mustard. Stir in the chopped raisins, prunes, and orange rind and their cooking liquid. The sauce can be used right away or kept, refrigerated, for many days.

Olive and Pickle Relish

(CONDIMENTO)

This is a wonderful accompaniment to any fairly simple selection of tapas that are not marinated. Keep it in mind whenever you are preparing a large variety of tapas—it will take less than 5 minutes to prepare. SERVES 6

40 very small cured black olives
16 tiny pearl onions, bottled, or marinated in sherry vinegar (see p. 51)
8 small sweet gherkins, cut in quarters lengthwise
20 strips bottled marinated hot red peppers

Combine all ingredients. Since everything is already marinated, you may serve right away (cold or at room temperature) or store in the refrigerator.

Tomato, Tuna, and Egg Salad

(EL MOJE)

This salad, really more of a condiment since its ingredients are finely chopped, is typical of the town of Motilla del Palancar in the province of Cuenca. SERVES 6

    2 medium tomatoes, finely chopped
    2 tablespoons flaked light meat tuna
    2 hard-boiled eggs, coarsely chopped
    4 tablespoons slivered onion
    2 tablespoons diced pimiento,
        home prepared (see p. 204)
        or imported
    4 black olives, cut in pieces
    2 cloves garlic, minced
    1 tablespoon minced parsley
    2 tablespoons fruity olive oil
    4 teaspoons wine vinegar,
        preferably white
    2 tablespoons water
    Salt
    Freshly ground pepper

Mix together gently in a bowl the tomatoes, tuna, eggs, onion, pimiento, olives, garlic, and parsley. In a separate bowl whisk the oil, vinegar, water, salt, and pepper and fold into the tomato mixture. Chill.

Sweet and Sour Marinated Onions

(CEBOLLAS EN ADOBO)

These onions are cooked and marinated in a delicious, slightly sweet sauce that includes raisins. They go well with any sauceless tapa, like Marinated Pork Loin (p. 99) and Marinated Broiled Quail (p. 94). SERVES 4

    3½ tablespoons olive oil
    1 small onion, chopped
    1 clove garlic, minced
    1 medium tomato, skinned
        and chopped
    1 sprig parsley
    1 bay leaf
    ¼ teaspoon basil
    ¼ teaspoon thyme
    Salt
    Freshly ground pepper
    ½ pound pearl onions,
        not more than 1½ inches
        in diameter, peeled
    ¼ cup white wine vinegar
    2 tablespoons raisins
    1 tablespoon sugar

Heat 2 tablespoons of the oil in a small skillet and sauté the chopped onion and garlic until the onion is wilted. Add the tomato, sauté for a minute, then add the parsley, bay leaf, ⅛ teaspoon of the basil, ⅛ teaspoon of the thyme, salt, pepper, and 2 tablespoons water. Cover and simmer for 20 minutes.

Place the pearl onions in a saucepan with ½ cup water, the vinegar, the remaining 1½ tablespoons of oil, the tomato mixture, the remaining ⅛ teaspoon of basil, the remaining ⅛ teaspoon of thyme, the raisins, salt, pepper, and sugar. Bring to a boil, reduce to a simmer, and cook, uncovered, for 45 minutes. Cool and refrigerate. The onions will keep for many days in the refrigerator.

Pepper Salad, Cádiz Style

(ENSALADA DE PIMIENTOS A LA GADITANA)

In Andalucía, and particularly in the city of Cádiz, this refreshing finely chopped salad is served as a relish to accompany almost any kind of grilled or fried fish. SERVES 4

2 red peppers
3 green peppers
1 small onion, finely chopped
1 medium tomato, finely chopped
2 tablespoons olive oil
1 tablespoon red wine vinegar
Salt
Freshly ground pepper

Place the red and green peppers in an ungreased roasting pan and cook in a 375°F oven for 17 minutes. Turn the peppers and continue roasting for another 17 minutes. Skin, seed, and chop finely.

Combine the chopped peppers in a bowl with the onion, tomato, oil, vinegar, salt, and pepper. Refrigerate for 1 hour.

Pearl Onions in Sherry Vinegar

(CEBOLLETAS AL JEREZ)

Sherry vinegar, from Jerez in southern Spain, gives these onions their distinctive flavor. SERVES 4

1/4 pound pearl onions, smallest available, but not larger than 3/4 inch
1 cup water
4 teaspoons salt
2/3 cup sherry vinegar
1/2 dried red chili pepper, seeded, or 1/4 teaspoon crushed red pepper
4 peppercorns
1 bay leaf
2 cloves
1/8 teaspoon thyme

For easy peeling, plunge the onions into boiling water and cook for 1 minute, then rinse in cold water. Trim off the stems and slip off the papery skin. (If your onions are a little too large, you may remove some extra layers to reduce size.)

Soak the onions in the cup of water and the salt for at least 30 minutes (this takes away the onions' sting). Drain. In a saucepan bring the vinegar to a boil. Add the onions and simmer for 2 minutes. Add the chili pepper, peppercorns, bay leaf, cloves, and thyme. Cool, then transfer to a covered container and refrigerate until ready to use. These can be eaten within 30 minutes or kept for weeks.

Stuffed Pickles

(PEPINILLOS RELLENOS)

There is a famous bar in Madrid that has been around for over a century and is called, simply, Los Pepinillos—The Pickles. And pickles it has by the thousands, home cured in barrels that fill this charming bar with the most pleasant aromas of damp wood and vinegar. The pickles come in several degrees of hotness and are often combined with olives, pickled fish, anchovy, and red pepper to form *banderillas* (see pp. 52–54). Clients are forewarned by owner Eulogio of a pickle's hotness through his numbering system—#5 is the most fiery and not for those of timid tastes.

This tapa (not of the hot variety) is the one for which Los Pepinillos is best known. It is typically washed down with the bar's special golden vermouth mixed with seltzer. MAKES 1

> 2 anchovy fillets, or a ¼-inch-thick strip
> of pickled herring or Marinated Smelts
> (p. 88)
> 1 very small dill gherkin, split lengthwise

Place the anchovy or herring over half of the pickle. Cover with the other half and secure with a toothpick.

BANDERILLAS

Banderillas, tidbits of marinated fish, olives, vegetables, and the like skewered on toothpicks, are a separate class of tapa. Some tapas bars will have none, while others, especially in the north of Spain, specialize in them and serve nothing else. To determine the price of what you have eaten, the custom is to count up the empty toothpicks. In the past I have belittled the *banderilla* as an almost too simple tapa of little interest—just an easy way out. But recently I have become very fond of them because of their interesting blends of tastes and because they are colorful and can be put together in minutes from ingredients in your refrigerator.

The trick when eating *banderillas* is to put everything that is on the toothpick in your mouth at once (it is usually not as much as it appears to be) so that as you chew the taste of each ingredient comes forth and merges with the rest. By the way, *banderillas* are so called because of their resemblance to the colorful ornamented darts used in the bullring.

For *banderillas* we will use mostly canned or bottled ingredients, but if you have on hand anything homemade that is appropriate, by all means use it. I have substituted pickled herring for Boquerones en Vinagre (marinated raw smelts, or other similar small fish), which would be used in Spain. There is a recipe (p. 88), however, if you wish to make them.

You may of course put together your own version of *banderillas*. Here are a few commonly found in Spain. (Each recipe is for one *banderilla*.) Skewer them on the toothpicks from top to bottom in the order given. [May be prepared ahead]

Banderilla Dressing

(PICADA)

This "picada," a finely chopped mixture of parsley, garlic, pickle, and oil, can be dabbed on any of the *banderillas* and gives an interesting added zest. The recipe comes from Tito of Madrid's Bar Cascabel, which specializes only in *banderillas*.

MAKES ENOUGH TO DRESS ABOUT 20 *BANDERILLAS*

> 3 tablespoons finely minced parsley
> 3 cloves garlic, finely minced
> 3 tablespoons dill or cornichon pickle, finely minced
> 3 tablespoons olive oil

Place the minced parsley, garlic, and pickle in the bowl of a processor or blender. With the motor running, add the oil gradually. Blend until as smooth as possible.

Banderillas

1 1 pitted green Spanish olive, with or without pimiento
A 1-inch piece of pickled herring
1 piece of pimiento
A ½-inch-thick crosswise slice dill or cornichon pickle
A marinated pearl onion, bottled or homemade (p. 51)
1 rolled anchovy, with or without caper

2 1 pitted green Spanish olive, with or without pimiento
A ¼-inch-thick crosswise slice dill or cornichon pickle
1 piece of pimiento
A ¾-inch chunk solid white meat tuna

3 1 small mushroom, stem removed
1 rolled anchovy, with or without caper
A dab of mayonnaise
½ very small potato (or an equivalent piece of a larger potato), boiled, peeled, and trimmed on the bottom to sit flat
Banderilla Dressing (preceding recipe)

Top the *banderilla* with a dab of the dressing (while optional on the other *banderillas*, it is an important part of this one).

4 1 cooked shrimp, shelled
1 cooked asparagus tip, about 2 inches long
A dab of mayonnaise
½ small hard-boiled egg, cut crosswise, trimmed on the bottom to sit flat

5 1 piece of pimiento
1 pitted green Spanish olive, with or without pimiento
A dab of mayonnaise
¼ small hard-boiled egg, cut in a wedge
A ¾-inch chunk solid white meat tuna

6 1 rolled anchovy, with or without caper
1 pitted cured black olive
A dab of mayonnaise
½ small hard-boiled egg, cut crosswise, trimmed on the bottom to sit flat

7   A marinated pearl onion, bottled
     or homemade (p. 51)
     A ¼-inch slice dill or
     cornichon pickle
     A 1-inch piece of pickled herring
     ¼ marinated artichoke heart

8   1 pitted green Spanish olive,
     with or without pimiento
     A 1-inch piece of pickled herring
     1 rolled anchovy
     A 1-inch chunk solid white meat tuna

9   1 small boiled shrimp, shelled
     1 piece of sliced cured ham
     1 piece of sliced boiled ham
     1 piece of lettuce
     ½ small hard-boiled egg,
     cut crosswise, trimmed
     on the bottom to sit flat
     A dab of mayonnaise and
     a sprinkling of parsley
     for garnish

The following *banderilla* from Los Pepinillos bar (see p. 52) can be made as hot as you wish by marinating the ingredients in the liquid of the hot red peppers.

10   1 rolled anchovy
     A 1-inch piece of marinated herring or
     Marinated Smelts (p. 88)
     1 strip bottled marinated hot
     red pepper
     1 pitted green Spanish olive

Potato and Seafood Banderilla

(PINCHO DE PATATA, HUEVO, ATÚN Y GAMBA)

This *banderilla* is bathed in an onion and oil dressing and gains in flavor when left refrigerated overnight, well covered, so that the tastes of the different ingredients have a chance to blend. Bring to room temperature before serving. SERVES 4 (MAKES 8)

3 tablespoons olive oil
Salt
1 slice onion, separated into rings
2 small boiled potatoes (about ¼ pound),
peeled and in ¼-inch slices
(you will need 8 slices)
1 hard-boiled egg, sliced (about 8 slices)
Solid white meat tuna, divided
into eight ½-inch chunks
8 small shrimp, cooked (see p. 73),
cooled, and shelled
Eight ½-inch pieces onion,
two layers thick
Mayonnaise, preferably homemade (p. 47)
Minced parsley

Coat the bottom of a serving dish, just large enough to hold the 8 potato slices, with the oil. Sprinkle with salt and cover with the onion rings. Arrange the potato slices in the dish and cover each with a slice of egg and a chunk of tuna. Skewer on 8 toothpicks a shrimp, then a piece of onion (the shrimp should be on top). Attach this to the potato-egg-tuna layers. Dab with mayonnaise and sprinkle with parsley.

Egg and Tuna Wrapped in Ham

(PINCHO DE HUEVO Y ATÚN ENVUELTO EN JAMÓN)

The city of Logroño, in the heart of Rioja wine country, has a very old, very narrow pedestrian street called Calle del Laurel, and it is *the* tapas street in the city. Every doorway is another bar, and at peak tapas hours the bars, as well as the street, are shoulder to shoulder with people. This is one of Logroño's tapas, a variation of a *banderilla*, that I found particularly attractive. SERVES 2–4 (MAKES 4)

2 small hard-boiled eggs
2 teaspoons mayonnaise, preferably
  homemade (p. 47)
4 teaspoons Marinated Tuna (p. 93)
1 large, thin slice boiled ham, cut in
  4 long strips
1 teaspoon minced parsley

Cut the eggs in halves crosswise and trim the ends so that the halves sit flat. Top each half with ½ teaspoon of the mayonnaise, then with 1 teaspoon of the tuna. Wrap a strip of ham around the sides of the egg, covering the white. Secure the seam of the ham with a toothpick. Sprinkle with parsley. [May be prepared ahead]

Manchego Cheese with Quince Preserves

(QUESO MANCHEGO CON MEMBRILLO)

Cheese with quince preserves is actually served as a dessert in Spain (the ideal end to a roast baby lamb dinner, for example), but I suspected the combination was tart enough to be a tapa, and so I served it as such at a recent tapas affair at my home. It was the hit of the evening, and I could not replenish the platter fast enough.

Quince is a relative of the apple and is the ideal complement to a sharp cheese. It is quite easy to find as a preserve, but better for a tapa when in paste form, because it can be sliced. The *membrillo* paste may be found in Spanish specialty shops. Spanish cheeses, until recently unavailable in the United States, are now here in several delicious varieties (see p. 203). Manchego cheese, made from sheep's milk, is perfect for this tapa, although some other well-cured cheese, like an Italian "table" cheese or a well-cured French sheep's milk cheese, also works well. SERVES 6

Two ¼-pound wedges well-cured Manchego
  cheese, or some other well-cured cheese
½ pound quince paste (membrillo)
  or quince marmalade

Trim the rind from each cheese wedge. Place the wedge on its side and slice into ¼-inch-thick triangles. Slice the *membrillo* paste into the same size triangles in the same manner and place on top of the cheese. (If using quince marmalade, spread it over the cheese.) [May be prepared ahead] Serve at room temperature.

Smoked Fish on Avocado Rounds

(AGUACATE CON PESCADO AHUMADO)

Sophisticated and attractive tapas need not be complicated, as illustrated by this appetizer, which is simplicity itself. I tasted it at El Faro in Cádiz, a restaurant where owner Gonzalo Córdoba is always looking for a creative new touch to complement his extraordinary seafood. You can put this tapa together in a matter of minutes. SERVES 4-6 (MAKES 12)

> 1 small avocado
> Mayonnaise, preferably homemade
>   (p. 47)
> 2 ounces smoked fish, such as salmon
> Parsley for garnish

Beginning at each end of the avocado, make as many 1/8-inch slices as you can before reaching the pit. With a 1½–1¾-inch cookie cutter, preferably with a scalloped edge, cut rounds from the center of the avocado slices. Dab each with about ½ teaspoon mayonnaise and place a piece of smoked fish, about the size of the avocado round, on top. Garnish with parsley.

NOTE: You can double the number of appetizers by cutting slices from the sides of the avocado and by using irregularly shaped pieces from the center portion. If you choose to do this, you will need another 2 ounces of smoked fish.

Endives Filled with Salmon

(ENDIVIAS CON SALMÓN)

This is an extremely simple and elegant tapa that was part of a tasting menu at one of Spain's most charming restaurants, El Molino, just outside of Santander. The décor at El Molino is an eclectic mixture of antiques and personal memorabilia, which exuberantly spill over into every niche and corner of this delightfully rustic stone house. SERVES 4-6 (MAKES 12)

> 2 ounces smoked salmon
> 12 small endive leaves
> 3 tablespoons olive oil
> 1 tablespoon fresh lemon juice
> Salt
> Freshly ground pepper,
>   preferably white

Place a piece of salmon in each of the endive leaves. In a small bowl whisk the oil, lemon juice, salt, and pepper and pour over the filled endive leaves. Serve immediately or keep chilled for a short while until ready to serve.

Pimientos in Vinaigrette

(PIMIENTOS EN VINAGRE)

These cooling and delicious peppers go well with almost any tapas assortment. They can be served right away, but gain in flavor if left overnight. SERVES 4

3 red peppers

DRESSING
1/2 teaspoon paprika,
   preferably Spanish style
1 tablespoon water
3 tablespoons olive oil
2 tablespoons red wine vinegar
Salt
Freshly ground pepper
1/8 teaspoon thyme
1 clove garlic, sliced
1 teaspoon minced parsley
1 bay leaf
1 tablespoon slivered onion

Roast the peppers and skin, core, and seed according to the instructions for pimiento on page 204. Cut in strips 1/2 inch wide.

To make the dressing, in a small bowl dissolve the paprika in the tablespoon of water. Whisk in the oil, vinegar, salt, pepper, and thyme, then stir in the garlic, parsley, bay leaf, and onion. Add the pimiento strips and marinate, refrigerated, until ready to use.

Pimiento and Dried Cod Salad

(ENSALADA DE PIMIENTOS Y BACALAO)

This dish of pimiento and cod in a tomato sauce (served at room temperature) was one of a very appealing selection of tapas at Venta L'Home (see p. 195). SERVES 6

START PREPARATION ONE DAY IN ADVANCE

1/4 pound dried salt cod
   (see p. 204)
4 red peppers
Tomato Sauce (p. 150)

Soak the cod for 24–36 hours at room temperature in cold water, changing the water occasionally.

Roast, skin, core, and seed the peppers according to the instructions for pimiento on page 204. Cut into 1/2-inch-wide strips.

Drain the cod and place it in a pot with water to cover. Bring to a boil, then remove from the heat and drain. Flake with your fingers. Combine the Tomato Sauce, flaked cod, and pimiento strips. Serve at room temperature or chilled. [May be prepared ahead]

Marinated Rice-Filled Pimientos

(CANUTILLOS DE PIMIENTOS CON ARROZ)

This is a wonderfully refreshing addition to any tapas spread. Use only short-grain rice (it will hold together better) and home-prepared pimientos (only they will have the fresh sweet taste needed here). SERVES 8

PREPARE ONE DAY IN ADVANCE

6 large red peppers
1/2 cup chicken broth
1/2 cup water
2 tablespoons butter
1/2 cup short-grain rice (see p. 204)
Salt
2 tablespoons fruity olive oil
2 scallions, finely chopped
1 small onion, finely chopped
1 clove garlic, minced
1 tablespoon minced parsley
1/4 teaspoon thyme
Freshly ground pepper
1 teaspoon fresh lemon juice
1 tablespoon chopped pine nuts
3 anchovy fillets, minced

DRESSING
6 tablespoons olive oil
3 tablespoons red wine vinegar
1/4 teaspoon Dijon-style mustard
Salt
Freshly ground pepper

Roast and peel the peppers according to the instructions for pimiento on page 204. Remove the stem and open carefully along one side and remove the seeds.

To make the rice, bring the chicken broth and water to a boil in a saucepan. Meanwhile, melt the butter in a small, deep casserole, stir in the rice, and let it absorb the butter. Pour in the hot broth and water, season with salt, cover, and bake at 400°F for 15 minutes. Remove from the oven and let sit for another 10 minutes, covered. Uncover and cool.

In a skillet heat 1 tablespoon of the oil and sauté the scallions, onion, and garlic slowly until the onion is wilted. Cover and continue cooking slowly until the onion is tender but not brown. Turn off the heat. Mix in the rice, parsley, thyme, salt, pepper, the remaining tablespoon of oil, lemon juice, pine nuts, and anchovy.

Cut each pepper in half lengthwise. Dry well. Place about 1 1/2 tablespoons of the rice mixture on each half and roll up. Arrange the rolled pimientos on a serving dish deep enough to hold the vinaigrette. Cut each roll carefully in half.

In a small bowl whisk together the Dressing ingredients. Pour over the pimientos, cover, and refrigerate overnight. Serve cold.

Green Pepper and Tomato Salad

(ENSALADA A LA VASCA)

Green olives give a touch of tartness to this tasty salad. SERVES 6-8

6 medium green peppers
Salt
4 small tomatoes, cubed
10 large cured green olives (such as Green Olives, Sevilla Style, p. 47), coarsely chopped
4 tablespoons fruity olive oil
2 tablespoons red wine vinegar

Roast the peppers and peel, core, and seed according to the instructions for pimiento on page 204.

Place the pepper strips on a platter and sprinkle with salt. Arrange the tomatoes on top and sprinkle on the chopped olives. Add a little more salt. Drizzle with the oil and vinegar when ready to serve.

Cumin-Flavored Mushroom Salad

(ENSALADA DE SETAS)

This is one of the most delicious mushroom salads I have ever eaten, combining wild and cultivated mushrooms, slivered red peppers, and a touch of cumin. The salad can be made in advance—the lemon juice keeps the mushrooms from turning dark—but don't keep for more than a couple of hours or the mushrooms will lose their crispness.
SERVES 4-6

**¼ pound cultivated mushrooms,
   stems trimmed, brushed clean
¼ pound wild mushrooms,
   such as puffballs or boletus (suitable for
   eating uncooked), stems trimmed,
   brushed clean (if unavailable,
   omit and double the amount of
   cultivated mushrooms)
½ fresh red pepper,
   in julienne strips**

DRESSING
**¼ cup fruity olive oil
2 tablespoons fresh lemon juice
1 clove garlic, mashed to a paste or
   put through a garlic press
1 tablespoon minced parsley**

**¼ teaspoon freshly
   ground cumin
Salt
Freshly ground pepper**

Leave the mushrooms whole if they are small; otherwise, cut in halves or quarters. Trim the light, fleshy interior from each of the red pepper strips. Combine in a bowl with the mushrooms. Whisk the dressing ingredients and fold gently into the mushrooms. Marinate for at least 1 hour and serve at room temperature or chilled.

Marinated Mushrooms

(CHAMPIÑONES EN ADOBO)

Rather than a marinade, these mushrooms are in *adobo*, which means the mushrooms—and the sauce —have first been cooked. I find these mushrooms especially appetizing and quite different from most marinated mushrooms. SERVES 4

PREPARE ONE DAY IN ADVANCE

2 tablespoons olive oil
3 tablespoons minced onion
1 clove garlic, minced
1 tablespoon tomato sauce
¼ cup dry white wine
¼ cup water
2 cloves
⅛ teaspoon saffron
Salt
Freshly ground pepper
½ pound very small mushrooms,
   stems removed, brushed clean

Heat the oil in a small, deep casserole. Add the onion and garlic and sauté until the onion is wilted. Stir in the tomato sauce, wine, water, cloves, saffron, salt, and pepper. Simmer, covered, for 45 minutes, adding more water if necessary.

Add the mushrooms to the cooking liquid and simmer 5 minutes more. Turn off the heat, cover, and let sit until cool. Refrigerate overnight. Serve cold or at room temperature.

Asparagus, Shrimp, and Mushroom Salad

(ENSALADA DE ESPÁRRAGO, GAMBA Y CHAMPIÑÓN)

Another creation from the talented young Madrid chef Tomás Herranz (see p. 173). SERVES 4

START PREPARATION TWO HOURS IN ADVANCE

¾ pound very thin green
   asparagus, ends snapped off
Chicken broth
12 very small shrimp or
   8 small-medium shrimp,
   unshelled
1 small tomato, diced
2 medium mushrooms, stems
   removed, brushed clean, sliced

DRESSING
2 tablespoons fruity olive oil
2 teaspoons fresh lemon juice
Salt
Freshly ground pepper
1 teaspoon minced parsley
⅛ teaspoon thyme

Bring the asparagus to a boil in a mixture of water and chicken broth, just barely to cover. Reduce the heat, cover, and simmer for about 5 minutes, or until the asparagus is just done. Do not overcook. Drain and cool. Bring the cooking liquid back to a boil, add the shrimp, and cook for a minute or two. Cool and shell.

To make the dressing, in a small bowl whisk the oil, lemon juice, salt, and pepper. Stir in the parsley and thyme. Place the asparagus and shrimp in a shallow bowl and mix gently with the dressing. Refrigerate for about 2 hours.

Arrange the asparagus attractively on individual dishes or on a serving platter. Place the shrimp on top, sprinkle with the tomato and mushroom, and drizzle on the dressing. Serve at room temperature.

Marinated Asparagus Wrapped in Ham

(ESPÁRRAGOS ALIÑADOS
ENVUELTOS EN JAMÓN)

Make sure you don't overcook the asparagus—the spears must be firm so that you can pick them up with your fingers. SERVES 6-8

1/2 pound thin asparagus, ends snapped off
Chicken broth
Salt
Dressing (p. 57), reducing the
   vinegar to 1 tablespoon
2 ounces boiled ham, very thinly sliced,
   in 1 1/4 × 3-inch strips

Place the asparagus in a skillet with a mixture of water and chicken broth just barely to cover. Bring to a boil, cover, and simmer for about 3–4 minutes—the asparagus should be tender but still crisp. Plunge into cold water to arrest further cooking. Drain well and arrange in a single layer in a shallow bowl. Sprinkle with salt.

Make the dressing and pour over the asparagus. Marinate, refrigerated, for several hours (but not overnight—the asparagus will lose its color). Remove the asparagus from the marinade and wrap a strip of the ham close to the stem end. Since the asparagus is marinated, you will want to pick it up at the point where the ham is wrapped around it.

Salad of Julienned Carrots

(ENSALADA DE ZANAHORIA O'MERLO)

Pontevedra, a Galician city of porticoed streets and intimate plazas, is slightly off the tourist track but well worth a visit to see its untouched Old Quarter, constructed from golden stone blocks, and to eat at one of the great tapas bars of Galicia, O'Merlo. Alfonso Merlo and his wife, Marisol, have just recently returned from a long sojourn in England to set up this bar in an old aristocratic stone house, which they lovingly restored. There are more than fifty tapas served at O'Merlo, in portions that are quite overwhelming.

This carrot salad is very simple and at first glance may not seem out of the ordinary. Notice, however, the large amount of vinegar in which the mayonnaise-coated carrots marinate, giving them a very special flavor. SERVES 4

PREPARE ONE DAY IN ADVANCE

3/4 cup mayonnaise,
   preferably homemade (p. 47)
2 tablespoons white wine vinegar
1/2 pound carrots
   (about 4 medium), scraped,
   ends trimmed, and cut in about
   2-inch-long julienne strips

In a small bowl mix until smooth the mayonnaise and vinegar. Place the carrots in a shallow bowl and fold in the mayonnaise mixture. Cover and refrigerate overnight.

Cumin-Flavored Carrot Salad

(ENSALADA DE ZANAHORIA BAR BAHÍA)

Here is a quite different carrot salad with Middle Eastern overtones—the carrots are lightly cooked and seasoned with garlic, oregano, and cumin. It comes from the exceptional Bar Bahía in Cádiz (see p. 37). SERVES 4

PREPARE SEVERAL HOURS IN ADVANCE

½ pound carrots (about 4 medium),
   scraped, ends trimmed
Chicken broth
Salt
2 tablespoons white wine vinegar
1½ tablespoons water
1 large clove garlic, mashed to a paste
   or put through a garlic press
¼ teaspoon oregano
¼ teaspoon freshly ground cumin
¼ teaspoon paprika, preferably
   Spanish style

Place the carrots in a saucepan with a mixture of water and chicken broth just barely to cover. Add a little salt. Bring to a boil, then cover and simmer for about 10 minutes (more or less depending on the thickness of the carrots), until just done but still slightly crisp. Cool and cut in ¼-inch slices.

In a cup mix together the vinegar, water, garlic, oregano, cumin, paprika, and salt. Fold gently into the carrots. Marinate for several hours or overnight.

Cauliflower Salad

(ENSALADA DE COLIFLOR)

A very refreshing—and very Spanish—way to prepare cauliflower. SERVES 6

START PREPARATION SEVERAL HOURS IN ADVANCE

1 small head cauliflower
2 teaspoons fresh lemon juice
3 tablespoons minced hard-boiled egg
1 tablespoon minced parsley

DRESSING
¼ cup olive oil
2 tablespoons red wine vinegar
1 clove garlic, mashed to a paste
   or put through a garlic press
1 tablespoon capers, preferably small
1 teaspoon paprika, preferably
   Spanish style
Dash of cayenne pepper
Salt

Cut off the thick stems of the cauliflower and break into small flowerets. Place in 1 inch boiling salted water to which the lemon juice has been added. Cover and simmer for about 10-12 minutes, or until just barely tender. Drain well. Cool. Trim off the stems very close to the flowerets.

Beat together lightly all the dressing ingredients. Pour over the cauliflower and mix with a rubber spatula until the dressing is absorbed. Add more salt if necessary. Marinate for several hours or overnight, sprinkle with the egg and parsley, and serve.

Cabbage, Green Pepper, and Raisin Salad

(ENSALADA DE REPOLLO)

A refreshing addition to any tapas menu. SERVES 8

PREPARE SEVERAL HOURS IN ADVANCE

1 pound green cabbage, shredded
2 medium carrots, scraped, in
   julienne strips
1 green pepper, in julienne strips
3 tablespoons raisins
4 tablespoons olive oil
2 tablespoons white wine vinegar
1½ teaspoons
   Dijon-style mustard
Salt
Freshly ground pepper

Combine the cabbage, carrot, green pepper, and raisins in a bowl. In a separate bowl whisk the oil, vinegar, mustard, salt, and ground pepper and fold into the cabbage mixture. Taste for salt, cover, and refrigerate for several hours.

Eggplant Salad

(ENSALADA DE BERENGENA)

Onion, eggplant, red pepper, and tomatoes are the main ingredients for this Catalán-style salad. SERVES 4-6

¼ pound large pearl onions, peeled
A 1-pound eggplant, cut in half
   lengthwise, stem removed
2 red peppers
¼ pound very ripe tomatoes
1 clove garlic, minced
1 tablespoon minced parsley
2 tablespoons olive oil
1 tablespoon red wine vinegar
¼ teaspoon Dijon-style mustard
Salt
Freshly ground pepper
Pinch sugar

Place the onions, eggplant halves (skin side up), and peppers in an ungreased roasting pan in a 375°F oven. Roast for 17 minutes, turn the peppers and onions, and continue roasting 17 minutes more.

Peel and seed the peppers. Peel the eggplant, removing some of the seeds. Chop the peppers, eggplant, onions (remove the outer skin if papery), and tomatoes in about ½-inch pieces. Combine gently in a bowl with the garlic and parsley.

In a small bowl beat together with a whisk the oil, vinegar, mustard, salt, pepper, and sugar. Mix gently into the vegetables. Chill and serve. The vegetables may be roasted in advance and the dressing mixed in advance. Do not combine, however, more than an hour before serving.

Anise-Flavored Beet Salad

(REMOLACHA AL ANÍS)

Beets are always a refreshing addition to a tapas menu, especially when flavored with a hint of anise. SERVES 4

2 medium fresh beets (about 1 pound), stems trimmed
6 tablespoons olive oil
3 tablespoons red wine vinegar
Salt
Freshly ground pepper
1 small onion, coarsely chopped
½ teaspoon crushed anise seeds

Cover the unpeeled beets with water, bring to a boil, then simmer, covered, for about 1 hour, or until tender. Peel, cool, and cut into ¾-inch slices. Cut each slice in quarters.

In a medium bowl beat together with a fork the oil, vinegar, salt, and pepper. Stir in the onion and anise, then mix in the beets gently. Cover and refrigerate until ready to serve. The salad gains in flavor when kept for several hours or days in the refrigerator.

Fresh Beets in Romesco Sauce

(REMOLACHA EN SALSA ROMESCO)

This tapa is a specialty of chef José María Llach at the wonderful Quo Vadis restaurant (see p. 182) in Barcelona. SERVES 6

3 medium fresh beets (about 1½ pounds), stems trimmed
½ recipe Romesco Sauce (p. 74), reducing the oil added at the end to 2 tablespoons and thinning with 4 tablespoons water
Minced parsley

Cook the beets according to the instructions in the preceding recipe. Peel, cool, and cut into 1-inch cubes. Combine with the *romesco* sauce and arrange in a serving dish. Sprinkle with parsley. The sauce and beets can be made in advance, but do not combine until close to serving time.

Vegetable Salad in Romesco Sauce

(ENSALADA EN SALSA ROMESCO)

Romesco sauce, made with dried sweet red peppers, garlic, and almonds, has many different uses in Cataluña—spread on toast as a canapé, as a sauce or dip for fish and shellfish (p. 74), with fresh beets (see preceding recipe), and here as an unusual dressing for a mixed vegetable salad.

SERVES 6-8

Romesco Sauce (p. 74), reducing the
    almonds to 5 and increasing the
    vinegar to 4½ tablespoons
1 medium-large potato, preferably red waxy
¼ pound green beans, cut in halves
1 medium zucchini (about 6 ounces), in
    ¼-inch slices, each slice cut in half
½ hard-boiled egg, sliced
4 thin slices onion
½ small cucumber, in ¼-inch slices,
    each slice cut in half
1 medium green tomato, in ¼-inch slices,
    each slice cut in half
10 small pitted green Spanish olives,
    with or without pimiento
½ pimiento, home prepared (p. 204)
    or imported, in strips
1 tablespoon minced parsley

Make the *romesco* sauce and let sit for 1 hour.

Place the potato in a saucepan with salted water to cover, bring to a boil, and cook for 15 minutes. Turn off the heat and let the potato sit in the hot water, covered, until tender. In a skillet barely cover the green beans and zucchini with salted water, and bring to a boil. Simmer until just tender but still a little crisp.

Arrange the vegetables in layers in a salad bowl or deep serving dish: first the potato, skinned, cut in ⅛-inch slices, and sprinkled with salt; then the green beans, zucchini, egg, onion, cucumber, tomato, olives, and pimiento. Pour the *romesco* sauce over the vegetables and sprinkle with the parsley. Let sit for at least 1 hour at room temperature or refrigerated before serving.

White Bean Salad

(ENSALADA DE JUDÍAS BLANCAS)

Here is a sprightly mix of tastes and colors. This bean salad works very well with good-quality canned beans (or chickpeas), rinsed, or prepare your own following the instructions for cooking chickpeas (see p. 43).

SERVES 4

PREPARE SEVERAL HOURS IN ADVANCE

¾ pound cooked white beans, or chickpeas
1 medium tomato, cubed
1 hard-boiled egg, sliced, each slice
    cut in half
4 pitted cured black olives, each
    cut in 4 pieces
1 tablespoon minced parsley
2 tablespoons fruity olive oil
1 tablespoon wine vinegar, preferably white
Salt
1 clove garlic, mashed to a paste or
    put through a garlic press

In a bowl combine gently the beans, tomato, egg, olives, and parsley. In a separate bowl whisk the oil, vinegar, salt, and garlic. Fold into the bean mixture and marinate in the refrigerator for several hours.

Vegetable Pâté

(PASTEL DE VERDURAS)

With the wave of "nouvelle" cuisine that has descended upon Spain, pâtés, such as this one of vegetables, have become standard fare in fashionable eating establishments. SERVES 8–10

½ pound small carrots, scraped, ends trimmed
¼ pound green beans, ends snapped off
6 very small leeks, well washed, green part trimmed
½ pound medium mushrooms, brushed clean
1¼ cups chicken broth
Salt
½ head cauliflower, stems trimmed, in small flowerets
½ cup plus 2 tablespoons heavy cream
5 eggs, lightly beaten
Freshly ground pepper
Butter
Bread crumbs

TOMATO SAUCE
1 tablespoon olive oil
1 small tomato, finely chopped

Cut the carrots, green beans, and leeks in half lengthwise. Separate the mushrooms into stems and caps. Cut the caps in halves. In a large skillet heat 1 cup of the chicken broth with 1½ cups water and salt. Bring to a boil, add the leeks and mushrooms, cover, and simmer until just tender, about 5 minutes. Remove, then add the carrots, green beans, and cauliflower to the broth and remove as they become tender, about 20–25 minutes. Drain and dry all the vegetables well.

To make the tomato sauce, in a small skillet heat the oil, then sauté the tomato over low heat for 2 or 3 minutes. Strain, pressing with the back of a wooden spoon to extract as much liquid as possible. Reserve 2 tablespoons of the purée and combine in a bowl with the cream and eggs. Season with salt and pepper and beat lightly with a fork.

Grease a 9¼ × 5¼ × 2¾-inch loaf pan well with butter. Sprinkle with bread crumbs. Arrange the vegetables lengthwise in the mold in the following order: first the carrots, cut side up (overlapping a little if necessary); then the cauliflower; green beans (lengthwise); and mushrooms. On top arrange the leeks in rows, changing direction so they will fit and trimming the green part as necessary. Pour on the cream mixture, tapping the mold so that the cream fills all the spaces between the vegetables.

Cover the loaf pan tightly with foil, place in a pan of boiling water (bain-marie), and bake at 350°F for 45 minutes. Loosen the foil to see if the custard has set. If there is still some liquid, continue cooking for another few minutes. Remove the loaf pan from the water, loosen the foil, and cool. Refrigerate till cold. Unmold and serve by cutting into slices.

Potato, Vegetable, and Tuna Salad
(ENSALADILLA RUSA)

A salad of potatoes, carrots, and peas, sometimes with additions of tuna and hard-boiled egg, all bathed in mayonnaise, is one of Spain's most popular and ever-present tapas. It is usually served as is, to be eaten with a fork, but it can also fill puff pastry (see p. 116) or tartlet shells. SERVES 6

1 pound red waxy potatoes
3 ounces light meat tuna, flaked
1½ teaspoons red wine vinegar
2 teaspoons grated onion
1 clove garlic, mashed to a paste or
    put through a garlic press
1 tablespoon minced parsley
1 teaspoon very small whole capers or
    chopped larger capers
2 tablespoons chopped dill or
    cornichon pickle
1 tablespoon diced pimiento,
    home prepared (see p. 204)
    or imported
2 hard-boiled eggs, coarsely chopped
3 tablespoons cooked peas
3 tablespoons chopped cooked carrots
Salt
½ cup mayonnaise, preferably
    homemade (p. 47)

Boil the potatoes in salted water until they are tender. Cool slightly, then peel and dice. In a bowl combine the tuna, vinegar, onion, garlic, parsley, capers, pickle, and pimiento. Add the potatoes, eggs, peas, and carrots. Salt to taste and let sit for about 30 minutes. Fold the mayonnaise gently into the potato mixture. Arrange in a smooth mound on a dish and decorate, if you wish, with strips of pimiento. [May be prepared ahead] If refrigerated, let sit at room temperature for a while before serving.

Potatoes in Garlic Mayonnaise
(PATATAS ALIOLI)

This is another very popular tapa at bars in Spain, of the kind that is often served compliments of the house when you order a drink. SERVES 4-6

¾ pound potatoes, preferably red waxy
½ cup mayonnaise, preferably
    homemade (p. 47)
3 cloves garlic, mashed to a paste or
    put through a garlic press
2 tablespoons minced parsley
Salt

Bring the potatoes to a boil in salted water (mixed with a little chicken broth, if you wish), cover, and simmer for 15 minutes. Turn off the heat and leave the potatoes in the water, covered, until the potatoes are tender, about 15 minutes. Peel and cut the potatoes into ¾-inch chunks.

In a bowl combine the mayonnaise, garlic, and parsley. The mayonnaise should be a little thin to combine smoothly with the potatoes—dilute with a little vinegar or fresh lemon juice if necessary. Fold in the potatoes gently, season with salt, and let sit for about 20 minutes at room temperature before serving. Or make ahead and refrigerate, then return to room temperature.

Potato Salad with Tuna and Egg

(PATATAS ALIÑADAS, BAR BAHÍA)

Bar Bahía in Cádiz (see p. 37) always has this lovely potato salad on hand. Chef Salvador serves it at room temperature, but it is also good chilled.
SERVES 4–6

3/4 pound all-purpose potatoes
Salt
1½ tablespoons white wine vinegar
3 tablespoons olive oil
Freshly ground pepper
1 tablespoon flaked light meat tuna
1 hard-boiled egg, sliced, each slice
   cut in half
½ small onion, slivered
1 tablespoon minced parsley
2 tablespoons diced tomato (optional)

Place the potatoes in salted water to cover, bring to a boil, cover, and cook for 10 minutes. Remove from the heat, keep covered, and let sit until the potatoes are tender, about 15 minutes. Peel and cut in 1/8-inch slices.

Whisk the vinegar, oil, salt, and pepper. Spread a thin coating of the dressing over the bottom of a deep serving dish. Arrange half of the potato slices on top, then sprinkle with salt, half of the tuna, half of the egg slices, half of the onion, and half of the dressing. Repeat for a second layer. Top with parsley and optional tomato and let sit (at room temperature or refrigerated, depending on how you are serving it) for at least 1 hour.

Potatoes with Capers and Dill

(PATATAS CON ALCAPARRAS Y ENELDO)

An interesting variation on potato salad (the dressing includes orange juice, capers, and fresh dill) and always a good addition to a tapas menu.
SERVES 6

3 medium potatoes (about 1½ pounds),
   preferably red waxy
½ cup olive oil
2 tablespoons fresh lemon juice
2 tablespoons orange juice
2 tablespoons minced onion
2 tablespoons minced parsley
1 tablespoon minced fresh dill
4 teaspoons small capers
Salt
Freshly ground pepper
Fresh dill for garnish

Boil the potatoes in their skins in salted water until tender. While the potatoes are cooking, make the dressing. In a small bowl mix together the oil, lemon juice, orange juice, onion, parsley, dill, capers, salt, and pepper. Let sit at room temperature.

Drain the potatoes, cool briefly, skin, then cut in slices about 1/8 inch thick. Arrange in layers in a serving dish, pouring some of the dressing over each layer and sprinkling with salt. Marinate for several hours at room temperature, carefully turning occasionally with a metal spatula. Serve at room temperature, decorated with a sprig of dill. [May be prepared ahead]

Salad of Tiny Potatoes and Tuna
(ENSALADA DE CACHELOS Y ATÚN)

Cachelos are the wonderfully fresh and delicious potatoes from Galicia, so important to the region's cuisine. SERVES 8

1 pound very small (about 1¼ inches)
   red waxy or new potatoes
Salt
½ cup flaked light meat tuna,
   preferably marinated (see p. 93)
3 tablespoons olive oil
4 teaspoons wine vinegar, preferably white
1 clove garlic, mashed to a paste or put
   through a garlic press
1 hard-boiled egg
2 tablespoons minced onion
3 tablespoons minced parsley
Cayenne pepper or hot pepper flakes to taste
2 tablespoons minced dill or
   cornichon pickle
8 small pimiento-stuffed green olives,
   cut in halves crosswise

Place the potatoes in salted water to cover, bring to a boil, and cook for 15 minutes. Turn off the heat and let sit, covered, for another 15 minutes, or until the potatoes are tender. Skin (or leave the skins on if you prefer) and cut in halves crosswise. Combine in a bowl with the tuna.

In a separate bowl whisk the oil, vinegar, salt, and garlic. Mash the egg yolk and finely chop the white. Stir into the dressing the onion, the mashed yolk, 2 tablespoons of the parsley, and the cayenne pepper. Fold gently into the potatoes. Transfer to a serving dish and sprinkle with the pickle, olives, the remaining tablespoon of parsley, and the chopped egg white. Serve at room temperature or chilled.

Potato Salad with Pickles and Capers
(PATATAS TÁRTARA)

An excellent variation on a mayonnaise potato salad from the O'Merlo tapas bar in Pontevedra (see p. 61). SERVES 4

PREPARE SEVERAL HOURS IN ADVANCE

1 pound potatoes, preferably new or
   red waxy
¾ cup mayonnaise, preferably homemade
   (p. 47)
1 tablespoon minced parsley
2 tablespoons finely chopped dill or
   cornichon pickle
1 teaspoon small whole capers or chopped
   large capers
¼ teaspoon tarragon
Salt

Place the potatoes in a saucepan with salted water to cover and boil for 10 minutes. Turn off the heat and let the potatoes sit in the hot water, covered, for 15–20 minutes, or until tender. Drain, peel, and cut in ½-inch cubes.

In a bowl combine the mayonnaise, parsley, pickle, capers, and tarragon. Fold in the potatoes gently and taste for salt. Refrigerate for several hours, then bring to room temperature before serving.

Rice Salad, Barcelona Style

(ENSALADA DE ARROZ A LA BARCELONESA)

Casa Tejada near the Turo Park in Barcelona has all the tapas you would expect from a first-rate tapas bar and then some—more than forty in all. It is extremely busy, catering mainly to a young crowd, and barmen deliver tapas at a furious pace. I particularly enjoyed their Garlic and Tomato Bread (p. 119), Shrimp in Garlic Sauce (p. 13), and this delicious rice salad, topped with a bit of mayonnaise.

SERVES 6-8

2 tablespoons olive oil
3 tablespoons minced onion
1 cup short-grain rice (see p. 204)
1 cup chicken broth
1 cup boiling water
Salt
1 sprig parsley
1/4 teaspoon thyme
1/8 teaspoon tarragon
2 tablespoons minced scallion
    (green part only)
3 tablespoons minced dill or
    cornichon pickle
2 tablespoons flaked light meat tuna
2 tablespoons minced green pepper
2 tablespoons minced raw carrot
1 tablespoon minced cucumber,
    preferably kirby
2 tablespoons minced romaine lettuce
    (white stem portion only)
2 tablespoons minced pimiento,
    home prepared (see p. 204)
    or imported
Mayonnaise (optional)

DRESSING
3 tablespoons olive oil
1 tablespoon red wine vinegar
2 teaspoons fresh lemon juice
1/4 teaspoon Dijon-style mustard
1/4 teaspoon thyme
1 clove garlic, mashed to a paste or
    put through a garlic press
1 tablespoon minced parsley
Salt
Freshly ground pepper
Pinch sugar

Heat the oil in a deep ovenproof casserole. Add 1 tablespoon of the onion and sauté until it is wilted. Add the rice, let it absorb the oil, then stir in the broth, boiling water, salt, parsley sprig, thyme, and tarragon. Cover and cook at 400°F for 15 minutes. Remove from the oven and let sit, covered, for 5-10 minutes. Uncover, discard the parsley, and cool.

Combine the dressing ingredients in a small bowl and fold gently into the rice. Then mix in the scallion, pickle, tuna, green pepper, carrot, the remaining 2 tablespoons of minced onion, the cucumber, lettuce, and pimiento. Let sit at room temperature for several hours.

Serve at room temperature and if desired cover each portion with a layer of mayonnaise.

Summer Rice Salad

(ARROZ DE VERANO)

Chef Luis Bejarano at the charming Enrique Becerra bar/restaurant in Sevilla has a typically Andalucian culinary philosophy that has served him well: "If you cook with lots of love, everything you make will turn out well." Indeed, Enrique Becerra has one of the most respected and popular tapas bars in Sevilla—the food is first class and always beautifully presented. ("Look at the joy and happiness here," remarks Chef Bejarano, gesturing to an appetizing display of fresh salads.) This "al dente" rice salad was one of my favorite tapas here.

SERVES 6-8

    2 tablespoons olive oil
    1 cup short-grain rice (see p. 204)
    3/4 cup boiling water
    3/4 cup boiling chicken broth,
        fat removed
    1/4 teaspoon thyme
    1/8 teaspoon tarragon
    Salt
    Half a 7-ounce can white meat
        tuna, flaked
    2 tablespoons minced parsley
    2 tablespoons minced pimiento,
        home prepared (see p. 204)
        or imported
    1 1/4 cups mayonnaise, preferably
        homemade (p. 47)
    6 tablespoons ketchup
    1/2 teaspoon Worcestershire sauce
    1 teaspoon pickle or caper juice
    Freshly ground pepper
    Parsley sprigs for garnish

Heat the oil in a deep casserole, add the rice, stir to coat with the oil, then add the water, broth, thyme, tarragon, and salt. Bring back to a boil, cover tightly, and cook at 400°F for 12 minutes. Remove from the oven and let sit, covered, for 10 minutes, then transfer the rice to a bowl and cool. Mix in the tuna, minced parsley, and pimiento.

In a small bowl mix together 1 cup of the mayonnaise, the ketchup, Worcestershire sauce, pickle juice, salt, and pepper. Fold into the rice mixture. To serve, arrange the rice in a smooth mound and cover with a thin coating of the remaining 1/4 cup of mayonnaise. Decorate with parsley sprigs. This is ready to eat right away, but gains in flavor when kept refrigerated for several hours or overnight.

Escarole Salad with Tuna and Sausage
(ENSALADA DE ESCAROLA CON ATÚN Y BUTIFARRA)

Butifarra is the typical Catalán sausage, for which a French garlic sausage or a Polish sausage could be substituted. SERVES 4-6

½ small head escarole, torn in pieces
2 scallions, coarsely chopped
1 ounce cured ham, in julienne strips
2 tablespoons flaked light meat tuna
4 anchovy fillets, coarsely chopped
2 ounces cooked sausage, such as butifarra, Polish, or saucisson cuit sausage, in ⅛-inch slices
¼ cup olive oil
2 tablespoons red wine vinegar
Salt
Freshly ground pepper
1 hard-boiled egg, sliced

In a salad bowl toss together the escarole, scallions, ham, tuna, anchovy, and sausage. In a small bowl whisk the oil, vinegar, salt, and pepper and combine with the escarole mixture. Fold in the sliced egg and serve slightly chilled.

Sliced Eggs with Garlic and Parsley
(HUEVOS DUROS EN ALIÑO)

A large amount of garlic and parsley makes these attractive eggs particularly tasty. SERVES 4-6

2 cloves garlic, peeled
4 tablespoons minced parsley
Salt
Freshly ground pepper, preferably white
⅛ teaspoon paprika, preferably Spanish style
6 tablespoons olive oil
5 hard-boiled eggs, thinly sliced crosswise (use an egg slicer)
Grated carrot and black or green olives for garnish

In a processor or blender beat the garlic, parsley, salt, pepper, and paprika. With the motor running, pour in the oil gradually.

Arrange the sliced eggs in a serving dish and sprinkle with salt. Pour on the sauce and decorate with some grated carrot and several olives. Refrigerate until chilled. It will keep for several hours or overnight.

Salmon-Stuffed Eggs

(HUEVOS RELLENOS DE SALMÓN)

SERVES 4-5

5 hard-boiled eggs
2 ounces fresh salmon, steamed or
   poached, boned, and flaked;
   or canned salmon, drained
   and flaked
4 tablespoons Tomato Sauce (p. 66)
¼ teaspoon Worcestershire sauce
1 tablespoon minced pimiento, home
   prepared (see p. 204) or imported
2 tablespoons minced dill or
   cornichon pickle
¼ teaspoon pickle juice
1 tablespoon minced onion
Salt
Freshly ground pepper
Dash of cayenne pepper
Mayonnaise
Green Spanish olives for garnish

Cut the eggs in half lengthwise and remove the yolks. Place 2 of them in a bowl and press another through a sieve and reserve. (The remaining 2 will not be used.) Mash the 2 yolks and mix in the salmon, tomato sauce, Worcestershire sauce, pimiento, pickle, pickle juice, onion, salt, pepper, and cayenne. Fill the egg whites with this mixture, forming a smooth mound. Dab with mayonnaise (about ¼ teaspoon each), cover with the reserved egg yolk, and decorate with a piece of green olive. The eggs can be kept refrigerated for several hours.

Shrimp in Green Mayonnaise

(GAMBAS EN MAYONESA VERDE)

This delicious tapa demands a creamy, freshly made mayonnaise. The recipe is equally good with other kinds of shellfish. SERVES 6

PREPARE SEVERAL HOURS IN ADVANCE

½ Cooking Liquid recipe (p. 77)
1 pound medium-large shrimp, unshelled

GREEN MAYONNAISE
⅔ cup Mayonnaise (p. 47)
4 anchovies, finely chopped
2 tablespoons minced parsley
¼ teaspoon thyme
½ teaspoon minced capers

Bring the cooking liquid to a boil, add the shrimp, and cook for about 2 minutes, until just done — do not overcook. Drain, cool, and shell.

In a bowl combine the mayonnaise, anchovies, parsley, thyme, and capers. Fold in the shrimp gently and marinate for several hours or overnight.

VARIATION
Use this same mayonnaise dressing, reducing the anchovies to 2; adding 2 cloves garlic, mashed; ½ teaspoon Dijon-style mustard; salt, and pepper to mix with ½ pound mushrooms that have been brushed clean, stems trimmed, marinated for a few minutes in the juice of 1 lemon, then cut in ¼-inch slices lengthwise. Combine the mushrooms and mayonnaise not more than 30 minutes before serving or the dressing will turn watery.

Shrimp with Romesco Sauce

(GAMBAS COCIDAS CON SALSA ROMESCO)

One of the most popular ways to serve shrimp in Spain is boiled and at room temperature—the shrimp in their shells and the heads on. They are sold in bars and restaurants by the kilo rather than by portion, often accompanied by mayonnaise (homemade, p. 47), salpicón sauce (p. 82) or this unusual and very typical dip from the Catalán province of Tarragona. *Romesco* can also be a sauce for a hot shellfish dish, and when visiting Tarragona, be sure to stop into the Sol Ric restaurant, where chef Simón Tomás makes the best *romesco* sauce found anywhere in Spain.

If dried sweet red pepper is unavailable, use home-prepared pimiento (see p. 204) for a sauce that will be good, but lacking the earthy flavor that the dried pepper imparts. SERVES 6

3/4 pound medium or large shrimp,
   unshelled, heads on, if possible
1/2 Cooking Liquid recipe (p. 77)

ROMESCO SAUCE
1 large ripe tomato
5 cloves garlic, peeled
1 dried sweet red pepper (such as
   "New Mexico" style)
1/2 dried red chili pepper, seeded,
   or 1/4 teaspoon crushed red pepper
1/2 cup water
3 tablespoons plus 1 teaspoon
   red wine vinegar
1/2 cup plus 1 tablespoon olive oil
A 1/4-inch slice long crusty loaf bread
10 blanched almonds
Salt
Freshly ground pepper

To make the *romesco* sauce, roast the tomato and garlic in an ungreased roasting pan at 350°F for 30 minutes. Place the dried red pepper and chili pepper in a saucepan with the water and 3 tablespoons of the vinegar. Bring to a boil, cover, and simmer for 5 minutes. (If using pepper flakes, add them later to the processor.)

Heat 1 tablespoon of the oil in a small skillet and fry the bread until golden on both sides. Transfer to a processor or blender. In the same oil fry the almonds until golden and add to the processor, along with the boiled red peppers (if using crushed red pepper, add here), garlic, and tomato. With the motor running, pour in gradually the remaining 1/2 cup of oil, the remaining teaspoon of vinegar, salt, and pepper. Strain, taste for salt, place in a serving bowl, and keep at room temperature.

To cook the shrimp, bring the cooking liquid to a boil, add the shrimp, and cook for about 2 minutes, until just done. Cool. Serve the shrimp in their shells, or shelled if you prefer, arranged around the rim of the sauce bowl. The sauce can be made a day in advance, the shrimp a couple of hours before. Reserve both at room temperature and serve at room temperature.

Shrimp in Caper and Pickle Vinaigrette

(SALPICÓN DE LANGOSTINO)

The best marinade ever for shrimp—forceful, but never overpowering the delicate taste of the shrimp. SERVES 6

PREPARE TWO HOURS IN ADVANCE

½ Cooking Liquid recipe (p. 77)
1 pound large shrimp, unshelled
½ cup olive oil
¼ cup red wine vinegar
1 small onion, minced
4 tablespoons minced dill or
   cornichon pickle
4 teaspoons tiny whole capers or
   chopped larger capers
1 hard-boiled egg, finely chopped
1 tablespoon minced parsley
Salt
Freshly ground pepper

Bring the cooking liquid to a boil, add the shrimp, and cook very briefly, until just done, about 2 minutes. Shell the shrimp and cut in halves crosswise.

In a bowl whisk the oil and vinegar. Stir in the onion, pickle, capers, egg, and parsley. Season with salt and pepper. Add the shrimp and marinate at room temperature for 2 hours and serve at room temperature. These shrimp are best if not refrigerated, but if you must, be sure to bring back to room temperature before serving.

Shrimp, Melon, and Apple Salad

(COCKTAIL GRAN CONCIERTO)

Here is an interesting mixture of tastes that makes a very attractive tapa, especially if presented in a melon shell. SERVES 6

½ Cooking Liquid recipe (p. 77)
½ pound small shrimp, unshelled
6 tablespoons mayonnaise, preferably
   homemade (p. 47)
2 tablespoons ketchup
¼ teaspoon Worcestershire sauce
Salt
Freshly ground pepper
3 pounds orange melon, such as
   Cranshaw or cantaloupe
1 apple, peeled and diced in
   ½-inch pieces

Bring the cooking liquid to a boil, add the shrimp, and cook for about 2 minutes. Cool and shell. In a small bowl mix together the mayonnaise, ketchup, Worcestershire, salt, and pepper.

Divide the melon in half crosswise and scoop out melon balls. Clean out any remaining loose flesh from the shell and reserve the shells and the melon balls. [May be prepared ahead]

Combine the shrimp with the melon and apple. Fold in the mayonnaise dressing gently. Spoon into the melon shells and present slightly chilled.

Boiled Lobster, Two Sauces

(LANGOSTA COCIDA DOS SALSAS)

Lobster, like shrimp, is most often prepared in Spain simply boiled and served at room temperature, with a choice of sauces. In this recipe the presentation is quite striking, for the lobster shell is kept intact and forms a centerpiece for this tapa. SERVES 4

> Green Mayonnaise (p. 73)
> Salpicón Sauce (p. 82), doubling all
>   ingredients except the oil and vinegar
> Cooking Liquid (p. 77)
> Two 1¼-1½-pound live lobsters
> Shredded lettuce
> Parsley sprigs or watercress for garnish

Prepare the green mayonnaise and salpicón sauce.

Bring the cooking liquid to a boil, cover, and simmer for 20 minutes. Add the lobsters, cover, and cook for about 15 minutes. Cool the lobsters right side up on a platter.

To serve, you will need to keep the head and tail of 1 lobster intact while extracting the meat. To do this, with kitchen scissors slit the underside of the tail, trim away the membrane and small bones covering the meat, and carefully lift out the tail meat in one piece with the aid of a small knife. Extract the meat from the other tail section also, but since the shell will not be used, there is no need for extra care. Cut the tail meat into 1-inch chunks. Remove the large claws from the lobsters (these shells will also be discarded), and extract the meat in large pieces. Separate and reserve the small claws, unshelled. [May be prepared ahead]

Cover a pretty serving dish, preferably of an oval shape, with a bed of lettuce and place the lobster carcass in the center. Arrange the lobster meat around it and decorate with the small claws. Garnish the lobster with parsley or watercress. Either spoon the sauces over the lobster (each covering half of the meat) or serve the sauces separately. This dish is best when lobster and sauces are at room temperature.

Three-Layer Omelet

Banderillas

Clockwise: Blood Sausage in Puff Pastry; Marinated Quail; Pâté with Turkey Breast; Cumin-Flavored Mushroom Salad; Manchego Cheese with Quince Preserves

Making potato nest for Zucchini, Peppers, and Tomato in Potato Nests

Spicy Boiled Octopus (*center*)

Frying Stuffed Mussels

Tapas in Spain   (*Photos by Luis Casas*)

Tapas in New York   *First row:* At the Ballroom   *Second and third rows:* Preparing tapas at home – for a Christmas party, for a buffet on the terrace, for a picnic on the dock   (*Photos by Luis and Elisa Casas*)

Left to right, first row: Scallop Pie; Pimientos in Vinaigrette; Green Olives, Sevilla Style   *Left to right, second row:*
Baby Eels in Garlic Sauce; Spinach Turnovers   *Left to right, third row:* Sweet and Sour Marinated Onions; Salpicón Sauce for Lobster; Snails in Green Sauce
Left to right, fourth row: Boiled Lobster, Two Sauces; Green Mayonnaise for lobster

Galician-Style Lobster Salad

(SALPICÓN DE LUBRIGANTE A LA GALLEGA)

I tasted this exceptional salad in Cedeira, a colorful fishing port in an idyllic setting on the upper Galician estuaries in La Coruña province. The restaurant El Náutico was along the waterfront promenade, and huge portions of food would emerge from the kitchen with incredible speed and efficiency. Our waitress was a bit startled by our request for the ingredients in the lobster salad, for to her this was "just" a salad that anyone could have made. Yet the Galician vinaigrette has its secrets, such as a goodly amount of paprika, a very light hand with the oil, and lots of chopped hard-boiled egg. SERVES 4

Two 1½-pound live lobsters
2 tablespoons minced parsley
1 hard-boiled egg, coarsely chopped
¼ cup finely chopped onion
¼ cup diced pimiento, preferably
   home prepared (see p. 204)
   or imported
1½ teaspoons paprika, preferably
   Spanish style
1 large clove garlic, peeled
2 tablespoons olive oil
4 tablespoons wine vinegar,
   preferably white
Salt

COOKING LIQUID
12 cups water
2 cups fish broth (p. 27) or clam juice
2 bay leaves
2 slices lemon
4 sprigs parsley
½ teaspoon thyme
Salt

10 peppercorns
2 slices onion

Bring the cooking liquid to a boil, cover, and simmer for 20 minutes. Add the lobsters, cover, and cook for about 15 minutes. Cool the lobsters on a platter and reserve 2 tablespoons of the cooking liquid. Shell everything except the small claws. Chop the meat to a coarse-medium consistency. Place in a bowl, adding the unshelled claws also, and mix in the parsley, egg, onion, and pimiento.

Dissolve the paprika in the reserved 2 tablespoons of cooking liquid. In a mortar, mash the garlic, then mix in the dissolved paprika.

In a small bowl whisk the oil, vinegar, salt, and the paprika mixture. Fold into the lobster mixture and taste for salt. You can serve this right away or refrigerate for several hours. Serve cold or at room temperature, as you prefer.

VARIATION

Since lobster is so expensive, you might want to extend it by mixing with some mild firm-textured fish. You can also make the salad without any lobster. Use ¾ pound of fish, ideally monkfish (see p. 86). Place the fish in a small amount of the cooking liquid, barely to cover, bring to a boil, cover, and simmer for about 10 minutes (more or less, depending on the thickness of the fish). Flake and combine with the other ingredients.

Lobster and Endive Salad
(ENSALADA DE BOGAVANTE CON ENDIVIAS)

We sampled this delicate dish as part of a tasting menu at Zalacaín (see p. 24) in Madrid. It was simple and elegant and masterfully prepared and presented. SERVES 4

Cooking Liquid (p. 77)
A 1¾-pound lobster
1 endive
Parsley or watercress for garnish

DRESSING
3 tablespoons fruity olive oil
1 tablespoon fresh lemon juice
Salt
Freshly ground pepper, preferably white

Bring the cooking liquid to a boil, then plunge the lobster into the liquid. Cover and simmer for about 20 minutes. Remove to a platter and cool.

In a small bowl combine the dressing ingredients with a wire whisk. Separate the endive into individual leaves. Stack them, then slice lengthwise into julienne strips.

Remove the shell from the lobster. Slice the tail meat into ½-inch-thick slices. Cut the rest into chunks. Use the small claws, if desired, to decorate the dish. [May be prepared ahead]

Place the endive on a serving platter or on individual serving dishes and arrange the lobster pieces attractively on top. Pour on the dressing and serve at room temperature, garnished with a sprig of parsley or watercress.

VARIATION
This recipe is also excellent using ½ pound fresh steamed salmon instead of lobster. See recipe on page 21 for cooking instructions. Sprinkle with salt. In this version I also add to the dressing 1 tablespoon finely minced chives or the green part of scallions, 1 teaspoon minced parsley, and ¼ teaspoon chervil.

Mussels in Escabeche
(MEJILLONES EN ESCABECHE)

The marinade for these mussels is well spiced and cooked (thus an *escabeche* rather than a *vinagreta*), giving the mussels a wonderfully rich flavor. SERVES 6

PREPARE TWO DAYS IN ADVANCE

1 small carrot, scraped, in thin
   julienne strips
⅜ cup white wine
2 dozen medium mussels (see p. 204)
½ cup olive oil
8 cloves garlic, peeled
¼ teaspoon paprika, preferably
   Spanish style
¼ teaspoon thyme
2 bay leaves
¼ teaspoon oregano
2 cloves
Salt
Freshly ground pepper
¼ cup red wine vinegar
2 dill or cornichon pickles, in thin
   julienne strips

To pickle the carrot, place the julienne strips in the liquid of a jar of pickles. Refrigerate until the following day.

Heat the wine in a skillet. Add the mussels, cover, and cook, removing the mussels as they open. Place the mussel meat in a bowl and discard the shells. Reserve ⅜ cup of the mussel cooking liquid.

Wipe out the skillet, heat the oil, and sauté the garlic cloves until lightly golden. Remove the garlic to the bowl with the mussels. Turn off the heat and stir into the skillet the paprika, thyme, bay leaves, oregano, cloves, salt, and pepper. Add the vinegar and the reserved cooking liquid. Simmer, uncovered, for 5 minutes. Cool a few minutes, then pour over the mussels. Fold in the pickles and carrots and refrigerate overnight. Remove from the refrigerator 20 minutes before serving.

Mussels Vinaigrette

(MEJILLONES A LA VINAGRETA)

There is nothing more colorful and inviting for a tapas party than a large tray of these exceptional mussels. Everyone has loved the recipe from my first book so much that I am repeating it here. The mussels should be made the day before and returned to their shells when ready to serve. SERVES 4-6

PREPARE ONE DAY IN ADVANCE

½ cup olive oil
3 tablespoons red wine vinegar
1 teaspoon small capers or chopped larger capers
1 tablespoon minced onion
1 tablespoon minced pimiento, home prepared (see p. 204) or imported
1 tablespoon minced parsley
Salt
Freshly ground pepper
2 dozen medium mussels (see p. 204)
1 slice lemon

In a bowl whisk the oil and vinegar, then add the capers, onion, pimiento, parsley, salt, and pepper.

Scrub the mussels well, removing the beards. Discard any that do not close tightly. Place 1 cup water in a skillet with the lemon slice. Add the mussels and bring to a boil. Remove the mussels as they open; cool. Remove the mussel meat from the shells and mix them into the vinaigrette. Cover and refrigerate overnight. Reserve half the mussel shells, clean them well, and place them in a plastic bag in the refrigerator. Before serving, replace the mussels in their shells and spoon a small amount of the vinaigrette over each.

Mussels and Shrimp in Avocado Vinaigrette

(MEJILLONES Y GAMBAS
EN VINAGRETA DE AGUACATE)

This tapa comes under the category of *nueva cocina vasca*—"nouvelle" Basque cuisine—and was found at an attractive new restaurant in Madrid called Restaurante Basque. SERVES 4

1 dozen medium mussels (see p. 204)
1 slice lemon
8 large shrimp, unshelled
Shredded lettuce
Minced parsley

DRESSING
A 1-pound avocado
2½ tablespoons fresh
   lemon juice
4 tablespoons olive oil
Salt
Freshly ground pepper
¼ teaspoon Dijon-style mustard
1 teaspoon grated onion
¼ teaspoon crushed red pepper

Place the mussels in a skillet with ½ cup water and the lemon slice. Bring to a boil and remove the mussels as they open. Cool. Discard the shells and, to keep the mussels moist, place them in a bowl with a little of the liquid in which they have cooked. Cook the shrimp in the remaining mussel liquid for a minute or two. Cool and shell.

To prepare the dressing, peel the avocado and remove the pit. Cut the avocado in pieces and place in a processor with the lemon juice. Blend until smooth. Gradually add the olive oil. Season very well with salt and pepper and add the mustard,

onion, and red pepper. [May be prepared ahead]

Arrange the mussels and shrimp attractively on a bed of shredded lettuce. Cover with the avocado dressing, and sprinkle with parsley. Serve cold or at room temperature.

Clams with Vinegar

(BERBERECHOS EN VINAGRE)

This extremely simple tapa is popular in *bodegas*, bars that specialize in drinks rather than food and where clients come to engage in conversation and to sip their favorite brew. The tapas are casual, almost incidental, accompaniments. Casa Sierra in Madrid, unchanged in its two-hundred-year existence, has the wonderful, lively old-world ambience of a Madrid long gone and is one of my favorite *bodegas* in the city. Their most popular tapas are these tiny canned clams, doused with a special white wine vinegar. SERVES 4-6

A 10-ounce can baby clams, drained
   and well chilled
1 tablespoon white wine vinegar

Simply mix the clams with the vinegar and serve cold.

Oysters in Escabeche

(OSTRAS ESCABECHADAS)

Galicia in northern Spain is famed for the quality of its oysters. In times past they were most often preserved in *escabeche* and packed in barrels, and they frequently found their way to the pubs of London. Today Spaniards prefer their oysters freshly opened with little more than a few drops of lemon. Nevertheless, marinated oysters are still a tradition in Spain during the Christmas season. This is an excellent way to prepare the shelled and canned (but fresh) oysters found in fish stores. SERVES 6-8

PREPARE TWO DAYS IN ADVANCE

2 dozen large oysters
1/2 cup olive oil
1 large clove garlic, sliced
1/2 cup dry white wine
3 tablespoons sherry vinegar
Salt
6 peppercorns
3 bay leaves

If the oysters are in their shells, remove them and dry well on paper towels. In a small skillet heat the oil until it is just tepid, not hot. Add the oysters and cook slowly for about 2 minutes. Transfer the oysters to a shallow serving bowl (earthenware is best and wood is most classic). Add the garlic to the oil in the skillet, turn up the heat, and cook the garlic until it is golden. Remove. Cool the oil slightly, then add the wine, vinegar, salt, peppercorns, and bay leaves. Bring to a boil, then simmer for about 10 minutes, or until the raw taste of the vinegar is gone. Cool, then pour over the oysters. Refrigerate for 2 days, then serve cold or at room temperature.

Octopus Vinaigrette

(SALPICÓN DE PULPO BAR MIAMI)

A tapas tour of Sevilla led us to Bar Miami, where the fried squid rings were cooked as they should be but rarely are—crisp and very tender—and this excellent octopus salad was prepared in a typically Andalucian manner. SERVES 4

PREPARE SEVERAL HOURS IN ADVANCE

1 1/2 pounds octopus, preferably small
1 small tomato, chopped (about 1/4 cup)
1/2 green pepper, diced
1/4 cup finely chopped onion
1/4 cup olive oil
2 tablespoons white wine vinegar
1/4 cup water
Salt
Freshly ground pepper

Cook the octopus according to the instructions on page 170. With scissors, cut the tentacles into 1-inch pieces. Combine in a bowl the octopus, tomato, green pepper, and onion. In a separate bowl whisk the oil, vinegar, water, salt, and pepper. Fold the dressing into the octopus mixture. Marinate for several hours or overnight.

Shellfish Salad in Orange Mayonnaise

(ENSALADA DE MARISCO AL PERFUME DE NARANJA)

What makes this salad out of the ordinary is the unusual hint of orange in the mayonnaise dressing. And do make your own mayonnaise. SERVES 8

> ¾ cup mayonnaise, preferably homemade (p. 47)
> 3 tablespoons freshly squeezed orange juice
> 1 tablespoon heavy cream
> ¼ teaspoon grated orange rind
> Cooking Liquid (p. 77)
> A 1¼–1½-pound live lobster
> 1 dozen mussels (see p. 204)
> ½ pound monkfish (see p. 86), or other firm fish, like halibut or fresh cod
> ½ pound large shrimp, unshelled
> Shredded lettuce
> Salt
> Two ¼-inch slices orange, each cut in 4 wedges
> 1 tablespoon minced parsley

Mix together the mayonnaise, orange juice, cream, and orange rind. Refrigerate. Bring the cooking liquid to a boil, immerse the lobster, and cook for about 15 minutes. Drain and cool. Discard (or save for future use) all but 1 inch of the cooking liquid, and in the remaining liquid cook the mussels, removing them as they open. Add the monkfish, cooking for about 8–10 minutes. Remove and cool. Then cook the shrimp for 2 or 3 minutes. Shell the lobster according to the directions on page 76, keeping the shell intact to use as garnish and cutting the meat into chunks. Discard the mussel shells, flake the monkfish, and shell the shrimp. [May be prepared ahead]

Arrange a bed of lettuce on a serving platter. Cover with the flaked fish and sprinkle with salt. Place the lobster, shrimp, and mussels on top and decorate the platter with the lobster shell and orange wedges. Sprinkle with parsley. Serve, passing the mayonnaise dressing separately.

Shellfish Vinaigrette

(SALPICÓN DE MARISCOS)

There is always a salpicón of some sort on a tapas menu and this one is by far the most elegant, containing only lobster, crab, and shrimp in a delicious vinaigrette of pickles, capers, onion, and pimiento. This tapa is always one of the stars at my tapas parties and, needless to say, is the first to disappear. If you can't find good-quality king crab meat, it is best to eliminate the crab and increase the lobster and shrimp. I also like to add a half dozen tiny mussels, steamed opened (see p. 164) and left in their shells, for an attractive contrast of colors. SERVES 6–8

PREPARE ONE DAY IN ADVANCE

> 1¼–1½ pounds live lobster, or lobster tails
> Cooking Liquid (p. 77)
> 1½ pounds medium-large shrimp, unshelled
> ½ pound cooked king crab meat, cut in chunks
> 6 very small cooked mussels (optional)
>
> SALPICÓN SAUCE
> ¾ cup olive oil
> 6 tablespoons tarragon vinegar

5 tablespoons chopped dill or
  cornichon pickles
2 tablespoons small whole capers or
  chopped larger capers
2 tablespoons minced onion
2 tablespoons chopped pimiento,
  home prepared (see p. 204)
  or imported
1 tablespoon minced parsley
Salt
Freshly ground pepper

Boil the lobster in the cooking liquid for about 15 minutes, remove, reduce the amount of liquid to about 4 cups, and cook the shrimp for about 2 minutes. Cool. Shell the lobster and shrimp and cut the lobster into chunks.

To make the salpicón sauce, in a large bowl whisk the oil and vinegar, then stir in the remaining sauce ingredients. Fold in the shrimp, lobster, crab meat, and optional mussels gently. Chill for a day, mixing occasionally.

Marinated Seafood

(SALPICÓN MESÓN BOTÍN)

Mesón Botín, a Spanish restaurant in the heart of Manhattan, features this excellent fish and shellfish salad on its menu. SERVES 8

START PREPARATION SEVERAL HOURS IN ADVANCE

¼ pound halibut or monkfish
  (see p. 86), or other fish
  of similar texture
Coarse salt
Cooking Liquid (p. 77)

A 1½-pound live lobster
1 dozen small mussels (see p. 204)
½ pound medium-large shrimp, unshelled
¼ pound small scallops, or large scallops
  cut in halves
¼ cup olive oil
2 tablespoons red wine vinegar
¼ teaspoon Dijon-style mustard
1 tablespoon minced parsley
1 green pepper, chopped
2 tablespoons finely chopped onion
1 tablespoon tomato sauce
Salt
Freshly ground pepper
Four ¼-inch slices cucumber,
  each cut in quarters
6 endive leaves, cut in pieces

Sprinkle the halibut with salt on both sides and let sit until ready to cook (this helps to firm the flesh).

Bring the cooking liquid to a boil, add the lobster, and cook for 15–20 minutes. Remove the lobster to a platter and cool.

Pour out all but 2 inches of the cooking liquid (save for future use), return to a boil, then add the mussels and remove as they open. Add the shrimp and the scallops to the broth and cook for about a minute or two. Remove the shrimp and scallops, then cook the halibut in the cooking liquid for about 6 minutes. Cut the fish into tapas-size pieces, removing any skin and bone. Shell the lobster and cut the meat into chunks. Shell the shrimp and leave the mussels in their shells, or on the half shell. Place all the seafood together in a bowl and sprinkle with salt, if necessary.

Whisk the oil, mustard, and vinegar. Add the parsley, green pepper, onion, tomato sauce, salt, and pepper. Pour over the seafood and stir gently.

Marinate in the refrigerator for several hours or overnight. One hour before serving, stir in the cucumber and endive gently.

Fish and Vegetable Salad

(SALPICÓN A LA VALENCIANA)

When I saw this colorful, glistening fresh salad in a huge bowl at the Cervecería Pema in Valencia it struck me as the most inviting salad I had ever laid eyes on. It tasted just as good as it looked. SERVES 4

PREPARE SEVERAL HOURS IN ADVANCE

1/4 pound cauliflower and/or broccoli, thick stems removed, cut in small flowerets
Salt
1 teaspoon fresh lemon juice
1 dozen medium mussels (see p. 204)
1 slice lemon
1/2 pound cleaned squid (see p. 204), or about 1 pound uncleaned, preferably very small, with tentacles
2 ounces baby eels (angulas) (optional; see pp. 127, 171)
2 tablespoons diced green pepper
3 tablespoons diced tomato
1 scallion, chopped
1 clove garlic, minced
1/4 cup slivered onion, preferably Spanish onion
4 pitted cured black olives, each cut in 3 or 4 pieces
1 tablespoon chopped dill or cornichon pickle

DRESSING
2 tablespoons olive oil
1 tablespoon fresh lemon juice
1/4 teaspoon Dijon-style mustard
Salt
Freshly ground pepper

Place the cauliflower in a skillet with 1 inch of salted water and the lemon juice. Bring to a boil, cover, and simmer for 5–10 minutes, or until just tender. Drain and discard the liquid.

Arrange the mussels in the same skillet with 1/2 inch water and the lemon slice. Bring to a boil and remove the mussels as they open—do not overcook. Discard the shells. In the same liquid place the squid and simmer for about 2 minutes. Leave them whole if they are tiny; otherwise, cut in halves or rings.

In a bowl mix together the cauliflower, mussel meat, squid, *angulas*, green pepper, tomato, scallion, garlic, onion, olives, and pickle.

Whisk the dressing ingredients together in a small bowl. Fold into the fish mixture and refrigerate for several hours.

VARIATION
I particularly like this salad as it is, but you may choose to substitute or add other fish, like monkfish, halibut, and/or shrimp.

Marinated Stuffed Squid

(CALAMARES RELLENOS A LA VINAGRETA)

Few of my guests who sampled these marinated, sliced squid (stuffed with pork, veal, nuts, and mushrooms) at a recent tapas party could identify what they were eating as squid, but all, nevertheless, found the tapa fascinating and delicious. SERVES 8

PREPARE ONE DAY IN ADVANCE

1 ounce (about 20) blanched almonds
3 tablespoons pine nuts
5 hazelnuts
2½ pounds cleaned squid
    (see p. 204), with tentacles,
    the bodies about 7 inches long
    (weight, uncleaned, about
    4½ pounds)
¼ pound slab bacon, cut in pieces
¼ pound lean pork, cut in pieces
¼ pound veal, cut in pieces
4 cloves garlic, chopped
1 tablespoon chopped parsley
1 ounce dried mushrooms (soaked for a
    few minutes in warm water, stems
    removed) or 3 ounces fresh wild
    mushrooms (if unavailable, use
    cultivated mushrooms)
1 egg, lightly beaten
1 slice bread, crusts removed, soaked
    in milk, then squeezed dry
½ teaspoon freshly ground pepper
2 teaspoons salt
1 tablespoon dry (fino) Spanish sherry
1 tablespoon brandy, preferably Spanish
    brandy or Cognac
1 tablespoon grated onion
1 teaspoon paprika, preferably Spanish style
2 tablespoons minced cured ham
2 tablespoons olive oil
1 small onion, chopped
1 small leek, carefully washed and
    coarsely chopped
1 carrot, peeled and coarsely chopped
½ cup dry white wine
1 cup fish broth (p. 27), clam juice, or
    chicken broth

DRESSING
½ cup olive oil
3 tablespoons red wine vinegar
½ teaspoon Dijon-style mustard

1 clove garlic, minced
¼ teaspoon thyme
1 tablespoon minced parsley
Salt
Freshly ground pepper

In the bowl of a processor grind the almonds, pine nuts, and hazelnuts until very fine. Remove to a small bowl. Place the fins (if available) and tentacles in the bowl of the processor. Add the slab bacon, pork, veal, garlic, parsley, and mushrooms and grind coarsely.

Transfer this mixture to a mixing bowl. Add the egg, bread, pepper, salt, sherry, brandy, ground almonds, pine nuts, and hazelnuts, grated onion, paprika, and ham.

Fill the squid bodies, not more than half full, with this mixture. Close with a toothpick. Heat the oil in a shallow casserole and sauté the chopped onion, leek, and carrot until the onion is wilted. Add the stuffed squid and sauté (but do not brown) for about 5 minutes. Pour in the white wine and fish broth, bring to a boil, then cover and simmer for 1 hour. Cool, then chill.

To make the dressing, combine all ingredients in a processor and beat until smooth and creamy. Remove the squid from the cooking liquid and drain well. Discard the liquid. Cut in ½-inch slices, arrange in a dish, and pour on the dressing. Marinate in the refrigerator overnight. (It can be kept for several days.) Bring to room temperature before serving.

Monkfish, "Lobster" Style
(RAP EN LLAGOSTAT)

Rape (*rap* in the Catalán language), known variously in this country as monkfish, angler, or lotte, is a startlingly ugly fish that bears an amazing resemblance in taste and texture to lobster and is often, in fact, used as a substitute for that expensive crustacean. It is an excellent fish for many purposes (particularly prized in Europe as a soup ingredient) and appears in several preparations elsewhere in this book. Monkfish has only one central bone, making it easy to separate the meat into two thick fillets, which even look like lobster tails.

Recently monkfish has gained many followers in this country and is no longer difficult to buy. Even your local fish store can probably find it for you. In this recipe the fish is sprinkled with paprika, increasing its lobsterlike appearance, and is served like lobster, chilled or at room temperature, with mayonnaise or a salpicón sauce on the side. Your guests will imagine that you spent the day shelling lobsters.
SERVES 6

>   ¾ pound monkfish fillet
>   (it should be about 1 inch thick)
>   Coarse salt
>   ½ teaspoon paprika,
>   preferably Spanish style
>   2 tablespoons butter, melted
>   Mayonnaise (p. 47)
>   Salpicón Sauce (p. 82), reducing the
>   oil and vinegar by half

Sprinkle the fish with salt and let it sit for about 20 minutes. Make about 4 incisions on top of the fillet and fill each with some of the paprika. Brush the fish with the butter, then sprinkle a little more paprika over the top. Bake at 350°F in a lightly greased shallow roasting pan for about 20 minutes. Cool, then chill.

Cut in chunks (as you would lobster) and arrange on a platter that has been garnished with, for example, lettuce, radish, olives, capers, and lemon wedges. Serve the mayonnaise and/or salpicón sauce on the side.

Monkfish and Clams in Fennel Vinaigrette
(RAPE CON ALMEJAS)

This dish comes from a tasting menu at the very popular Cabo Mayor restaurant in Madrid, which serves seafood of refined and quite "nouvelle" preparations. The monkfish and clams in this recipe are not cooked, just bathed in a delicate vinaigrette. Monkfish (see discussion in preceding recipe) is ideal because it has a firm flesh and can be sliced very thin. SERVES 4

>   ¼ pound monkfish, skinned and boned,
>   in 1 long, thick piece
>   ¼ cup fruity olive oil
>   4 teaspoons fresh lemon juice
>   ¼ teaspoon crushed fennel seed
>   Salt
>   Freshly ground pepper, preferably white
>   8 clams, shucked, at room temperature

Partially freeze the fish, then slice lengthwise as close to paper thin as possible (you could do this with a slicing machine). In a small bowl whisk the oil, lemon juice, fennel, salt, and pepper. To make in advance, keep the dressing at room temperature and refrigerate the fish and clams (bring them to room temperature before continuing).

This is best served on individual dishes. Heat the dishes, then place the raw monkfish slices on them (with the heat the fish will stick slightly to the dish, thereby keeping its shape and cooking a little). Arrange the whole shucked clams on top and spoon on the dressing. Serve at room temperature.

VARIATION

A similar dish is served at Casa Fermín in Oviedo (see p. 122), with shrimp and crisp green beans accompanying the monkfish. To prepare, freeze and slice the monkfish according to instructions, then marinate the fish in the dressing (substituting ¼ teaspoon thyme for the fennel) for at least 1 hour. Arrange the monkfish in overlapping rows around the edge of a serving platter or individual dishes. (It is not necessary to heat the dishes for this version.) Place lightly cooked green beans (smallest and thinnest available) in the center of the dish(es) and arrange 20 very small cooked and shelled shrimp (5 shrimp each portion) over the green beans.

Monkfish and Shrimp "Snails"

(CARACOLES DE RAPE Y GAMBA)

A shrimp salad, seasoned with rosemary, is rolled in a strip of fish, making a very attractive and delicately flavored tapa. It is adapted from a dish on the menu of the spectacularly beautiful Parador de Segovia (see p. 9). SERVES 6 (MAKES 12)

½ pound monkfish fillet (see p. 86),
   or other firm-fleshed fish like halibut
Cooking Liquid (p. 157)
8 medium-large shrimp, unshelled
4 teaspoons mayonnaise, preferably
   homemade (p. 47)
½ teaspoon crushed rosemary
Parsley sprigs for garnish

DRESSING
2 tablespoons mayonnaise
2 teaspoons ketchup
Dash of Worcestershire sauce
¼ teaspoon pickle or caper juice
Salt
Freshly ground pepper

Partially freeze the fish and slice in very thin strips about 5 inches long and 1¾–2 inches wide. Bring the cooking liquid to a boil and add the fish strips, cooking just until they turn white, less than a minute. Cool. Add the shrimp to the same liquid and cook for about 2 minutes. Cool and shell. Chop the shrimp finely and mix with the mayonnaise and rosemary.

Spread about 2 teaspoons of the shrimp mixture on each fish slice. Roll, slice in half crosswise, and turn the rolls on their sides. Secure the fish seam with a toothpick.

Combine the dressing ingredients in a small bowl. Dab about ¼ teaspoon on each tapa and garnish with a small sprig of parsley. Serve right away, or refrigerate (preferably without the dressing on top) until ready to use.

Marinated Smelts

(BOQUERONES EN VINAGRE)

These tiny fish, marinated in vinegar, garlic, and parsley, are found everywhere in Spain as a tapa. They are also often found as an ingredient for *banderillas* (see pp. 52–54). SERVES 4-6

PREPARE ONE DAY IN ADVANCE

> ¾ pound smelts, fresh anchovies,
> or other very small fish, cleaned;
> heads, tails, and fins removed
> Salt
> ½ cup white wine vinegar
> 3 cloves garlic, minced
> 1 tablespoon minced parsley

Soak the cleaned fish in cold water to cover for 1 hour. Drain, then butterfly the fish, leaving the bone in. Arrange skin side up in a shallow, flat-bottom bowl in one layer. Sprinkle with salt and pour on the vinegar. Cover and refrigerate overnight (the fish will not be cooked, only marinated).

Drain the fish and discard the vinegar. Pull out the spine bone and split the fish in halves, trimming away any ragged edges. Return to the bowl, sprinkle with the garlic and parsley, and refrigerate a few more hours.

Marinated Trout Fillets

(ESCABECHE DE TRUCHA)

Near the immense and most impressive cathedral of Sevilla is the attractive bar/restaurant Figón del Cabildo, which serves an excellent assortment of tapas. Particularly good is this trout, marinated with onion and raw carrot. SERVES 4

PREPARE SEVERAL HOURS IN ADVANCE

> 1 small onion, peeled
> A ½-pound trout, in 2 fillets,
> skin on
> 1 carrot, in julienne strips
> 6 tablespoons olive oil
> 3 tablespoons white wine vinegar
> Salt
> Freshly ground pepper, preferably white

Place the onion in a roasting pan and bake at 350°F for about 45 minutes, or until tender. Cut in slivers. Meanwhile, steam the trout (see p. 21), cool, skin, and place in a shallow bowl. Sprinkle with the onion and carrot.

In a small bowl whisk the oil, vinegar, salt, and pepper and pour over the trout. Cover and refrigerate for at least 8 hours, spooning the marinade over the fish occasionally. Serve cold or at room temperature.

Smoked Salmon Pâté

(PASTEL DE SALMÓN AHUMADO)

This lovely pâté, combining fresh and smoked salmon, has a delicate flavor and a smooth texture. The avocado halves, buried in the salmon, are sliced with the pâté for a beautiful presentation and an outstanding combination of tastes. SERVES 10-12

1 tablespoon olive oil
1 medium tomato, finely chopped
Salt
1/2 pound smoked salmon
  (not too salty)
1/2 pound fresh salmon,
  skinned and boned
2 eggs
White pepper, preferably freshly ground
1 1/2 cups heavy cream
2 tablespoons diced cured ham,
  cut from a 1/4-inch-thick slice
Butter
Bread crumbs
A 1/2-pound avocado, cut in half
  lengthwise, peeled, and pitted

To make a simple tomato sauce, heat the oil in a small skillet. Add the tomato and salt and cook over low heat for 2–3 minutes, until the tomato is softened. Strain, pressing with the back of a wooden spoon to extract as much liquid as possible. Reserve 4 tablespoons.

Put the smoked and fresh salmon in the bowl of a processor or blender and beat until smooth. Beat in the eggs, reserved tomato sauce, and pepper. With the motor running, pour in the cream gradually.

With an on-off motion, blend in the ham. Taste for salt.

Butter a 9 1/4 × 5 1/4 × 2 3/4-inch loaf pan generously, then dust with bread crumbs. Pour half of the salmon mixture into the pan. Arrange the avocado halves cut side down (if the halves seem to protrude too far for the rest of the salmon to cover them, trim the cut side) and cover with the rest of the salmon.

Cover the pan tightly with foil and place in a larger pan of hot water (bain-marie). Bring to a boil on top of the stove, then lower the heat to medium-low and continue cooking for 1 1/2 hours. Remove the mold from the water, loosen the foil, and cool. Refrigerate until cold. Unmold and serve chilled and sliced.

Marinated Salmon

(SALMÓN EN ESCABECHE)

The San Miguel bar/restaurant in the Galician city of Orense is a tremendously successful father-son operation, which highlights all the best that Galicia has to offer—in particular, seafood. Whatever is served in the restaurant can also be ordered at the bar, which is where I tasted this delicious marinated salmon. SERVES 4-5

PREPARE SEVERAL HOURS IN ADVANCE

1 pound thick fillets of fresh salmon,
   skin on
4 tablespoons olive oil
2 tablespoons white wine vinegar
1 tablespoon minced parsley
Salt
Freshly ground pepper, preferably white
20 marinated cocktail onions
1 dill gherkin pickle, in thin
   lengthwise slices
Strips of pimiento for garnish,
   preferably home prepared (see p. 204)

Steam the salmon (see p. 21), remove the skin, and cool. Place in a shallow casserole.

In a small bowl whisk the oil, vinegar, parsley, salt, and pepper. Pour over the fish, then scatter in the onions and arrange the pickle slices and pimiento strips over the fish. Refrigerate for several hours or overnight. Divide into tapas-size portions and serve at room temperature.

Fish Mousse, Santa Catalina Style

(PUDIN DE MERLUZA SANTA CATALINA)

The stunning Parador Castillo de Santa Catalina crowns the Santa Catalina mountain high above the Andalucian city of Jaén. From up here the whitewashed houses of Jaén look like toy reproductions, and olive trees dotting the surrounding mountains (the city is in the heart of Spain's olive groves) run in dizzying rows into infinity. The *parador* is a modern structure, although it looks for all the world like an ancient castle. Within, the old and the new have been blended in an extraordinary fashion, creating a fantasy land as surrealistic and extravagant as it is old and austere.

Food at the *parador* also has a modern touch, exemplified by this light and delicious cold fish mousse. As a tapa this dish may be served in a slice, or spread on a piece of bread or a cracker (in which case you can eliminate the mayonnaise dressing). SERVES 8

1 tablespoon olive oil
1 medium onion, sliced
2 cloves garlic, peeled
1 medium tomato, skinned
   and chopped
1 cup dry white wine
1¼ pounds fresh cod steaks,
   or other mild fish steaks
1 bay leaf
2 sprigs parsley
1 small leek, well washed
Salt
Pinch saffron
1 carrot, scraped
1 pimiento, preferably home prepared
   (see p. 204), chopped

½ cup tomato sauce,
   preferably homemade (p. 66, using
   2 medium tomatoes)
7 eggs
Freshly ground pepper
½ cup heavy cream
Bread crumbs
Lettuce leaves
Parsley or watercress as garnish

MAYONNAISE DRESSING
Mayonnaise (p. 47)
2 large cloves garlic, mashed to a paste
   or put through a garlic press
3 tablespoons chopped green
   Spanish olives

Heat the oil in a large, shallow casserole. Sauté the onion and garlic until the onion is wilted. Add the fresh tomato and sauté 5 minutes more. Pour in the wine and boil down to half.

Arrange the fish in one layer in the casserole. Barely cover with water. Add the bay leaf, parsley, leek, salt, saffron, and carrot. Bring to a boil, reduce the heat, cover, and simmer for about 15 minutes.

Remove all skin and bones from the fish and flake into small pieces. Strain and reserve the cooking liquid, discarding the leek, carrot, and bay leaf and placing the rest of the vegetables in the bowl of a food processor. Blend to a medium consistency.

Measure the cooking liquid to ¾ cup (if there is more, boil down). Add the fish and the ¾ cup reserved cooking liquid to the processor and blend briefly. Add the pimiento, tomato sauce, eggs, salt, and pepper. Process just until blended—the mixture should be well chopped but not too smooth. With the motor running, pour in the cream gradually.

Transfer the fish mixture to a well-buttered 9¼ × 5¼ × 2¾-inch loaf pan that has been dusted with bread crumbs. Cover tightly with foil and place in a larger pan of hot water (bain-marie).

Place on top of the stove and bring to a boil, then bake at 225°F for 80 minutes. Remove the loaf pan from the pan of water and loosen the foil. Cool, then chill.

Mix the mayonnaise dressing ingredients and let sit at room temperature.

To serve the fish loaf, loosen the sides and shake the loaf pan until the mousse is free. Invert and unmold. Cut in ¾–1-inch slices. Arrange attractively on lettuce leaves and garnish with parsley or watercress. Serve the mayonnaise dressing separately.

Trout and Monkfish Mousse
(PUDIN DE RAPE Y TRUCHA)

We paid a return visit to Casa Irene in the tiny village of Artiés and found owner and chef Irene as charming and creative as we had remembered her. She serves this extraordinary fish combination sliced, topped with mayonnaise, and broiled. I find it as good, if not better, as a cold spread. It can be made a day in advance. SERVES 6

> 3 tablespoons butter
> ½ pound monkfish (see p. 86)
>   or halibut, skinned and boned,
>   coarsely cut up
> A ¾-pound trout, skinned
>   and boned, coarsely cut up
> ½ cup plus 2 tablespoons
>   heavy cream
> Salt
> Freshly ground pepper
> Butter
> Bread crumbs

Heat the 3 tablespoons of butter in a skillet and sauté the monkfish and trout until just done. Transfer to a processor or blender and blend with an on-off motion until finely chopped. Quickly blend in the cream, salt, and pepper.

Grease a 7¾ × 3⅝-inch mold well with butter and sprinkle with bread crumbs. Pour in the fish mixture and cover tightly with foil. Place in a larger pan of hot water (bain-marie), and bring the water to a boil on top of the stove, then bake at 350°F for 40 minutes. Remove the loaf pan from the water and continue baking for another 10 minutes. Loosen the foil, cool, then chill.

Loosen the fish loaf from the pan and turn out. To serve, you may slice the loaf, spread with mayonnaise, and serve cold, or run it under the broiler until the top is golden. It can also be served as a spread for bread or crackers—top the canapé with a dab of mayonnaise and garnish with a piece of pimiento or parsley.

Marinated Sardines
(SARDINAS EN ESCABECHE)

Decades ago, when there was little refrigeration, *escabeches* were a very practical way to preserve perishables. In Spain this method remains one of the best and most popular preparations for sardines —and as convenient now as in times past, because the dish can be made up to a week in advance. SERVES 8

PREPARE TWO DAYS IN ADVANCE

> 2 pounds small sardines,
>   cleaned, heads on
> Salt
> Flour for dusting
> ¾ cup olive oil
> 6 cloves garlic, peeled
> ¾ cup red wine vinegar
> ¾ cup dry white wine
> ¾ cup fish broth (p. 27)
>   or clam juice
> 2 bay leaves
> ¼ teaspoon thyme
> 6 peppercorns
> Lemon slices

Sprinkle the fish inside and out with salt and dust with flour. Heat ¼ cup of the oil in a skillet with 1 clove of the garlic and sauté the sardines until golden and cooked through. Arrange the fish in a shallow serving casserole (Spanish earthenware is ideal) and discard the garlic. Heat the remaining ½ cup of oil in the skillet and cook the remaining 5 garlic cloves until they are golden. Stir in the vinegar, wine, fish broth, bay leaves, thyme, peppercorns, and salt. Boil for a few minutes to reduce the liquid and remove the raw vinegar and wine taste. Cool and pour over the fish. Arrange lemon slices on top, cover, and refrigerate for at least 2 days. Be sure to bring to room temperature before serving.

Marinated Tuna

(ATÚN ESCABECHADO)

PREPARE ONE DAY IN ADVANCE

In Spain marinated tuna is packed in cans and ready for use. It is simple to make yourself, however, and will give added character to any number of cold dishes calling for canned tuna. Simply combine a 7-ounce can light or white meat tuna, drained and flaked, with 1 tablespoon white wine vinegar and marinate for at least 1 day (makes about 1 cup).

Cod Salad with Tomato and Onion

(ESQUEIXADA)

You will surely stump your guests with this delicious Catalán tapa, for it is neither salty nor fishy and gives little hint that it even contains dried cod.
SERVES 6

START PREPARATION ONE DAY IN ADVANCE

> ¾ pound skinned and boned
>   dried salt cod (see p. 203)
> 1 medium onion, peeled and quartered
> 1 red pepper, cut in thin strips
> 12 cured black olives
> 9 tablespoons olive oil
> 4½ tablespoons
>   red wine vinegar
> Salt
> Freshly ground pepper
> 1 medium tomato, diced

Soak the cod at room temperature in cold water to cover for 24–36 hours, changing the water occasionally. Soak the onion in salted water for 1 hour. Drain the cod and the onion well.

Shred the cod with your fingers into a serving bowl. Coarsely chop the onion and add it to the cod along with the red pepper and olives. In a small bowl whisk the oil, vinegar, salt, and pepper. Fold this dressing into the salad. Mix in the tomato gently and chill well. You can make this several hours in advance or even the night before, in which case you should add the tomato closer to serving time and check the vinegar, which seems to lose its punch after a few hours.

Marinated Quail

(CODORNICES "MARQUÉS DE VILLENA")

Spain is game country, and quail, pheasant, and partridge are almost as common as chicken. One of the most delicious ways to serve these birds is marinated. Tiny quail in particular, when attractively arranged and garnished, make a spectacular tapa for a party. The recipe comes from the Parador Marqués de Villena in Alarcón (see p. 149).

It is important to marinate the quail for several days to develop its flavor fully and, equally important, to bring the quail to room temperature before serving. SERVES 8

PREPARE SEVERAL DAYS IN ADVANCE

4 tablespoons olive oil
8 quail, trussed
20 very small pearl onions, peeled
1 head garlic, separated and peeled
3 carrots, scraped then cut in half
  crosswise and in quarters lengthwise
1 leek, well washed,
  or 2 large scallions
3 bay leaves
2 sprigs parsley
1½ teaspoons thyme
Salt
12 peppercorns
½ stalk celery with leaves
Pinch saffron
½ cup red wine vinegar
2 cups dry white wine
½ cup chicken broth,
  all fat removed

GARNISH
1 lemon, sliced
Parsley sprigs
Dill or cornichon pickles, sliced
  decoratively into "fans"
Strips of red pepper or pimiento,
  preferably home prepared (see p. 204)
  or imported

Heat the oil in a large casserole. Sauté the quail slowly until they are well browned on all sides. Transfer the birds to a warm platter. In the same casserole sauté the onions, garlic, carrots, and leek until the onions are wilted. Add the bay leaves, parsley, thyme, salt, peppercorns, celery, and saffron. Stir in the vinegar, wine, and broth. Return the quail to the casserole. Cover and simmer for 45 minutes.

Arrange the quail in a round, shallow serving casserole, preferably Spanish earthenware. Pour the cooking liquid over them and cool. Cover and refrigerate for 3–4 days, turning occasionally.

To serve, bring the quail to room temperature and cut in halves with scissors for easier eating. Discard the leek, parsley, peppercorns, and celery. Julienne the cooked carrots and reserve. Return the quail skin side up to the marinade and arrange attractively with the carrots, pearl onions, lemon slices, parsley sprigs, pickles, and red pepper strips.

Pâté with Turkey Breast

(PATÉ CAFÉ SAN MARTÍN)

This is one of the best pâtés I have ever eaten, devised and elaborated by chef Tomás Herranz (now heading his own restaurant in Madrid; see p. 173) and served at the Café San Martín in New York City. A roll of white meat turkey, wrapped in ham, is cooked into the pâté, so that each slice has an attractive cross section of turkey at its center.

The Café San Martín is one of my favorite restaurants, owned and expertly supervised by the most gracious of hosts, our good friend Ramón San Martín. SERVES AT LEAST 10-12

PREPARE SEVERAL DAYS IN ADVANCE

A ½-pound piece turkey breast, the length of the pâté pan and 1½ inches wide
Chicken broth
3 very thin slices boiled ham
¾ pound veal, cut in pieces
¾ pound lean boneless pork, loin or shoulder, cut in pieces
½ pound chicken livers
¼ pound pork fat
½ pound canned imported liver pâté or domestic liverwurst
1 teaspoon thyme
½ teaspoon freshly ground nutmeg
4 teaspoons salt
¼ teaspoon freshly ground pepper
5 ounces semisweet (oloroso) Spanish sherry
1 egg
Pork fatback, in thin slices

½ cup whole shelled pistachio nuts, papery outer skin removed
3 bay leaves

Tie the turkey breast at intervals with string. Place in a shallow casserole with chicken broth barely to cover. (You can season this, if you wish, with some salt, a few peppercorns, a bay leaf, some thyme, and a sprig of parsley.) Bring to a boil, cover, and simmer for 10 minutes. Remove from the liquid and cool. Cut off the string and wrap in the ham slices.

Combine in the bowl of a processor the veal, pork, chicken livers, pork fat, canned pâté or liverwurst, thyme, nutmeg, salt, and pepper. Blend to a medium consistency. With an on-off motion, incorporate the sherry and egg.

Line a 9¼ × 5¼ × 2¾-inch loaf pan with strips of fatback and extend them over the side. Pour in half of the pâté mixture, sprinkle with half of the pistachio nuts, then place the turkey roll down the center. Add the rest of the pâté mixture, then the remaining nuts, pushing them gently into the pâté. Place the bay leaves in a row down the middle and fold over the strips of fatback to cover the pâté. (If they do not cover, add more strips.) Cover tightly with foil.

Place the loaf pan in a larger pan of hot water (bain-marie) and bake at 350°F for 1¾ hours. Remove from the oven and from the pan of water, loosen the foil, and pour off any fat. Weigh down with a heavy object (a brick covered with foil is ideal) and cool. Refrigerate for several days but bring to room temperature before serving. Serve, if desired, with Onion Marmalade (p. 49).

Duck and Cured Ham Pâté

(PATÉ DE PATO)

The stately and exclusive Ritz Hotel has been an institution in Madrid since the turn of the century. Most of the world's heads of state and royalty have been guests there, for the Ritz maintains its standards and knows how to treat people who expect the very best.

In the hotel's exceptionally elegant restaurant, which spills over into a lush outdoor garden in summer, duck pâté has been served for many years as part of a traditional menu served with impeccable style. And, by the way, if you ever have occasion to visit the hotel's bar, be sure to try their exceptional homemade potato chips as a tapa.

SERVES AT LEAST 10-12

PREPARE SEVERAL DAYS IN ADVANCE

½ pound chicken livers
1 duck liver (optional)
A 3½-pound duck, skinned and boned,
   fat removed, cut in pieces
¾ pound lean boneless pork,
   loin or shoulder
¼ pound pork fat
2 eggs
2 tablespoons salt
½ teaspoon freshly ground pepper
¾ teaspoon thyme
½ cup dry (fino) Spanish sherry
¼ cup brandy, preferably Spanish
   brandy or Cognac
2 large cloves garlic, minced
2 tablespoons minced parsley
⅓ cup (about 2 ounces) cured ham
   (not salty), in ¼-inch cubes

Pork fatback, in thin slices
4 bay leaves

Place in the bowl of a processor the chicken and duck livers, the boned duck, pork, and pork fat. Blend to a medium consistency. With an on-off motion, mix in the eggs, salt, pepper, thyme, sherry, brandy, garlic, and parsley. Stir in the ham.

Line a 9¼ × 5¼ × 2¾-inch loaf pan with strips of fatback and extend them over the side. Pour in the pâté mixture, arrange the bay leaves in a row down the center, then fold over the strips of fatback to cover the pâté. (If they do not cover, add more strips.) Cover tightly with foil and place in a large pan of boiling water (bain-marie) and bake at 350°F for 2 hours.

Remove the loaf pan from the water, loosen the foil, and pour off any fat. Weigh down with a heavy object (a brick covered with foil is an ideal size and weight) and cool. Remove the weight, cover, and refrigerate for several days. Bring to room temperature before serving. Onion Marmalade (p. 49) complements the pâté beautifully.

Partridge and Liver Pâté

(TERRINA DE PERDIZ)

This has for many years been one of my favorite pâté recipes. It is a pâté that is less coarse in texture than most, and I like to serve it with pumpernickel bread. To make it easier to serve as a tapa, I slice the pâté down the center lengthwise, so that each half then slices into small squares that fit perfectly on cocktail-size pieces of bread. SERVES AT LEAST 10-12

PREPARE SEVERAL DAYS IN ADVANCE

1/4 pound slab bacon, coarsely chopped
Meat from a 1-pound partridge or pheasant, coarsely chopped
1 partridge liver (optional)
1 pound chicken livers, cut in pieces
1/4 cup flour
1/4 cup dry (fino) Spanish sherry
2 tablespoons brandy, preferably Spanish brandy or Cognac
6 tablespoons heavy cream
2 eggs
4 teaspoons salt
1/4 teaspoon freshly ground pepper
1/2 teaspoon freshly ground nutmeg
1 tablespoon chopped truffles (optional)

In a processor place the bacon, partridge meat, and the partridge and chicken livers. Blend until finely chopped. Add the flour and beat until smooth. With the motor running, pour in the sherry, brandy, cream, eggs, salt, pepper, and nutmeg. With an on-off motion, mix in the truffles, if desired.

Pour into a well-greased 9¼ × 5¼ × 2¾-inch loaf pan, cover tightly with foil, and place in a larger pan of hot water (bain-marie). Bake at 325°F for 2 hours. Remove from the hot water, loosen the foil, and cool for 20 minutes. Place a weight (a brick wrapped in foil is the perfect size) on the pâté and let sit about 1 hour more. Remove the weight and refrigerate for several days, then serve at room temperature, accompanied, if you wish, by Onion Marmalade (p. 49).

Pâté with Fresh Figs

(PÂTÉ CON BREVAS)

For this simple and interesting tapa you can use a homemade or good-quality canned pâté, preferably liver-based and fairly smooth textured. SERVES 4

4 fresh figs, in ½-inch crosswise slices
2 ounces pâté, in ¼-inch slices
4 tablespoons heavy cream
Parsley sprigs for garnish

Arrange the fig slices on a serving dish. Put pieces of pâté of about the same size over the fig slices and secure with a toothpick. Pour the cream around— not over—the tapa (the cream lends a pleasant contrast of texture and flavor). Decorate with parsley sprigs. You can put together the figs and pâté in advance, but arrange on the dish with the cream at the last minute. Serve at room temperature.

Head Cheese Vinaigrette

(CABEZA DE JABALÍ A LA VINAGRETA)

What we call "head cheese" translates literally from Spanish as "wild boar's head." Both are improbable names for a very delicious cold cut made from calf head, which is much easier to buy already prepared than to make at home. When head cheese is mixed with this vinaigrette of pickle, red pepper, carrot, and olives, it is cool, crisp, refreshing, and quick to prepare. You may serve it right away or refrigerate overnight. SERVES 4

½ pound head cheese, in thin slices,
   then in julienne strips

DRESSING
4 tablespoons olive oil
2 tablespoons red wine vinegar
2 teaspoons minced parsley
2 tablespoons very thin julienne
   strips of dill or cornichon pickle
2 tablespoons 1-inch-long julienne
   strips of red pepper
2 tablespoons minced carrot
8–12 very small cured black olives
Salt
Freshly ground pepper

In a small bowl combine all the dressing ingredients. Place the head cheese in a shallow serving bowl and mix in the dressing gently. Chill.

Fresh Ham with Orange and Walnut Sauce

(JAMÓN FRESCO CON MERMELADA DE NARANJA Y NUECES)

Here is a great way to serve fresh ham, as I ate it at the Virrey Palafox restaurant in the old Castilian city of Burgo de Osma. It is an especially convenient dish if you have the ham left over—just be sure the meat is juicy and at room temperature. The sauce is enough for about 6 tapas-size servings, so adjust the recipe according to the amount of fresh ham you have. The same sauce is also excellent with the Orange-Flavored Sautéed Chicken Pieces (p. 182). SERVES 6

Six ¼-inch slices fresh ham

ORANGE AND WALNUT SAUCE
¾ cup orange marmalade,
   preferably imported English
1 tablespoon raisins
2 pitted prunes, cut in pieces
¼ cup broken walnut meats
3 tablespoons fresh orange juice
1 tablespoon water

Combine in a small saucepan ¼ cup of the marmalade with the raisins and prunes. Cover and simmer for 10 minutes. Uncover and cook 5 minutes more. Cool, then add the remaining ½ cup of marmalade, the walnuts, orange juice, and water. This can be used right away or kept for many days. To serve, arrange the meat slices attractively on a serving platter and pass the sauce separately.

Marinated Pork Loin

(LOMO DE ORZA)

Travelers driving between Madrid and Barcelona usually reach the old Arab town of Calatayud (named after its Moorish ruler, Kalat Ayub, and crowned by an impressive castle built for him) just around tapas time. Therefore the main street is lined with bars with a selection of tapas quite out of proportion to the town's population. This pork, cooked, then preserved in an oil marinade (in an earthenware pot called an *orza*), is one of those local tapas specialties that suddenly appear in this region and then rarely reappear elsewhere in Spain.

SERVES 6

PREPARE ONE DAY IN ADVANCE

1–1¼ pounds lean boneless
    pork loin, in 1-inch-thick slices
Salt
Freshly ground pepper
1 cup plus 2 tablespoons olive oil
1 tablespoon fresh lemon juice
¼ teaspoon thyme
⅛ teaspoon crushed rosemary
4 cloves garlic, lightly crushed and peeled

Sprinkle the pork with salt and pepper. Heat 2 tablespoons of the oil in a skillet. Brown the meat quickly on both sides over medium-high heat. Lower the heat and continue cooking for about 15 minutes, or until the pork is just cooked through but still juicy. (It is very important not to let the meat get dry.)

Transfer the meat to a shallow casserole, preferably earthenware, in which it fits snugly. Add the remaining cup of oil. (The oil should just cover the meat. Depending on the size of your dish, you may need a little more or less.) Add the lemon juice, thyme, rosemary, garlic, salt, and pepper and shake the dish to blend.

Cover the dish with foil and leave at room temperature for 24 hours. Serve at room temperature, each meat slice cut on the bias into ¼-inch strips, with a dribbling of the oil marinade.

Fried Pork Skins with Rolled Anchovy

(CORTEZA DE CERDO CON ANCHOA)

In Salamanca's arcaded Plaza Mayor, one of Spain's most beautiful city squares, the swallows swoop by the hundreds, and every evening's *paseo*, or stroll, in summer is a major event. Residents, especially from the large university population, circulate by the thousands around the square, and university singing groups (*tunas*), dressed in medieval garb, entertain. Everyone takes advantage of some fine tapas in the square and in the streets radiating from it. Fried pork rinds with anchovy, an excellent combination, are a very common tapa in Salamanca, as are a variety of batter-fried fish and vegetables.

The preparation of this tapa needs no recipe—simply top a small piece of fried pork rind (usually found in the potato chip section of your store) with a rolled anchovy, or if the rind is curled, fit the anchovy inside. Figure at least two per person.

Mortadella and Ham Salad

(ENSALADA DE MORTADELA Y JAMÓN)

I have sampled two versions of this salad, one with a vinaigrette dressing and the other with *salsa rosada* — mayonnaise and tomato. Although I prefer the vinaigrette, which is slightly tart, family and friends who have sampled both seem to like the slight sweetness of the other version. This salad may be served right away, but I think it gains in flavor when left to marinate overnight. The main recipe is for the vinaigrette version. SERVES 6

PREPARE ONE DAY IN ADVANCE

¼ pound mortadella, in thin slices, then in 2-inch-long julienne strips
¼ pound boiled ham, in thin slices, then in 2-inch-long julienne strips
1 pimiento, home prepared (see p. 204) or imported, in julienne strips
4 tablespoons minced dill or cornichon pickle
½ cup minced onion
2 tablespoons minced parsley

DRESSING
¼ cup olive oil
2 tablespoons red wine vinegar
¼ teaspoon Dijon-style mustard
Salt
Freshly ground pepper

In a bowl mix together the mortadella, ham, pimiento, pickle, onion, and parsley. In a small bowl whisk the dressing ingredients, then fold gently into the mortadella mixture. Serve immediately or let marinate for several hours at room temperature, or longer in the refrigerator.

VARIATION
Omit the onion and add 1 small carrot, scraped, in 1-inch-long julienne strips. Reduce the pickle to 2 tablespoons. Fold in ¼ cup mayonnaise blended with 2 tablespoons ketchup, salt, pepper, and a dash of Worcestershire sauce.

Stuffed Pig's Feet Vinaigrette

(MANOS DE CERDO RELLENOS A LA VINAGRETA)

A delicious and most unusual tapa, these pig's feet are boned, filled with pork, raisins, mushrooms, and spinach, then sliced and bathed in a caper vinaigrette. The list of ingredients is long, but everything can be done days in advance. The pig's feet must be whole, not split as they usually are when packaged in the supermarket. SERVES 8

PREPARE ONE DAY IN ADVANCE

3 small whole pig's feet
Two 1-inch cubes slab bacon
½ carrot, scraped and cut in thick slices
1 small onion, peeled and studded with 4 cloves
1 sprig parsley
¼ teaspoon thyme
1 bay leaf
1 cup dry red wine
3 cups chicken broth
4 peppercorns

Salt
1 hard-boiled egg, minced

FILLING
2 teaspoons raisins
1½ cups finely chopped
   spinach leaves
1 tablespoon bread crumbs
2 teaspoons white or red wine
¼ pound ground pork
½ teaspoon minced truffles
   (optional)
⅛ teaspoon salt
Freshly ground pepper
1 clove garlic, mashed to a paste
   or put through a garlic press
1 tablespoon minced parsley
4 tablespoons minced mushroom
1 tablespoon minced cured ham

VINAIGRETTE
4 tablespoons olive oil
4 teaspoons red wine vinegar
Salt
Freshly ground pepper
1 teaspoon small capers or chopped
   larger capers
4 teaspoons minced onion
2 teaspoons minced parsley

Tie each pig's foot with string so it will hold together in cooking. Place in a deep pot with the bacon, carrot, peeled onion, parsley sprig, thyme, bay leaf, red wine, broth, peppercorns, and salt. Bring to a boil, cover, and simmer for about 3½ hours.

To make the filling, soak the raisins in warm water for 15 minutes. Drain and chop coarsely. Place the spinach with some salt and a few drops of water in a saucepan, cover, and cook slowly for 4 minutes. Drain and dry on paper towels. Soak the bread crumbs in the wine. Combine in a bowl the ground pork, raisins, bread crumbs, optional truffles, salt, pepper, garlic, parsley, mushroom, ham, and spinach.

While the pig's feet are still warm, remove the string, butterfly, and remove the bones carefully, doing your best not to break the skin of the pig's feet. Cut out the pieces of firm cartilage, chop them finely, and add to the ground pork mixture.

Fill each pig's foot with about 3 tablespoons of the filling. Tie at intervals with string and wrap tightly in foil. Return to the cooking liquid and add enough water to cover. Bring to a boil, then simmer, covered, for 2 hours. Remove from foil, drain, cool, and refrigerate for several hours until firm. Reserve 4 teaspoons of the cooking liquid.

To make the vinaigrette, whisk the oil, vinegar, the reserved 4 teaspoons of cooking liquid, salt, and pepper. Stir in the capers, onion, and parsley.

Cut the filled pig's feet into ¼-inch slices and cover with the vinaigrette. Marinate overnight. Sprinkle with the minced egg when ready to serve.

3

TAPAS
WITH
BREAD
OR
PASTRY

A party would not be a party without bread- and pastry-based tapas, so easy to pick up with your fingers and so well suited to accompany cocktails and other aperitifs. But the tapas in this chapter are never the overworked themes that are part of every caterer's repertoire. Here are savory pies and turnovers, with fillings of scallops, squid, green olives, and spinach with raisins; puff pastries and tartlets with frogs' legs, chorizo, wild mushroom, blood sausage, and red pepper fillings; and canapés, hot and cold, of anchovy, dried cod, and olive paste. Even when more traditional fillings and toppings of shellfish and cheese appear, they will of course have an added Spanish flair.

Bread and pastry tapas generally turn soggy when left assembled for any length of time (the savory pies are the exception), so do whatever preparations are possible in advance, but try not to put the tapas together more than an hour before serving.

EMPANADAS AND EMPANADILLAS

Empanadas, large savory pies, and *empanadillas*, small turnovers with fillings often similar to those of the *empanadas*, are always popular tapas and are great party fare because they can be filled, then kept refrigerated or frozen until baking time. The *empanadas* in particular are excellent served at room temperature.

Savory Pie and Turnover Dough
(MASA HOJALDRADA)

This is an excellent puff pastry–style dough for *empanadas* and *empanadillas*. The lard, I feel, produces a more flavorful and flaky pastry, but shortening also works well. MAKES 1 LARGE TWO-CRUST PIE, TWO 10-INCH PIES, OR ABOUT 40 TURNOVERS

> 3 cups unbleached flour
> 1 1/2 teaspoons salt
> 3/4 cup cold water
> 4 1/2 teaspoons vinegar
> 2 egg yolks
> 1 cup lard, softened, or
>   vegetable shortening

Mix the flour in a large bowl with the salt, then incorporate the water, vinegar, and egg yolks and work with your hands until the dough forms a smooth ball. Let sit for 30 minutes covered with plastic wrap.

Roll the dough into a 10 × 15-inch rectangle. With a rubber spatula spread 1/3 cup of the lard over the dough. With the aid of a knife, fold one side over the top, then fold over the other side, business-letter fashion. Wrap again in plastic wrap and refrigerate for 15 minutes. Repeat, using another 1/3 cup of the lard, refrigerate 15 minutes more, and repeat a third time, leaving the dough refrigerated this time for 1 hour. The dough is better still if refrigerated overnight. [May be frozen]

Pork and Green Pepper Pie

(EMPANADA DE CERDO Y PIMIENTOS)

Pork and green peppers are a favorite filling for these pies from Galicia, the home of *empanadas*. A large amount of onion makes the filling juicy and very flavorful. SERVES 8-10

START PREPARATION SEVERAL HOURS IN ADVANCE

4 teaspoons paprika, preferably
   Spanish style
8 tablespoons olive oil
1 tablespoon minced parsley
1 large clove garlic, minced
Salt
3/4 pound pork shoulder or
   loin, in less than 1/8-inch-thick
   strips about 2 1/2 inches wide
2 green peppers, in thin strips
2 medium onions (about 3/4 pound),
   thinly sliced
2 tablespoons dry white wine
Savory Pie and Turnover Dough
   (preceding recipe)
1 egg, lightly beaten with
   1 teaspoon water

In a bowl combine the paprika, 4 tablespoons of the oil, the parsley, garlic, and salt. Add the meat and stir to coat well. Marinate for several hours or overnight.

Heat 2 tablespoons of the oil in a skillet. Add the peppers and stir fry for 1 minute. Add 1 tablespoon water, lower the heat, cover, and cook until the peppers are tender, about 15 minutes. Remove the peppers from the skillet.

Heat the remaining 2 tablespoons of oil in the same skillet and sauté the onions over low heat, covered, until tender but not brown. Remove the onions. Turn the heat up to high and add the marinated meat, with its oil, to the skillet and stir fry until it loses its color. Add the white wine and cook for another minute. Return the onions and peppers to the skillet and mix well. Taste for salt (the mixture should be well seasoned).

Roll the dough into a 10 × 15-inch rectangle, fold in thirds as directed, then roll into a rectangle 14 × 28 inches. Cut into two 14-inch squares, then trim each of these squares into a 14-inch circle. (If you prefer smaller pies, divide the dough in half and roll each half into a rectangle 10 × 20 inches. Cut into two 10-inch squares and trim each into a 10-inch circle to make two pies.) Place one circle on a dampened cookie sheet and cover with the pork filling, not quite reaching to the edges. Top with the remaining dough circle, rolling up the edges and pressing to seal. Slit in several places [May be prepared ahead and frozen], brush with the beaten egg, and bake at 350°F for about 35 minutes, or until golden. Allow to cool before serving. (It is also excellent at room temperature.)

Scallop Pie

(EMPANADA DE VIEIRAS)

This delicious and most unusual savory pie is made in Galicia with the region's exceptional scallops (see p. 167). If the ingredients are chopped finely, the filling is perfect for *empanadillas*. SERVES 8-10

Savory Pie and Turnover Dough (p. 105)
4 tablespoons olive oil

2 medium onions, chopped
1 large clove garlic, minced
1 green pepper, chopped
1 bay leaf
1 large pimiento, home prepared
(see p. 204), chopped
2 tablespoons minced parsley
2 tablespoons skinned and finely
chopped tomato
1 pound bay scallops, whole,
or sea scallops, cut up
2 tablespoons minced cured ham
Salt
1 egg, lightly beaten with
1 teaspoon water

Make the dough according to instructions.

Heat the oil in a large skillet, then sauté the onion, garlic, green pepper, and bay leaf slowly for 5 minutes. Lower the heat, cover, and continue cooking for 10 minutes. Add the pimiento and cook, covered, 5 minutes more, until the onion is tender but not colored and the peppers are softened. Uncover, turn up the heat, add the parsley and tomato, and sauté for a minute or two, until the tomato is softened.

Stir in the scallops, ham, and salt to taste (the mixture should be well seasoned). Cook 5 minutes more, then discard the bay leaf. Assemble and bake the pie as for Pork and Green Pepper Pie (preceding recipe), brushing with the beaten egg before baking. Or for individual turnovers, follow the instructions on page 105.

Squid Pie

(EMPANADA DE CHIPIRONES)

Squid with lots of onion and pimiento makes a wonderfully sweet and tasty filling for another typically Galician pie. It also is perfect for small turnovers, in which case the ingredients should be finely chopped. SERVES 8-10

Savory Pie and Turnover Dough (p. 105)
10 tablespoons olive oil
3 medium onions, chopped
2 large pimientos, home prepared
(see p. 204), chopped
Few strands saffron
Salt
1 pound cleaned squid (see p. 204), or
about 1¾ pounds, uncleaned,
with tentacles, coarsely chopped
1 egg, lightly beaten with
1 teaspoon water

Make the dough according to instructions.

Heat the oil in a skillet and sauté the onion for a minute or two. Cover and slowly "stew" the onion until tender, about 20 minutes. Uncover and add the pimientos, saffron, and salt, cooking for another 3 minutes. Turn up the heat and sauté the squid for about 2 minutes—don't overcook, or the squid will toughen.

Assemble and bake the pie according to the instructions for Pork and Green Pepper Pie (p. 106), brushing with the beaten egg before baking. For individual turnovers, follow the instructions on page 109.

Spinach Turnovers

(EMPANADILLAS DE ESPINACA)

Spinach, anchovy, pine nuts, and raisins make a distinctive and typically Spanish filling for turnovers.
SERVES 20 (MAKES 40)

Savory Pie and Turnover Dough (p. 105)
4 tablespoons raisins
3 tablespoons olive oil
2 pounds spinach leaves, washed and
    very finely chopped
Salt
Freshly ground pepper
12 canned anchovies, drained
    and chopped
4 cloves garlic, minced
4 tablespoons finely chopped pine nuts
1 egg, lightly beaten with
    1 teaspoon water

Make the dough according to instructions.

Soak the raisins in warm water to cover for 10 minutes. Drain and chop. Heat the oil in a skillet, add the spinach, stir to coat with the oil, then cover and cook slowly for 2 minutes. Uncover and turn up the heat to evaporate the liquid. Add the salt, pepper, anchovy, and garlic and cook for a minute. Turn off the heat and stir in the pine nuts and raisins.

Roll the dough to a 10 × 15-inch rectangle, fold in thirds as directed, then roll again to less than ⅛-inch thickness. Cut into 3-inch circles and place about 2 teaspoons of filling in the center of each. Bring up the sides and seal well with your fingers, then press with the tines of a fork. Brush with the beaten egg. Bake on a lightly greased cookie sheet at 350°F for about 15 minutes, or until a deep golden color.

Chicken, Pork, and Pimiento Turnovers

(EMPANADILLAS DE POLLO)

If you leave the chicken in larger pieces and cut the pork and pimiento in strips, this also makes a very good pie. The filling can be used right away, but gains in flavor when left for several hours or overnight. MAKES ABOUT 40 TURNOVERS OR 1 LARGE PIE

Savory Pie and Turnover Dough (p. 105)
3 tablespoons olive oil
Meat from one side of a chicken breast and
    a whole chicken thigh, finely chopped
Salt
Freshly ground pepper
1 pork chop, boned and finely chopped
2 ounces (about ⅓ cup) cured ham,
    finely chopped
1 small onion, finely chopped
2 cloves garlic, minced
¼ teaspoon paprika, preferably
    Spanish style
Few strands saffron
2 medium tomatoes (about ½ pound),
    skinned and finely chopped
1 pimiento, home prepared (see p. 204)
    or imported, chopped
1 egg, lightly beaten with 1 teaspoon water

Make the dough according to instructions.

In a skillet heat 2 tablespoons of the oil and sauté the chicken quickly until it just turns white, seasoning with salt and pepper. Add the pork and ham and continue cooking until the pork loses its color.

In a separate skillet sauté the onion and garlic in the remaining oil until the onion is wilted. Stir in the paprika and saffron, add the tomato and salt, cover, and cook slowly for 20 minutes.

Add the tomato mixture and the pimiento to the chicken mixture. Check the seasoning and cook slowly, uncovered, for 10 minutes.

To assemble and bake the turnovers, see page 108, and brush with the beaten egg before baking.

Spicy Meat Turnovers

(EMPANADILLAS DE CARNE)

These turnovers have both Arab and Catalán overtones, with the strong presence of cumin as well as the sweet contrast of the raisins.

SERVES 20 (MAKES 40)

Savory Pie and Turnover Dough (p. 105)
4 tablespoons raisins
4 tablespoons olive oil
2 medium onions, finely chopped
2 large cloves garlic, minced
½ pound ground veal
½ pound ground pork
½ pound ground beef
Salt
Freshly ground pepper
2 tablespoons minced parsley
¼ teaspoon oregano
½ teaspoon paprika,
    preferably Spanish style
2 teaspoons ground cumin,
    preferably freshly ground
4 tablespoons dry white wine
4 teaspoons tomato sauce
1 hard-boiled egg, minced
2 eggs, lightly beaten with 2 teaspoons water

Make the dough according to instructions.

Soak the raisins in warm water to cover for about 10 minutes.

Heat the oil in a skillet and sauté the onion and garlic until the onion is wilted. Add the ground veal, pork, and beef and cook over moderately high heat, stirring, until the meat loses its color. Season well with salt and pepper.

Drain the raisins and add to the skillet with the parsley, oregano, paprika, cumin, wine, tomato sauce, and hard-boiled egg. Cover and cook slowly for about 5 minutes.

To assemble and bake the turnovers, see page 108, brushing with the beaten egg before baking.

Green Olive Turnovers

(EMPANADILLAS DE ACEITUNAS)

This very simple filling of olives, egg, and cured ham requires no cooking. SERVES 20 (MAKES 40)

Savory Pie and Turnover Dough (p. 105)
1 cup (about 6 ounces) minced cured ham
4 hard-boiled eggs, minced
40 pitted green Spanish olives, cut in halves
1 egg, lightly beaten with 1 teaspoon water

Make the dough according to instructions.

In a bowl combine the ham and the minced egg. Roll and bake the dough as in the preceding recipe, placing 2 teaspoons of the egg and ham mixture and 2 olive halves in each turnover.

To assemble and bake the turnovers, see page 108, brushing with the beaten egg before baking.

Chorizo Wrapped in Bread and Leaves

(CHORIZO ENVUELTO EN PAN Y HOJA DE BERZA)

In the Galician dialect this tapa is called Bica da Folla and was a treat given to children when their mothers took unbaked corn breads or meat roasts to the village ovens for baking.

Wrapping the dough in a leaf is a wonderful baking method because the *chorizo* becomes very juicy and the bread stays soft, absorbing the flavor of the *chorizo*. SERVES 4

> ½ pound bread dough (you can use
>   any kind, but pizza dough works
>   particularly well)
> ¼ pound chorizo sausage, cut in 8 pieces
> 8 fairly flat large green leaves, such as
>   Swiss chard, collard greens,
>   large spinach leaves, or even lettuce
>   leaves, washed and dried

Divide the bread dough into 8 balls and roll each into a circle large enough to enclose the *chorizo*. Place the *chorizo* in the center and close the dough around it, pinching well to seal. Wrap in a leaf, covering the dough completely, and tie lengthwise and crosswise with string, like a package. [May be prepared ahead and refrigerated] Bake at 400°F for 20 minutes. To serve, remove the string and the leaves.

Puff Pastry

(HOJALDRE)

I have yet to find any other puff pastry recipe that is as simple to make and that produces such an outstanding pastry as this one from Julia Child's *Julia Child & Company*. Puff pastry can be kept for many weeks in your freezer, ready for any tapas emergency that may arise. MAKES 2¾ POUNDS

> 3 cups unbleached all-purpose flour
> 1 cup cake flour
> 1½ teaspoons salt
> 6½ sticks sweet butter, chilled
> 1 cup iced water

Mix together the all-purpose and cake flours and stir in the salt. Cut the sticks of butter in half lengthwise, then in half again, lengthwise. Now cut into ½-inch cubes and add to the flour. Rub the cubes of butter between your fingers to flatten them into flakes, combining them at the same time with the flour. Refrigerate the mixture for 10 minutes (the butter must be kept firm throughout the process). Add the cold water and stir until the dough holds together roughly.

Turn the dough onto a lightly floured work surface. Pat into a rectangle about 18 inches long and 8 inches wide. Sprinkle the top of the dough with flour. With the aid of a knife, fold one side over the top, then fold over the other side, business-letter fashion. Lift the dough, flour the work surface again, flour the top of the dough, then roll out with a rolling pin to the previous size, making the folded sides the width and the open ends the length. (Remember, all this must be done rapidly—if the butter softens, refrigerate briefly.) Fold up a second time in the same manner, roll out again, then repeat two more times, flouring surfaces as necessary and ending with the dough folded. Cover with plastic wrap and refrigerate for 40 minutes. Roll and fold twice more, and the dough is ready to use or to store for future use in the refrigerator or freezer.

Mushrooms in Puff Pastry

(TARTA DE HONGOS)

The earthy taste of wild mushrooms combines exquisitely with sherry, shallots, and puff pastry. If wild mushrooms are unavailable, cultivated mushrooms will also work beautifully. SERVES 8 (MAKES 8)

½ pound Puff Pastry dough
   (preceding recipe)
5 tablespoons butter
3 ounces wild mushrooms, such as
   chanterelles, boletus, or puffballs,
   or cultivated mushrooms
   (about 12 medium), stems trimmed,
   brushed clean, and sliced
1½ teaspoons minced shallots
2 tablespoons dry (fino) Spanish sherry
½ cup veal broth, or a mixture of
   chicken and beef broth
1½ teaspoons heavy cream
Salt

Make the Puff Pastry dough according to instructions. Roll to ⅛ inch and cut into 3-inch rounds. Bake at 425°F on a dampened cookie sheet on the upper rack of the oven for about 7 minutes, or until a deep golden color.

Heat the butter in a skillet and sauté the mushrooms for about 1 minute. Remove the mushrooms, leaving any remaining butter in the pan. Add the shallots and sauté briefly until they are softened, then deglaze the pan with the sherry. Stir in the broth and cream and cook down until slightly thickened. Salt if necessary. Return the mushrooms to the sauce. [May be prepared ahead]

Warm the puff pastry rounds and split in halves, hollowing out the center a bit for the filling. Fill the bottom halves with the warm mushroom mixture, pour on some sauce, cover with the other half, and serve right away.

Mushrooms and Pimientos in Puff Pastry

(HOJALDRE DE CHAMPIÑÓN)

Here is another tasty mushroom filling for puff pastry. SERVES 6-8 (MAKES ABOUT 18)

¼ pound Puff Pastry dough (p. 110)
1 tablespoon olive oil
1 tablespoon minced onion
1 clove garlic, minced
2 tablespoons minced pimiento, preferably home prepared (see p. 204) or imported
¼ pound mushrooms, brushed clean, finely chopped
½ dried red chili pepper, seeded and crumbled, or ¼ teaspoon crushed red pepper
Salt
Freshly ground pepper
2 teaspoons grated cheese, such as Manchego (see p. 203) or Parmesan

Make the puff pastry dough according to instructions.

Heat the oil in a skillet and sauté the onion and garlic until the onion is wilted. Add the pimiento and cook for a minute, then add the mushrooms, chili pepper, salt, and pepper and sauté until the mushrooms are softened. Remove from the heat and stir in the cheese.

Roll the puff pastry to ⅛ inch. Cut into 1¾-inch circles and place 1 teaspoon of filling on half of the circles. Moisten the edges with water, cover with the remaining pastry circles, and press with the tines of a fork to seal. [May be prepared ahead and refrigerated] Place on a dampened cookie sheet and bake at 425°F on the upper rack of the oven for 7–10 minutes, or until golden. To cut down on work, you could make this appetizer in a larger size—4½-inch circles, for example—and cut into portions when done (bake for about 20 minutes).

Frogs' Legs and Shrimp in Puff Pastry

(HOJALDRE DE ANCAS DE RANA Y GAMBAS)

Here is another enchanting filling for puff pastry, created by Príncipe de Viana, a first-rate and very elegant Basque restaurant in Madrid. The food is served, as is the custom in the Basque country, by waitresses rather than waiters, dressed in traditional Basque costume.

If frogs' legs are unavailable, you can make this tapa with shrimp only, tripling the amount. SERVES 8 (MAKES 8)

½ pound Puff Pastry dough (p. 110)
2 ounces (about 4–5 medium) shrimp, shelled
½ pound medium frogs' legs
1 ounce (about 4 medium) mushrooms, brushed clean
3 tablespoons butter
1 scallion, in julienne strips
1 teaspoon minced shallots
2 tablespoons dry (fino) Spanish sherry
6 tablespoons well-flavored veal broth, or a mixture of chicken and beef broth
2 teaspoons heavy cream

Make the puff pastry dough according to instructions. Roll to ⅛ inch and cut in 3-inch rounds. Place on a dampened cookie sheet and bake at 425°F on the upper rack of the oven for about 7 minutes, or until a deep golden color.

Split the shrimp in half, then cut into thin strips. Bone the frogs' legs and cut the meat into long, thin strips. Cut the mushrooms (stems on) into thin slices lengthwise (with stems), stack, then slice into julienne strips.

Heat 2 tablespoons of the butter in a skillet and sauté the scallion and shallots briefly until just softened. Turn up the heat and sauté the frogs' legs and shrimp for a minute. Add the mushrooms and sauté a minute more. Remove to a warm platter.

Melt the remaining tablespoon of butter in the skillet and deglaze with the sherry, allowing it to boil down for a few seconds. Stir in the broth and cream and simmer until the sauce is slightly thickened. Return the frogs' leg mixture to the skillet, turn up the heat, and cook until most of the sauce has been incorporated into the mixture—it should be neither dry nor saucy. [May be prepared ahead]

Heat the puff pastry rounds and split, hollowing out the center a little to make room for the filling. Fill with about 2 teaspoons of the frogs' legs mixture, heated, cover with the remaining pastry halves, and serve.

Red Peppers in Puff Pastry

(HOJALDRE DE PIMIENTOS MORRONES)

Raco d'en Binu is one of the most highly regarded restaurants in Cataluña. Located in the small town of Argentona, it attracts crowds of Barceloneses, especially on weekends. This combination of fresh red peppers and hollandaise sauce in puff pastry is one of the restaurant's star appetizers. The peppers should be very sweet and have a nice deep red color.

Since you will need only a small amount of hollandaise sauce for this recipe, plan at the same time to cook something else that calls for it, or you can store it in the refrigerator for several days. SERVES 4

½ pound Puff Pastry dough (p. 110)
1 egg yolk, lightly beaten with
    1 teaspoon water
4 red peppers
Olive oil for brushing
Hollandaise Sauce (p. 127)
Salt
Freshly ground pepper

Make the puff pastry dough according to instructions. Roll to ⅛ inch and cut into 4 rectangles, about 5 × 3 inches each. Brush with the egg yolk and place on a dampened cookie sheet. Bake at 425°F on the upper rack of the oven for about 10–11 minutes, or until golden. Cool.

Place the peppers in an ungreased roasting pan and brush them all over with the olive oil. Bake at 375°F for 17 minutes, turn the peppers, and bake 17 minutes more. Cool slightly, then peel off the skin, and core and seed them. While the peppers are cooking, make the hollandaise sauce.

Cut two of the peppers into 1-inch-wide strips and keep them warm. Place the other two peppers in a processor or blender and purée. Strain and transfer to a very small saucepan. Mix with a little water to a thick sauce consistency, season with salt and pepper, and simmer for a minute. [May be prepared ahead]

Split the puff pastry rectangles in halves. Hollow out a depression in the center of the bottom halves and fill with the purée. Arrange the pimiento strips on top, sprinkle with salt, then cover each with 1 tablespoon hollandaise sauce. Bake on a cookie sheet at 450°F for 2 minutes. Cover with the reserved pastry tops and return to the oven for another minute.

Spinach and Pear in Puff Pastry

(HOJALDRE DE ESPINACA Y PERA)

Spinach and pear make a wonderful blend of flavors. The puff pastry may be made (and baked, if you wish) far in advance, then frozen. Heat and fill the pastry just before serving. I discovered this combination at Madrid's latest "in" restaurant, La Gabarra, where it was served as a garnish for a *magret* of goose. SERVES 4

3/4 pound Puff Pastry dough (p. 110)
1/2 pound spinach, washed, stems removed,
  and coarsely chopped
1 pear, peeled, cored, and chopped
Salt
Freshly ground pepper
Dash of nutmeg

WHITE SAUCE
2 tablespoons butter
2 tablespoons flour
1/2 cup milk
1/2 cup chicken broth

Make the puff pastry dough according to instructions. On a floured surface, roll to a thickness of 1/4 inch. Cut into 2 1/4-inch circles. With a knife or a smaller round pastry or cookie cutter, mark a smaller circle within the 2 1/4-inch circles. Do not cut all the way through. Refrigerate the circles as they are ready — the dough must stay cold until baked.

Bake the pastry shells at 425°F on the upper rack of the oven for about 10 minutes, or until baked through and golden. Remove the "marked" center of the circle to form a hollow for the filling. Keep the pastry warm until ready to use, or reheat quickly before using.

Sprinkle the spinach leaves with water and mix them in a pot with the pear. Season lightly with salt and pepper. Cover and simmer very briefly until *just* tender — do not let the spinach or pears get soggy. Drain off any liquid that may remain.

To make the white sauce, melt the butter in a saucepan and stir in the flour. Cook for a minute or two, stirring constantly. Gradually stir in the milk and chicken broth and cook, stirring constantly, until thickened and smooth.

Mix the white sauce with the spinach mixture and season well with salt, pepper, and nutmeg. [May be prepared ahead] Fill the pastry shells and serve.

Blood Sausage in Puff Pastry

(HOJALDRE DE MORCILLA)

Who would ever dream of combining delicious but plebeian blood sausage with elegant puff pastry? That is exactly what chef Tomás Herranz (see p. 173) did, with exceptional results. SERVES 4 (MAKES 10)

> ¼ pound Puff Pastry
>   dough (p. 110)
> 3 tablespoons olive oil
> 3 tablespoons minced onion
> 3 ounces morcilla (blood sausage) (see
>   p. 204), skin removed, finely chopped
> ¼ teaspoon oregano
> ¼ teaspoon paprika,
>   preferably Spanish
>   style
> **Salt**
> **Freshly ground pepper**

Make the puff pastry dough according to instructions. Heat 2 tablespoons of the oil in a skillet and sauté the onion until it is wilted. Add the *morcilla*, and mash with a wooden spoon. Turn off the heat and stir in the remaining tablespoon of oil, the oregano, paprika, salt, and pepper (the mixture should be well seasoned).

Roll the puff pastry to a 3½ × 9-inch rectangle. It should be about ⅛ inch thick. Place the filling in a narrow strip down the center of the pastry. Wet the edge of one long side with water, bring the two long sides up, and pinch well to seal. Wet and pinch the ends to seal also. [May be prepared ahead and refrigerated] Place seam side down on a dampened cookie sheet. Bake at 450°F for 7 minutes, reduce to 350°F and bake 4 minutes more, or until well browned. To serve, cut in 1-inch-wide slices.

Chorizo in Puff Pastry

(CHORIZO EN HOJALDRE)

This tapa, often found at Madrid's most elegant affairs, has always been one of my very favorite ways to prepare *chorizo*. I usually make and freeze it well in advance, so it is on hand for impromptu gatherings. SERVES 5-6 (MAKES 16)

> ½ pound puff pastry dough,
>   preferably homemade (p. 110)
> ¼ pound chorizo sausage,
>   in ¼-inch slices
> 1 egg yolk, lightly beaten

Roll the puff pastry to a thickness of ⅛ inch. Cut into circles ¼ inch larger than the *chorizo* slices. Center a slice of *chorizo* on each circle, paint the edges of the dough with the egg yolk, and cover with another circle of pastry. Seal the edges well with a fork. Refrigerate each puff as it is made so that the pastry does not soften. [May be frozen]

Place the puffs on an ungreased cookie sheet and bake at 450°F on the upper rack of the oven for about 7 minutes, or until lightly browned and puffed.

115

Potato, Tuna, and Vegetables in Puff Pastry

(PASTEL DE ENSALADILLA RUSA)

This beautiful pastry, filled with a mayonnaise-dressed salad, glazed with gelatin, and decorated with pickle slices and shrimp, caught my eye at Mora, an elegant Barcelona gourmet take-out shop. Everything can be made in advance, but try to assemble close to serving time. SERVES 6

> 1 pound Puff Pastry dough (p. 110)
> Potato, Vegetable, and Tuna Salad
>   (p. 67)
> ½ Cooking Liquid recipe (p. 77)
> 12 medium-large shrimp, unshelled
> Pickles, in thin lengthwise slices
>
> GLAZE (OPTIONAL)
> 1½ teaspoons unflavored gelatin
> 1 cup clarified vegetable or
>   chicken broth, chilled

sides with the pickle slices, pressing them to the salad so that they adhere.

If you wish, you may make a gelatin glaze to cover just the shrimp or the entire top of the pastry. (To glaze the pastry, soften the gelatin in ¼ cup of the broth. Add the remaining ¾ cup of broth and heat until the gelatin is dissolved. Cool and chill until the mixture just begins to thicken slightly. Spoon over the pastry top and chill until set—but do not serve the pastry very cold.)

Make the dough and salad according to instructions. Bring the cooking liquid to a boil, add the shrimp, and cook for about 2 minutes. Drain, cool, and shell the shrimp.

Roll the puff pastry to a 6 × 15-inch rectangle. Place on a dampened cookie sheet and prick well with a fork all over, except for a 1-inch margin on each long side. Bake at 425°F for 15 minutes, pricking the center of the pastry occasionally to keep it from puffing. Lower the heat to 400°F and bake 5 minutes more, or until golden. Cool.

Fill the pastry shell with the salad and arrange the shrimp in rows along the top. Decorate the

Puff Pastry Tartlet Shells

(TARTALETAS)

Homemade puff pastry tartlet shells are a bit of work, but make a tremendous difference in the taste of your tapas. The puff pastry, of course, can be made well ahead and refrigerated or frozen, and the tartlets can be baked, stacked, and frozen in plastic bags. They are fragile, however, so be careful not to put anything on top of them in the freezer (the safest way is to put the tartlets in a box). MAKES ABOUT 65 TINY TARTLETS

1 pound Puff Pastry dough (p. 110)

Roll the puff pastry dough (using only 1/4 pound at a time because the dough must stay chilled) to less than 1/8-inch thickness. Cut rounds with a 1 1/2-inch pastry or cookie cutter and press into 1 1/2-inch tartlet molds (I like the ones that are fluted and rounded on the bottom), stretching the dough slightly so it extends a little over the top of the mold. Prick the dough, cover with another tartlet mold, and weigh it down (you can use dried beans, or metal pellets sold for this purpose). If the dough has softened, place for a couple of minutes in the freezer before baking.

Bake at 425°F on the upper rack of the oven for about 7 minutes. Remove the weights and the top mold, prick the tartlets, and bake for 1 minute, uncovered. Prick again and bake for another minute, or until golden.

Shrimp Tartlets

(TARTALETAS DE GAMBAS)

Simmering the shrimp for these tartlets slowly in onion, garlic, and tomato gives them a very special flavor. And when the shrimp are then mixed with mayonnaise, you have an exceptional tartlet filling. Make the effort to use homemade mayonnaise and homemade puff pastry tartlet shells—they make a noticeable difference. SERVES 6-8 (MAKES 24)

24 puff pastry tartlet shells, preferably
   homemade (preceding recipe)
2 tablespoons fruity olive oil
1/2 pound small-medium
   shrimp, unshelled
1/4 cup chopped onion
2 cloves garlic, minced
1 medium tomato, finely chopped
3/4 cup water
3/4 cup fish broth (p. 27)
   or clam juice
Salt
Freshly ground pepper
About 6 tablespoons mayonnaise,
   preferably homemade (p. 47)

Heat the oil in a skillet and sauté the shrimp, turning once, until they just turn pink. Remove to a warm platter. In the remaining oil sauté the onion and garlic until the onion is wilted. Add the tomato and cook 5 minutes more. Return the shrimp to the skillet and stir in the water, broth, salt, and pepper. Bring to a boil, then simmer, uncovered, for 30 minutes. Let the shrimp sit in the liquid until cool.

Shell the shrimp and chop finely. Combine with the mayonnaise [May be prepared ahead] and fill the tartlet shells shortly before serving. Serve, preferably at room temperature.

Crab Tartlets
(TARTALETAS DE CANGREJO)

This is one of my favorite tartlet fillings, first sampled as a before-dinner tapa in a fine Bilbao restaurant, Machinventa. SERVES 6 (MAKES ABOUT 15)

5 medium shrimp, cooked and shelled
5 tablespoons cooked shredded crab meat
2 tablespoons minced dill or
   cornichon pickle
4 tablespoons minced hard-boiled egg
2 tablespoons minced pimiento,
   home prepared (see p. 204)
   or imported
2 tablespoons minced onion
Several tablespoons mayonnaise,
   preferably homemade (p. 47)
About 15 puff pastry tartlet shells,
   preferably homemade (p. 117;
   1/4 pound dough necessary)
Pimiento or parsley for garnish

In a bowl mix together the shrimp (finely chopped), crab, pickle, egg, pimiento, and onion. Incorporate enough mayonnaise to make a smooth, creamy mixture. [May be prepared ahead] Not more than an hour before serving, spoon this mixture into the tartlet shells and garnish with pimiento or parsley. Leave at room temperature until ready to serve.

VARIATION

A very simple version of this tapa calls for 6 tablespoons shredded crab meat, 3 tablespoons mayonnaise, and 3 tablespoons chopped romaine lettuce. Sprinkle the lettuce into the tartlet shells, cover with mayonnaise, and then arrange the crab meat on top. Garnish with parsley.

Tuna Tartlets
(TARTALETAS DE ATÚN)

Mallorca, an elegant gourmet shop in Madrid, may lack the ambience of a typical tapas bar, but it is one of the most outstanding places in Madrid for tapas. Although most of the store's business is take-out, their huge variety of fabulous tapas can be purchased by the piece and eaten wherever there is room to stand, accompanied by a cold beer or a glass of wine. Mallorca's tapas tend toward the easy-to-serve varieties, such as those enclosed in pastry, crisply fried, sandwiched between bread slices, or in tartlet shells. Of the dozens of kinds of tartlets on display, I particularly like this one of pickled tuna. SERVES 4-6 (MAKES ABOUT 12)

Half a 7-ounce can light meat tuna,
   drained and flaked
3 teaspoons minced dill or
   cornichon pickle
1/4 teaspoon pickle juice
2 tablespoons tomato sauce
1/4 teaspoon wine vinegar, preferably white
1 teaspoon minced onion
2 tablespoons minced hard-boiled egg
1/2 teaspoon chopped capers
1/8 teaspoon cayenne pepper
Salt
Freshly ground pepper
About 12 puff pastry tartlet shells,
   preferably homemade (p. 117;
   1/4 pound dough necessary)
Green olives with pimiento,
   sliced crosswise, for garnish

Combine in a bowl all ingredients except the tartlet shells and olives. You can use right away, but the

118

mixture gains in flavor when allowed to sit, refrigerated, for a few hours or overnight. Fill the pastry shells (not much more than an hour before serving) and garnish with the olive slices.

VARIATION

Use this same mixture to spread on bread as a canapé. Garnish with chopped hard-boiled egg (makes about 8~10 canapés).

Garlic and Tomato Bread

(PÀ AMB TOMAQUET)

At Paco Alcalde in Barcelona's Barceloneta (see p. 10), long, thick slices of good Catalán country bread are stacked high on the bar, just waiting to be transformed into this delicious regional specialty. SERVES 4

5 tablespoons very fruity olive oil
4 cloves garlic, mashed to a paste
    or put through a garlic press
Four 3/4-inch slices cut from a
    coarse-textured round bread or
    a long loaf
1 very ripe, juicy tomato,
    cut in half

Combine in a cup the oil and garlic. Toast the bread slices lightly, then brush with the oil and garlic and rub well with the cut tomato. Repeat for the other side of the bread. [May be prepared ahead] Toast again briefly to crisp, and serve warm.

Green Olive Paste Canapé

(CANAPÉ DE PASTA DE ACEITUNA VERDE)

Olives, capers, anchovy, almonds, and garlic, the ingredients in this recipe, are the very essence of the flavor of Spain. This canapé always reminds me of the endless olive groves of Jaén, the plains of Castilla, the taverns of Madrid, Sevilla ...

The paste is wonderful spread on a slice of bread, but it could also serve as a condiment, enlivening the taste of, for example, meatballs, *empanadilla* fillings, and salad dressings. SERVES 4 (MAKES ABOUT 12)

40 pitted green Spanish olives,
    coarsely chopped
1 teaspoon capers
4 anchovies from a freshly opened can,
    coarsely chopped
1 teaspoon finely ground blanched almonds
1 clove garlic, mashed to a paste or put
    through a garlic press
4 tablespoons fruity olive oil
1/8 teaspoon ground cumin
1/4 teaspoon paprika, preferably
    Spanish style
1/4 teaspoon thyme
Freshly ground pepper
About twelve 1/4-inch slices long crusty
    loaf bread
Pimiento for garnish

Place all ingredients except bread and pimiento in the bowl of a processor and mix until as finely chopped as possible. Transfer to a mortar and pound until the mixture forms a paste. [May be prepared ahead] Spread very thinly on the bread and garnish with pieces of pimiento.

Olive Paste and Blue Cheese Canapé

(CANAPÉ DE PASTA DE ACEITUNA NEGRA Y QUESO CABRALES)

This paste of black olives, garlic, and pine nuts is a lovely complement to a robust blue cheese, such as the outstanding Cabrales (see p. 204) from Asturias in northern Spain. The black olives must be cured to give the proper flavor. SERVES 4-6 (MAKES ABOUT 12-14)

1/4 pound pitted cured black olives
1 large clove garlic, mashed to a paste
    or put through a garlic press
2 tablespoons pine nuts
3 tablespoons olive oil
1/4-inch slices long crusty loaf bread
1/4-1/2 pound blue cheese, such as
    Cabrales, Roquefort, or Gorgonzola
Black olives for garnish

Place the olives, garlic, pine nuts, and olive oil in the bowl of a processor and chop as finely as possible. [May be prepared ahead] Spread thinly on bread slices. Cover with blue cheese. Decorate with a piece of black olive.

Creamed Blue Cheese with Brandy

(CREMA DE CABRALES AL COÑAC)

Even such a small touch of brandy gives a whole new dimension to a blue cheese spread. The success of this tapa depends on the quality and flavor of your blue cheese. I find it best with Spanish Cabrales cheese (see p. 204). SERVES 5-6 (MAKES 16)

Sixteen 1/4-inch slices long crusty loaf bread
1/2 pound blue cheese, such as Cabrales,
    Gorgonzola, or Roquefort, at
    room temperature
1 teaspoon brandy, preferably Spanish
    brandy or Cognac
Minced parsley for garnish

Place the bread slices on a cookie sheet in a 350°F oven until lightly browned and crisp, about 5 minutes. Cool.

In a bowl, mash the cheese well with a fork. Mix in the brandy. You may serve this right away, but it definitely gains in flavor sitting overnight at room temperature. Spread the cheese on the bread and garnish with parsley, or serve the bread and cheese separately and let guests do the work for you.

Mushroom Toast

(TOSTA DE CHAMPIÑÓN)

There are several ways this tasty mushroom mixture can be served—broiled, fried, or enclosed in puff pastry. SERVES 4 (MAKES 8)

1 tablespoon olive oil
1/2 pound mushrooms,
   stems trimmed, brushed clean,
   and coarsely chopped
1 clove garlic, minced
1 tablespoon minced parsley
1 tablespoon minced cured ham
Salt
Freshly ground pepper
2 tablespoons grated cheese, preferably
   Manchego (see p. 203) or Parmesan
4 slices good-quality sandwich bread,
   crusts removed

WHITE SAUCE
3 tablespoons butter
3 tablespoons flour
1/2 cup plus 3 tablespoons milk
1 tablespoon dry white wine
Salt
Freshly ground pepper
A generous grating of nutmeg
A generous sprinkling of cayenne pepper

To make the white sauce, melt the butter in a saucepan and add the flour. Cook for a couple of minutes, then add the milk and wine gradually and cook, stirring constantly, until thickened and smooth. Season with salt, pepper, nutmeg, and cayenne.

In a skillet heat the oil until it is very hot. Sauté the mushrooms over high heat for about 2 minutes. (If the mushrooms give off liquid, evaporate it before continuing.) Add the garlic, parsley, ham, salt, and pepper and turn off the heat. Combine the white sauce with the mushroom mixture and stir in the cheese. [May be prepared ahead]

Toast the bread very lightly. Cut each slice into two triangles and cover with the mushroom mixture. Broil until golden, about 1 minute. If you wish to fry the triangles, place them face down in about 1/2 inch hot oil. To enclose in puff pastry, you will need about 1 pound Puff Pastry dough (p. 110), which you may cut in long 3-inch-wide strips and wrap around small horns (2 teaspoons filling per horn; bake at 400°F for about 8 minutes). Or you can make small puff pastry pies (see p. 112).

Canapé of Eggs, Hake, and Zucchini

(CANAPÉ DE REVUELTO DE MERLUZA Y CALABACÍN)

Casa Fermín is our favorite restaurant in the northwestern region of Asturias. Although Luis Gil Lus has moved his restaurant to new and more elegant quarters in Oviedo, his menu always includes the traditional Asturian dishes for which he is famous: *fabada* (bean stew), hake in cider sauce, and the creamiest rice pudding you have ever eaten. (Recipes for these dishes appear in *The Foods and Wines of Spain*.) Mr. Gil Lus, however, is always up on the latest trends in dining and adjusts his menu accordingly. Some of his recent additions include a salad of monkfish, green beans, and shrimp (see p. 87), and this excellent egg dish, which I have made into a canapé. SERVES 4-6

2 eggs
2 teaspoons milk
Salt
Freshly ground pepper,
   preferably white
1 tablespoon olive oil
2 tablespoons minced onion
½ cup zucchini,
   cut in ¼-inch slices,
   then diced
2 ounces hake or fresh cod,
   finely chopped
¼-inch slices long crusty
   loaf bread

In a bowl beat the eggs lightly with the milk, salt, and pepper. Heat the oil in a skillet and sauté the onion slowly until it is wilted. Add the zucchini,

salt, and pepper, sauté for another minute, then cover and continue cooking until the zucchini is tender, not more than 5 minutes. Uncover, add the fish, and cook for another minute or two until the fish turns white.

Half fill a slightly larger skillet with water and bring to a boil. Reduce to a simmer and place the skillet with the zucchini mixture inside the larger skillet, double-boiler fashion. Add the eggs and stir constantly with a wooden spoon until the eggs are set but are still quite soft. [May be prepared ahead] Pile onto the bread slices and serve warm or at room temperature.

Egg and Mushroom Canapé

(PINCHO DE REVUELTO DE SETA)

I never expected to find scrambled eggs on bread as a tapa, but it is more common than I had realized, especially in the north of Spain, where they like their tapas hearty and very substantial. (I was once served a "canapé" that turned out to be a huge slice of bread with an entire pig's ear on top!) In the Basque city of Vitoria, tapas are of this order, and the best one I found was this garlicky egg and mushroom mixture. SERVES 4-6 (MAKES 8-12)

2 eggs
4 teaspoons milk
Salt
Freshly ground pepper
2 tablespoons olive oil
8 medium mushrooms (about 6 ounces),
    wild or cultivated, brushed clean,
    coarsely chopped
2 tablespoons minced parsley
2 cloves garlic, minced
Eight-twelve ½-inch slices
    firm-textured long crusty loaf

Half fill a skillet, slightly larger than the one in which the eggs will cook, with hot water. Bring to a boil, then keep at a simmer. Beat the eggs lightly in a bowl with the milk, salt, and pepper.

Heat the oil in a skillet and sauté the mushrooms over high heat for a minute. Stir in the parsley and garlic, cook for a few seconds, then remove from the heat. Add the eggs and place the skillet in the larger skillet of water. Stir constantly with a wooden spoon until the eggs are set but still soft. [May be prepared ahead] Pile the mixture onto the bread and serve. This is excellent at room temperature.

Canapé of Fried Fish with Asparagus

(PINCHO DE MERLUZA)

All over Spain you will find fried foods—at room temperature, on bread slices, and often combined with vegetables—as tapas. When the flavors are well meshed, they make fine tapas indeed. SERVES 4 (MAKES 8)

½ pound thin fillets
    of hake or fresh cod
Salt
Flour for dusting
Oil for frying
1 egg, lightly beaten with
    1 teaspoon water
Eight ¼-inch slices long
    crusty loaf bread
Mayonnaise, preferably
    homemade (p. 47)
8 pimiento strips, preferably home
    prepared (see p. 204) or imported
8 cooked asparagus spears

Cut the fish into 8 tapas-size pieces. Sprinkle the fish with salt and dust with flour. Heat the oil in a skillet to a depth of ½ inch. Dip the fish in the beaten egg, then place directly in the hot oil. Fry until golden on both sides. Drain.

Spread the bread slices generously with mayonnaise and cover with the fish pieces, then with the pimiento strips, and last with the asparagus spears. This tapa is as good hot as at room temperature.

Fresh Fish Spread

(ENSALADILLA DE PESCADO)

Any mild fish can be used for this tasty spread that I discovered in Nou Manolín, a tapas bar and restaurant on the sunny Alicante coast. SERVES 4 (MAKES 8–10)

> Eight–ten ¼-inch slices
>   long crusty loaf bread
> 1 very small potato (about 2 ounces),
>   skin on
> ¼ pound fresh cod, scrod, tilefish,
>   or other mild fish
> Cooking Liquid (p. 157)
> 3 tablespoons mayonnaise, preferably
>   homemade (p. 47)
> ½ hard-boiled egg, minced
> 2 tablespoons shredded lettuce
>   (white rib portion only)
> Salt
> Freshly ground pepper
> Minced parsley for garnish

Place the bread slices on a cookie sheet and bake at 350°F until lightly golden and crisp, about 5 minutes. Cool.

Boil the potato in salted water until tender. Meanwhile, place the fish in cooking liquid to cover, bring to a boil, cover, and simmer for 10 minutes, turning once. Shred, removing all skin and bone.

Rice the potato, then mix with the fish, mayonnaise, egg, lettuce, salt, and pepper. [May be prepared ahead] Either spread on bread or serve in a bowl with the bread on the side. Garnish with parsley.

Fish, Mayonnaise, and Lettuce Spread

(MERLUZA BAR PARISIENNE)

From a bar of the same name in Cádiz comes this simple fish spread. SERVES ABOUT 6

PREPARE SEVERAL HOURS IN ADVANCE

> ¾ cup dry white wine
> 2 sprigs parsley
> 1 scallion, cut in 3 pieces
> 2 slices onion
> 1 bay leaf
> 3 peppercorns
> Salt
> ¼ teaspoon thyme
> 1 cup water
> ½ pound hake or
>   fresh cod steak
> 4 tablespoons minced romaine lettuce
>   (white stem portion only)
> 6 tablespoons mayonnaise, preferably
>   homemade (p. 47)
> Freshly ground pepper
> Slices long crusty loaf bread
>   and/or crackers

In a skillet bring to a boil the wine with the parsley, scallion, onion, bay leaf, peppercorns, salt, and thyme. Boil down to half, then add the water and the fish. Return to a boil, cover, and simmer for 10 minutes, turning the fish once. Drain and cool.

Shred the fish with your fingers into a bowl. Mix in the lettuce, mayonnaise, salt, and ground pepper. Refrigerate for several hours for the flavor to develop. Serve in a bowl and provide bread rounds and/or crackers for guests to help themselves.

Clam Toast

(TOSTA DE BERBERECHOS)

This is my mother-in-law's recipe, a tapa that she likes to make at home as a light evening snack. SERVES 3-4 (MAKES 8)

6 medium-large fresh clams (see p. 203) or one 10-ounce can
2 tablespoons olive oil
1 medium onion, finely chopped
2 cloves garlic, minced
4 tablespoons minced parsley
½ dried red chili pepper, seeded and crumbled, or ¼ teaspoon crushed red pepper
4 teaspoons flour
4 slices good-quality sandwich bread, crusts removed, each slice in two triangles, and very lightly toasted

Shuck the clams over a dish to catch the juices. Strain the liquid and reserve ⅓ cup—if there is less, add some bottled clam juice or water. Chop the clams.

Heat the oil in a skillet and sauté the onion slowly until it is wilted. Cover and continue cooking for another 20 minutes, or until the onion is tender but has not colored. Uncover, turn up the heat a little, and add the garlic, parsley, and chili pepper. Cook for a couple of minutes, then stir in the flour. Add the reserved clam juice and the clams and cook over medium-high heat until the mixture is thick enough to spread. [May be prepared ahead] Spread on the bread and serve, or spread, then reheat quickly in a 400°F oven when ready to serve.

Anchovy Toast

(TOSTADA DE ANCHOA)

If anchovy is one of your favorites, this tapa of fried bread, topped with an assertive lemon dressing, then anchovy fillets, brings out its best qualities. Make everything in advance and assemble shortly before serving. SERVES 6-8 (MAKES 12-16)

4 tablespoons fruity olive oil
2 tablespoons fresh lemon juice
2 tablespoons minced parsley
2 tablespoons minced onion
2 cloves garlic, minced
Freshly ground pepper
Oil for frying
Twelve-sixteen ¼-inch slices long crusty loaf bread
Three freshly opened 2-ounce tins good-quality flat anchovy fillets

To make the dressing, beat together lightly in a small bowl the olive oil, lemon juice, parsley, onion, garlic, and pepper.

Heat the oil about ¼ inch deep in a skillet and fry the bread until golden all over. (The bread should be crunchy all the way through.) Drain on paper towels. [May be prepared ahead]

Spread about 1 teaspoon of the dressing on each slice of bread and cover with about 2 anchovy fillets (depending on the size of the fillets and your taste for anchovy).

Smoked Fish Salad on Garlic Toast

(ENSALADILLA DE AHUMADOS)

Tapas bars almost always have a casual atmosphere and serve down-to-earth dishes. Not so at two of Madrid's most fashionable tapas bars, Bar Hevia and José Luis, which face each other on Serrano Street. The "beautiful people" go here for their before-meal snacks and socializing, and limousines line up, waiting for their owners, who are sampling such tapas as caviar, prawns, crab, wild mushrooms, and baby eels, all served by tuxedoed waiters. Most popular of all are smoked fish tapas, in particular salmon, and I was especially fond of this elegant smoked fish salad at Bar Hevia.

You should use three different smoked fish for this tapa, which can vary according to what is available. Some good choices are salmon, sturgeon, trout, and sable. SERVES 4 (MAKES 8)

3 tablespoons plus 1 teaspoon fruity olive oil
1 clove garlic, mashed to a paste or put through a garlic press
4 slices good-quality sandwich bread, crusts removed
2 ounces each of three varieties of smoked fish, not too salty and very coarsely chopped
4 tablespoons shredded romaine lettuce (white stem portion only)
4 teaspoons chopped pimiento, home prepared (see p. 204) or imported
2 teaspoons mayonnaise, preferably homemade (p. 47)
1/2 hard-boiled egg, sieved

Combine 2 tablespoons of the oil with the garlic. Brush the bread on both sides with this mixture. Place on a cookie sheet and bake on each side at 350°F for about 4 minutes, until golden. Cool.

In a bowl mix together the fish, lettuce, and pimiento. Blend the mayonnaise and the remaining 4 teaspoons of the oil in a cup until smooth, then fold into the fish mixture. [May be prepared ahead] Pile onto the bread and cut each in two triangles. Sprinkle with the sieved egg. Serve at room temperature.

Baby Eel Toast

(TOSTADA DE ANGULAS)

Baby eels, no thicker than spaghetti strands, are most typically eaten in Spain in a garlic sauce (see p. 171), but their delicate flavor makes them ideal for several other tapas, such as this delicious recipe that bathes them in hollandaise sauce and then broils them.

Angulas are usually sold precooked and can be added to recipes as is. If they are not cooked, plunge into boiling water and remove immediately. SERVES 4 (MAKES 8)

4 slices good-quality sandwich bread,
    crusts removed
2 teaspoons butter plus butter for bread
3 ounces angulas (available in some
    specialty shops, such as Casa Moneo
    in New York)
Salt
Bread crumbs

HOLLANDAISE SAUCE
3 egg yolks
2 tablespoons fresh lemon juice
1/4 teaspoon salt
Dash of cayenne pepper
8 tablespoons sweet butter, melted

To make the hollandaise sauce, place in the bowl of a blender or processor the egg yolks, lemon juice, salt, and cayenne. With the motor running, add the butter in a thin stream.

Butter the bread and toast lightly. Cut each piece in two triangles. Heat the 2 teaspoons of butter in a skillet and sauté the *angulas* quickly, about 30 seconds. Salt if necessary. [May be prepared ahead]

Pile the *angulas* on the bread triangles, cover each triangle with about 1 tablespoon of sauce, sprinkle lightly with bread crumbs, and run under the broiler. Watch carefully; it will take only about a minute.

Tuna on Fried Toast

(TOSTADA DE ATÚN A LA DONOSTIARRA)

In San Sebastián tapas on fried bread, attractively displayed and eaten by the honor system, are especially popular (see p. 130). The fried bread gives what could otherwise be a fairly ordinary tapa a very special taste. SERVES 6 (MAKES 16)

Oil for frying
Sixteen 1/4-inch slices long
    crusty loaf bread
A 7-ounce can light meat tuna, flaked
4 teaspoons white wine vinegar
2 tablespoons minced onion
Salt
4 teaspoons mayonnaise,
    preferably homemade (p. 47)
1 hard-boiled egg yolk
Dill or cornichon pickles,
    sliced lengthwise, for garnish
Mayonnaise

Heat the oil about 1/4 inch deep in a skillet and fry the bread slices quickly until golden, adding more oil as necessary. Drain on paper towels.

In a bowl combine the tuna, vinegar, onion, salt, and mayonnaise. [May be prepared ahead] Pile onto the fried bread and sieve the egg yolk over the top. Garnish with a pickle slice and a dab of mayonnaise.

Tuna Canapé

(CANAPÉ DE ATÚN "CHARITO")

A good friend in Madrid, Charito Romero, slipped me this carefully hand-printed recipe just as I was leaving the city, with a note saying that it was a tapa she frequently made and thought I might enjoy. It certainly is a tasty tapa—and simplicity itself. SERVES 7-8 (MAKES ABOUT 14)

2 tablespoons fruity olive oil
1 tablespoon wine vinegar, preferably white
1 teaspoon Dijon-style mustard
½ cup ketchup
A 7-ounce can white or light meat tuna, flaked
2 tablespoons minced onion
Freshly ground pepper
Salt
About fourteen ¼-inch slices long crusty loaf bread, toasted

In a small bowl mix together the oil, vinegar, mustard, and ketchup. In another bowl combine the tuna and onion, then stir in the ketchup mixture, seasoning with pepper and salt, if necessary. [May be prepared ahead] Spread on the toasted bread.

Tuna Butter Canapé

(CANAPÉ DE ATÚN)

This spread is also delicious made with skinned and boned canned sardines. SERVES 4-6 (MAKES 12)

Half a 7-ounce can light meat tuna, drained
2 tablespoons sweet butter, softened
Freshly ground pepper
1 teaspoon fresh lemon juice
1 teaspoon grated onion
12 thin crustless bread rounds
12 very thin slices beet, cucumber, or tomato
Parsley sprigs

In the bowl of a processor or blender chop the tuna finely. Add the softened butter, pepper, lemon juice, and grated onion. Blend to form a smooth paste. [May be prepared ahead]

Spread about 1 teaspoon of this mixture on each bread round. Top with a slice of beet, cucumber, or tomato, then place a small ball of the tuna spread in the center of each canapé and top with a small sprig of parsley.

Canapé of Mackerel and Cured Ham

(MONTADITO DE CABALLA Y JAMÓN)

Although this is a very simple canapé, the taste of mackerel with ham is exceptional. It's one of my husband's favorites. SERVES 4 (MAKES 8)

¼ pound cured ham, in thin slices (but
    not paper thin), each slice cut in pieces
    the size of the bread slices
Eight ¼-inch slices long crusty loaf bread
A 4½-ounce can mackerel
    fillets, imported from Spain

Simply fit pieces of the ham over the bread slices and top with a piece of mackerel fillet.

Garlicky Cod and Potato Spread

(AJO ARRIERO AL ESTILO DE CUENCA)

Cuenca, in eastern Castilla, is one of Spain's most beautiful towns, known for its "hanging houses" (*casas colgadas*). Cuenca's homes are built straight up on soaring cliffs, and the views are, needless to say, vertiginous. A prospering artists' colony resides here, and there is an interesting museum of abstract art in one of the most spectacular of the hanging houses.

This salt cod spread is popular throughout the province, but prepared especially well at Mesón Los Arcos on Cuenca's main square. SERVES 6-8 (MAKES 18)

¼ pound skinned and boned dried
    salt cod (see p. 203)
½ pound potato (1 medium-large),
    skin on, cut in half
½ cup olive oil
4 cloves garlic, mashed to a paste or
    put through a garlic press
Salt
Eighteen ¼-inch slices long
    crusty loaf bread
2 hard-boiled eggs, finely chopped
5 walnuts, chopped

To desalt the cod, place in cold water to cover for 24~36 hours, changing the water occasionally.

Cut the cod into 2 or 3 pieces and place in a pot with the potato. Cover with water, bring to a boil, and simmer, covered, until the potato is tender. Transfer the cod to the bowl of a processor or blender, peel the potato, and reserve the cooking liquid.

While the potato is still hot, pass it through a ricer or strainer into a bowl. (This cannot be done in the processor because the potato will turn sticky.) Warm ¼ cup plus 2 tablespoons of the olive oil in a small pot, then gradually stir it into the potato. Mix in 3 cloves of the mashed garlic.

In the processor or blender beat the cod until it forms a paste. With the motor running, add 3 tablespoons of the cooking liquid. Stir the cod mixture into the potato. Season well with salt.

To make the garlic bread, combine in a cup the remaining 2 tablespoons of oil and the remaining clove of mashed garlic. Bake the bread slices on a cookie sheet at 350°F for about 5 minutes, until golden and crisp. Turn and bake 5 minutes more. Brush with the oil and garlic mixture and return to the oven for another minute. Cool. [May be prepared ahead]

To serve, spread the cod mixture on the bread, then sprinkle with the egg and walnuts.

Canapé of Dried Cod and Potatoes

(PINCHO DE AJO ARRIERO)

The seaside city of San Sebastián, in the northern region of Spain known as the Basque country, has a very strong tapas tradition. Most of the bars along the porticoed promenade of the old port, where gaily painted and immaculately kept fishing boats vie for position, are now casual al fresco seafood restaurants. But nearby, in the heart of the city's Old Quarter on Calle del Puerto, tapas bars are end to end, and the tapas are of great variety and beautifully presented. Tapas in San Sebastián are mostly *pinchos*, that is, foods that you can easily pick up with your fingers and eat without the need for a plate. And you serve yourself—on the honor system. This spicy cod tapa was one of my favorites at the Bar Aralar. SERVES 4 (MAKES 8)

START PREPARATION ONE DAY IN ADVANCE

¼ pound skinned and boned
   dried salt cod (see p. 203)
3 tablespoons olive oil
¼ pound all-purpose potatoes,
   peeled and cut in ½-inch cubes
Salt
2 cloves garlic, minced
2 tablespoons diced pimiento,
   home prepared (see p. 204)
   or imported
1 small tomato (about 3 ounces)
½ dried red chili pepper,
   seeded, in 2 pieces, or ¼ teaspoon
   crushed red pepper
1 tablespoon minced parsley
Eight ¼-inch slices long crusty
   loaf bread

Soak the cod at room temperature in cold water to cover for 24~36 hours, changing the water occasionally.

Heat 1 tablespoon of the oil in a skillet, add the potatoes, sprinkle with salt, cover, and cook slowly until tender, about 15 minutes. While the potatoes are cooking, place the cod in a pot with water to cover, bring to a boil, then remove right away. Drain and shred the cod.

In another skillet heat the remaining 2 tablespoons of oil and sauté the garlic and cod for a couple of minutes. Add the pimiento, cook for another minute, then stir in the tomato, chili pepper, and parsley. Cover and cook slowly for 10 minutes. Add the potatoes and cook 5 minutes more. Discard the chili pepper. [May be prepared ahead]

Pile the cod mixture onto the bread slices and serve warm.

Spicy Dried Cod

(PERICANA)

Cod and dried red peppers make a robust blend to serve on garlic toast. SERVES 6 (MAKES 12)

START PREPARATION ONE DAY IN ADVANCE

¼ pound skinned and boned
   dried salt cod (see p. 203)
2 dried sweet red peppers
   (such as "New Mexico" style)
5 tablespoons olive oil
2 cloves garlic, mashed to a paste
   or put through a garlic press
Twelve ¼-inch slices long
   crusty loaf bread
4 cloves garlic, minced
Crushed red pepper (optional)

Soak the cod in cold water to cover at room temperature for 24–36 hours, changing the water occasionally. Soak the red peppers in warm water for 1 hour to soften.

To make the garlic bread, combine 3 tablespoons of the oil with the mashed garlic. Brush the bread on both sides with this mixture. Place on a cookie sheet and bake at 350°F for about 4 minutes to a side, or until golden. Cool.

Drain the cod and place in a pot of water. Bring to a boil and remove right away. Drain well and flake with your fingers. Scrape all of the flesh from the peppers and discard the skin. Heat the remaining 2 tablespoons of oil in a skillet. Add the minced garlic, stir, then blend in the cod and the flesh from the peppers. Season with the crushed red pepper, if desired. [May be prepared ahead] Pile the cod mixture on the bread and serve warm.

Veal and Cured Ham in Pita

(EMPAREDADOS DE TERNERA PALACIO DE LA BELLOTA)

El Palacio de la Bellota (Palace of the Acorn) is one of the best tapas bars in Valencia and takes its name from the incredibly nutty-flavored cured ham it serves, which comes from pigs raised on acorns. At Palacio de la Bellota tapas range from a variety of fresh Valencian shellfish to many dishes in sauces and marinades, as well as this popular "fried sandwich," all arranged in a long line of *cazuelas* across the bar. Owner Enrique Grau is one of Valencia's great paella chefs, and has made paella for two thousand in his special twelve-foot paella pan. SERVES 4 (MAKES 8)

¼ pound veal, in very thin slices
Salt
3 tablespoons olive oil
Two 5–6-inch pita breads, cut in halves
2 thin slices cured ham
Milk
Oil for frying
1 egg, lightly beaten with 1 teaspoon water

Sprinkle the veal on both sides with salt. Heat the olive oil in a skillet until very hot. Sauté the veal very quickly until brown on both sides.

Split open the pita bread halves completely. Divide the veal into 4 portions and place on 4 pita pieces. Cover with a slice of ham, then cover with the other 4 pieces of bread. Cut each half in half again.

Pour a little milk into a dish. Heat the frying oil about ¼ inch deep in a skillet. Dip the pita quarters in the milk to moisten, then coat with the beaten egg. Fry till golden on both sides. Drain and serve right away.

Canapé of Béchamel-Coated Veal

(CANAPÉ DE TERNERA EMPANADA VILLEROY)

Preparing foods Villeroy style—coated with white sauce, breaded, and fried—is a favorite method in Spain for serving chicken (see p. 183) and works equally well with veal. This tapa comes from the lovely old city of Oviedo, which because of its university population has many tapas bars, called *chigres*. At peak tapas hours traffic circulates with difficulty through the Old Quarter, for some streets are clogged with spirited tapas clients, holding a glass in one hand and a tapa in the other. This tapa comes from the busy La Gran Taberna. SERVES 6 (MAKES 12)

¾ pound beef, such as round,
   or veal, in very thin slices
Salt
1 cup bread crumbs
1 clove garlic, mashed to a paste or
   put through a garlic press
1 tablespoon minced parsley
Salt
Freshly ground pepper
¼ teaspoon thyme
2 eggs, lightly beaten with
   1 teaspoon water
4 tablespoons olive oil
Twelve ¼-inch slices long
   crusty loaf bread
Mayonnaise
Thin slices tomato

WHITE SAUCE
5 tablespoons butter
6 tablespoons flour
¾ cup chicken broth

¾ cup milk
Salt
Freshly ground pepper

To make the white sauce, melt the butter in a saucepan. Stir in the flour and cook for a minute or two. Add the chicken broth, milk, salt, and pepper gradually and stir constantly until thickened and smooth.

Sprinkle the meat with salt. Heat a lightly greased skillet until it is very hot. Sear the meat on both sides, then drain on paper towels. Spread the white sauce in a flat dish and coat the meat lightly on both sides. Place on a greased platter and refrigerate for at least 1 hour, or until the sauce solidifies.

Mix the crumbs, garlic, parsley, salt, pepper, and thyme. Dip the coated meat in the beaten egg, then in the crumb mixture. Heat the oil in the skillet and brown the meat quickly on both sides.

Spread the bread slices lightly with mayonnaise. Cut the meat into pieces and fit them on the bread slices. Cover with a slice of tomato and serve at room temperature.

Marinated Pork Canapé

(MONTADITO DE LOMO EN ADOBO)

You can walk into almost any bar in Spain and order this canapé—invariably they will have it, even if it is not on the menu. It is one of my favorites, and when I am in Spain I always ask for it. SERVES 4-6 (MAKES ABOUT 8)

1 tablespoon paprika, preferably
   Spanish style
3 cloves garlic, mashed to a paste
   or put through a garlic press
3 tablespoons olive oil
1 tablespoon fresh lemon juice
1/2 teaspoon thyme
1/2 teaspoon oregano
1 bay leaf, crushed
Salt
Freshly ground pepper
3/4 pound boneless pork loin,
   in 1/4-inch slices
1/4-inch slices long
   crusty loaf bread
Pimiento pieces, preferably
   home prepared (see p. 204)
   or imported, for garnish
   (optional)

In a small bowl combine the paprika, garlic, olive oil, lemon juice, thyme, oregano, bay leaf, salt, and pepper. Arrange the meat slices in a shallow bowl, pour on the marinade, coating each slice well with it. Cover and refrigerate for at least 1 hour, or up to 2 days.

Coat a skillet lightly with oil and heat until it is very hot. Drain the pork slices slightly and fry very quickly. Place on the slices of bread and serve warm, garnished, if you wish, with pimiento.

VARIATION

I have also enjoyed this tapa when topped with a piece of batter-fried pimiento (see p. 146).

Chorizo Canapés

(BANDERILLAS DE CHORIZO)

Here is an easy-to-assemble and tasty canapé, done in *banderilla* style (see pp. 52–54). SERVES 4 (MAKES 8)

> 2 slices good-quality sandwich bread
> Butter
> 1 ounce chorizo sausage, in
> 　1/8-inch slices, skin removed
> 1 hard-boiled egg, sliced
> 8 rolled anchovies
> 8 pimiento-stuffed green Spanish olives

Toast the bread very lightly, remove the crusts, and spread with a little butter. Cut each bread slice into 4 squares. Cover each with a slice of *chorizo*, a slice of egg, then an anchovy, and top with the olive. Spear everything together with a toothpick. [May be prepared ahead]

Chorizo Speared on Bread Cubes

(PINCHO DE CHORIZO)

Nothing could be simpler than this tapa, but it is always a popular one—in Spain and at my tapas parties. SERVES 4

> 1 teaspoon olive oil
> 1/4 pound chorizo sausage, in 8 pieces
> 　(see Note)
> 1 tablespoon dry red or white wine
> 8 pieces long crusty loaf bread, 1/2 inch
> 　thick and 1 1/2 inches square

Heat the oil in a skillet and cook the *chorizo* until brown on all sides and heated through. Deglaze the pan with the wine and let it evaporate. Spear the sausage to the bread cubes with toothpicks.
NOTE: You can cut the *chorizo* into slices if you wish, in which case more bread pieces will be necessary.

VARIATION
This same tapa can be made with *morcilla* (blood sausage), preferably of the kind that is made with rice (see p. 204). Decorate each tapa with a strip of pimiento.

Grilled Marinated Meat "Sandwiches"

(PRINGÁ)

I am fascinated with the name of this typical tapa from Sevilla. The spelling, first of all, should be *pringada*, but in exuberant Andalucian speech, word endings always seem to disappear, thus *pringá*. The word means "greasy," and although this dish isn't, its ingredients originally were the meats left over from the great Spanish chickpea stew, *cocido*. I have eaten this tapa in a variety of Sevillian bars, but nowhere does anyone prepare it as well as my friend Ruperto (see p. 34) does at Bar Casa Ruperto, marinating the meats first in coriander and cumin.

SERVES 5-6 (MAKES 10)

START PREPARATION SEVERAL HOURS IN ADVANCE

3 ounces fresh pork loin, finely chopped
1½ ounces morcilla (blood sausage)
    (see p. 204), finely chopped
1 chorizo sausage (2 ounces), skinned
    and finely chopped
1 ounce bacon, finely chopped
1 tablespoon olive oil
Twenty ¼–⅜-inch slices long
    crusty loaf bread
Softened butter

MARINADE
1 large clove garlic, minced
¼ teaspoon crushed coriander seed
¼ teaspoon freshly crushed cumin seed
¼ teaspoon paprika, preferably
    Spanish style
½ dried red chili pepper, seeded
    and crumbled, or ¼ teaspoon
    crushed red pepper
1 tablespoon olive oil

In a bowl combine the marinade ingredients, then mix in the pork loin, *morcilla*, *chorizo*, and bacon. Marinate for several hours or, better still, overnight.

Heat the oil in a skillet and sauté the marinated mixture over medium heat, stirring, for about 5 minutes. [May be prepared ahead] Spread about 1 tablespoon of this mixture on half of the bread slices, then cover with the remaining slices. Butter the outside of the bread, then cook, pressed flat in a sandwich grill or in a skillet. Turn once (place a weight over the sandwich if using a skillet) and continue grilling until golden on the other side.

4

TAPAS
WITH SOME
LAST-MINUTE
PREPARATION

Don't be put off by the words "last minute," for this chapter includes many of Spain's very finest and most popular tapas, and very few must be served literally the minute they leave the range. Under this heading you will find a potpourri of tapas that are fried, broiled, grilled, baked, and sautéed. They include many varieties of croquettes and Spanish-style omelets, vegetables, lots of shellfish, fish of all kinds, and an assortment of chicken, quail, and other meat-based tapas.

To avoid too much "last-minute" work, be sure to do as much advance preparation as possible (each recipe will indicate how much). Even the fried tapas can usually be made 30 minutes in advance and kept warm in a 200°F oven. But in the few cases where a recipe says to serve right away, please do so.

Fried Salted Almonds

(ALMENDRAS FRITAS)

Almond trees grow in many parts of Spain, but almonds as tapas seem to be more popular in Sevilla than elsewhere. When almonds are freshly fried, as they often are in Sevilla, they are really something special. SERVES 4-6

Oil for frying
4 ounces blanched whole almonds
Coarse salt

In a skillet heat the oil at least ½ inch deep to about 400°F and fry the almonds until lightly golden. Or, better, use a deep-fryer. Drain and sprinkle with coarse salt.

Fried Cheese with Shallot Dressing

(QUESO FRITO ALIÑADO CON SALSA DE ESCALONA)

Make this tapa even more delicious with one of the exciting soft Spanish cheeses now available in America (see p. 203). SERVES 6

½ pound fairly mild melting cheese,
   such as Spanish Tetilla, Mahón,
   or goat cheese, ½ inch thick,
   then cut in 1-inch squares
Flour for dusting
2 eggs, lightly beaten with
   2 teaspoons water
Bread crumbs
Oil for frying

DRESSING
2 tablespoons olive oil
2 teaspoons vinegar
4 teaspoons minced shallot
2 teaspoons minced parsley
½ teaspoon small whole
   or chopped large capers

In a cup combine the dressing ingredients. Dust the cheese pieces with flour, dip in the egg, then in the crumbs. [May be prepared ahead] In a skillet heat the oil at least ½ inch deep to about 380°F and fry the cheese quickly until golden on both sides. Or, better, use a deep-fryer. Drain.

Sprinkle the dressing over the cheese and serve immediately.

Chorizo-Filled Dates in Bacon

(FRITOS DE DÁTILES Y CHORIZO)

In 1983 Toronto was the scene of *¡Viva España!*, an elaborate two-week celebration of Spain and Spanish food. Gregorio Camarero came from Los Monteros hotel in Marbella, Spain, as guest chef at the Truffles restaurant in the sophisticated Four Seasons Hotel, where he delighted diners with a wide variety of elegant Spanish specialties. Among them, this simple and absolutely irresistible tapa. SERVES 4-6

> 1 chorizo sausage
>   (about 2 ounces)
> 12 pitted dried dates
> 3 slices bacon, cut in
>   quarters crosswise
> Oil for frying
> Flour for dusting
> 1 egg, lightly beaten with
>   1 teaspoon water

Cut off the ends of the *chorizo* and slice the sausage crosswise into 3 equal pieces, about ¾ inch each in length (remove the skin if tough). Cut each of these pieces in half lengthwise and in half again, to make a total of 12 "sticks." (If your *chorizo* is thick, these pieces may be too large for the dates, in which case cut in half again.) Insert each *chorizo* piece into a date and close the date around it. Wrap a strip of bacon around each date. Secure, if necessary, with a toothpick. [May be prepared ahead]

Place the wrapped dates in a skillet with the seam side of the bacon down and sauté until the bacon is golden. Turn and brown on the other side. Drain on paper towels. You may now serve the dates, or proceed to coat and fry them. If you are continuing, this step may also be done in advance.

Wipe out the skillet, then heat the oil at least ½ inch deep to about 380°F. Dust the dates with flour, then dip them into the egg and immediately into the hot oil. Fry until golden, turning once. Or, better, use a deep-fryer. Drain and serve right away.

Skewered Mushroom and Bacon with Alioli

(PINCHO DE CHAMPIÑÓN Y TOCINO AL ALIOLI)

I am very fond of this attractive and simple-to-make tapa. SERVES 4-6

> 1 tablespoon fruity olive oil
> Twelve ½-inch cubes slab bacon
>   (about 2 ounces)
> 12 small-medium mushroom caps,
>   brushed clean
> Alioli Sauce (p. 191)

Heat the oil in a skillet until very hot. Add the bacon and mushrooms and stir fry briefly, just until the mushrooms are softened and the bacon is a little crisp. Spear a cube of bacon on a mushroom cap (right side up) and either dab with the Alioli sauce or pass it separately.

Mushrooms Stuffed with Soft-Set Eggs

(CHAMPIÑONES RELLENOS DE REVUELTO)

This is a wonderful tapa, eye-catching and delicious. The eggs, mixed with shrimp, ham, and crab, blend beautifully with the flavor of the mushrooms. SERVES 6-8

2 eggs
2 teaspoons milk
Salt
Freshly ground pepper
18 small-medium mushrooms,
 brushed clean
1 tablespoon butter
1 tablespoon minced parsley
1 tablespoon minced pimiento,
 preferably home prepared (see
 p. 204) or imported
1 tablespoon minced cured ham
1 medium-large shrimp,
 shelled and minced
1 tablespoon flaked crab meat
Olive oil for brushing mushrooms

In a small bowl beat the eggs lightly with the milk, salt, and pepper. Separate the mushroom stems from the caps and chop the stems finely, reserving 1 tablespoon.

Half fill a skillet, larger than the skillet that will be used to cook the eggs, with water and bring to a boil. Keep at a simmer until ready to use.

In a small skillet heat the butter. Add the parsley, the reserved tablespoon chopped mushroom, pimiento, ham, shrimp, and crab meat and sauté for a minute or so. Pour in the eggs and place the skillet in the larger skillet of simmering water, double-boiler fashion. Stir with a wooden spoon until the eggs are set but still quite soft.

Brush the mushroom caps with oil and fill with the egg mixture, using the cupped side of a spoon to make a smooth dome. [May be prepared ahead] Bake at 400°F for no more than 5 minutes.

Ham-Filled Mushroom Caps

(CHAMPIÑONES RELLENOS DE JAMÓN)

Cava Baja Street, near the Plaza Mayor in Old Madrid, was one of my favorite haunts as a student in Madrid. It was always alive with people and the sound of flamenco singing and guitar music floating from the many bars and *mesones* (simple centuries-old eating establishments) that line the narrow cobbled street. Things are little changed today, and it was along this same street that I recently spotted these stuffed mushrooms. SERVES 4

3 tablespoons finely diced cured ham,
 cut from a 1/8-inch-thick slice
2 large cloves garlic, minced
2 tablespoons minced parsley
1/2 dried red chili pepper,
 seeded and crumbled, or
 1/4 teaspoon crushed red pepper
2 teaspoons fruity olive oil
12 medium mushroom caps,
 brushed clean

In a bowl mix together the ham, garlic, parsley, chili pepper, and olive oil. Fill the mushroom caps with this mixture, arrange in a baking dish [May be prepared ahead], and bake at 350°F for 15 minutes.

Mushrooms Stuffed with Pork and Pine Nuts

(CHAMPIÑONES RELLENOS)

There are endless versions of baked stuffed mushrooms, but I have never found any others quite so unusual and tasty as these, which first appeared in my book *The Foods and Wines of Spain*. SERVES 4-6

3/4 pound medium mushrooms,
    brushed clean
Fresh lemon juice
5 tablespoons butter
3 tablespoons minced onion
1 clove garlic, mashed to a paste
    or put through a garlic press
1/4 pound lean ground pork
Salt
Freshly ground pepper
3 tablespoons bread crumbs
1/2 teaspoon brandy, preferably
    Spanish brandy or Cognac
1 tablespoon minced parsley
1 tablespoon chopped pine nuts

Separate the mushroom stems and chop finely. Sprinkle the caps with lemon juice. Heat 4 tablespoons of the butter in a medium skillet and sauté the onion and garlic slowly until the onion is wilted. Add the meat, salt, and pepper and cook until the meat loses its color. Add 1/3 cup chopped stems (save rest for future use) and cook 3 minutes more. Turn off the heat and stir in the bread crumbs, brandy, parsley, pine nuts, and more seasoning if necessary (it should be very well seasoned).

Pile this mixture into the mushroom caps, forming a smooth dome with the cupped side of a teaspoon. Dot with the remaining butter. [May be prepared ahead] Bake at 350°F for 15 minutes.

Fried Stuffed Mushrooms

(CHAMPIÑONES RELLENOS Y FRITOS)

A great mushroom tapa—crunchy on the outside, juicy and flavorful within. These mushrooms should be fried rather quickly, before they have a chance to release any of their liquid. SERVES 4-6 (MAKES 12)

12 medium mushrooms, brushed clean
3 tablespoons butter
3 tablespoons minced onion
2 cloves garlic, minced
3 tablespoons minced cured ham
2 tablespoons bread crumbs, plus
    bread crumbs for coating
1 teaspoon dry (fino) Spanish sherry
1/2 teaspoon paprika,
    preferably Spanish style
1 tablespoon minced parsley
1 egg, lightly beaten with
    1 teaspoon water
Oil for frying

Separate the mushroom caps from the stems and chop the stems finely. Reserve 3 tablespoons. Melt the butter in a small skillet and sauté the onion and garlic slowly until the onion is wilted. Add the ham and the 3 tablespoons mushroom stems and cook for another minute. Remove from the heat and stir in the bread crumbs, sherry, paprika, and parsley.

Stuff the mushroom caps with a small amount of the mushroom filling (the filling should just be level with the caps). Coat the mushrooms carefully with egg, then roll in the bread crumbs. Heat the oil at least 1/2 inch deep to 380°F and fry quickly until a deep golden color. Or, better, use a deep-fryer. [May be kept warm in 200°F oven up to 30 minutes]

Mushrooms Sautéed with Garlic and Parsley

(CHAMPIÑONES SALTEADOS)

In Spain this is the most popular and, I think, one of the most delicious ways to prepare mushrooms, wild or cultivated. They take less than 5 minutes to cook and should be served immediately. SERVES 4

2 tablespoons fruity olive oil
1/2 pound wild mushrooms, such
    as boletus or chanterelles, or
    cultivated mushrooms, whole if
    small, halved or quartered
    if larger, brushed clean
Salt
Freshly ground pepper
1 clove garlic, minced
1 tablespoon minced parsley

In a skillet heat the oil until it is very hot. Add the mushrooms and stir fry over high heat for about 4 minutes, sprinkling with salt and pepper. Do not overcook or allow the mushrooms to give off any juices. Sprinkle with the garlic and parsley and serve right away.

VARIATION
Substitute 1/2 small onion, slivered, for the garlic, and stir fry the onion with the mushrooms, salt, and pepper. When the mushrooms are done, add 2 very thin slices cured ham, cut in 1 1/2-inch pieces, and cook for another minute. Sprinkle with parsley and serve.

Mushroom and Cheese Timbale

(TERRINA DE CHAMPIÑÓN Y QUESO)

I love these creamy, ever so subtly seasoned vegetable timbales. They may be made in individual portions for small parties or in a larger mold for bigger groups. If you make them in advance, reheat by covering with foil and returning to the bain-marie for 10 minutes. SERVES 6

2 tablespoons butter
1/2 cup very finely chopped carrots
2 large scallions, finely chopped
1 1/2 cups (about 1/4 pound) finely
    chopped mushrooms
1 1/3 cups heavy cream
3 eggs
1 teaspoon salt
1/4 teaspoon paprika, preferably
    Spanish style
A generous grating of nutmeg
1/2 cup grated cheese, such as
    Spanish Manchego (see p. 203)
    or Parmesan

Melt 1 tablespoon of the butter in a skillet and sauté the carrots and scallions slowly for about 5 minutes, until the carrots are tender. Turn up the heat, add the remaining tablespoon of butter, and sauté the mushrooms for a minute or so.

In a bowl beat together lightly the cream, eggs, salt, paprika, and nutmeg. Stir in the cheese and the sautéed vegetables. Butter 6 individual custard cups, divide the vegetable mixture among them, and place in a pan of hot water (bain-marie). Bake at 325°F for 25 minutes, or until a knife inserted in the custard comes out clean. Unmold and serve warm.

Wild Mushrooms with Brains and Cured Ham
(SETAS CARMINA)

It is always exciting to find a great tapas bar where you least expect it. The city of Albacete, on Spain's arid central plains, is more often avoided than visited. It was here that we stumbled upon Nuestro Bar, which serves an incredible one hundred varieties of tapas. For a sampling, you might try what they call Nuestras Cosicas—Our Little Things—a delicious selection of seven or eight special tapas.

The most inspired of their tapas, however, was this one, named after Carmina Useros, a local resident who traveled all over the province of Albacete collecting recipes, which she published privately in a cookbook that is now a collector's item. Mushrooms, brains, and ham, with a little garlic and parsley, is one of the greatest mixtures of tastes I have ever experienced. SERVES 4

1/2 pound calf, lamb, pork,
    or beef brains
5 tablespoons fruity olive oil
6 ounces large wild mushrooms with
    flat leafy caps, such as large tree
    oysters or chanterelles, stems trimmed,
    brushed clean
2 ounces diced cured ham, cut
    from a 1/8-inch-thick slice
2 cloves garlic, minced
2 tablespoons minced parsley
Salt

Cook the brains as directed on page 194 up to the point where they are cooled in the cooking liquid. You can use the brains right away or keep them refrigerated in the cooking liquid until you are ready to use them. Cut the brains into 3/4-inch pieces and dry on paper towels.

Heat 3 tablespoons of the oil in a skillet. Add the mushrooms and sauté quickly until just done, about 2 minutes. Add the remaining oil, the ham, and brains. Stir fry for a minute, sprinkle with the garlic, parsley, and salt, and serve immediately.

Fried Eggplant with Garlic and Egg
(BERENJENAS FRITAS CON AJO Y HUEVO PICADO)

Fried eggplant with the added flavor of garlic and egg is one of my favorites. I like it hot or at room temperature, just as long as it is recently fried. SERVES 4-6

1/2 pound eggplant,
    peeled or unpeeled, in
    1/4–3/8-inch slices
Coarse salt
Flour for dusting
Oil for frying
2 cloves garlic, minced
1 hard-boiled egg, finely chopped
2 tablespoons minced parsley

Sprinkle the eggplant slices well with salt and let drain in a colander for 30 minutes. Dry well on paper towels and dust lightly with flour. Heat the oil at least 1/2 inch deep in a skillet and fry until the slices are golden on both sides. Or, better, use a deep-fryer. Drain.

To serve, arrange on a dish and sprinkle with salt, the garlic, egg, and parsley.

Artichoke Hearts with Shrimp and Cured Ham

(ALCACHOFAS RELLENAS DE GAMBA Y JAMÓN)

El Amparo is one of Madrid's finest and most stylish new restaurants, and although the menu is seasonal and eclectic, more traditional Spanish cuisine is never ignored. A tasting menu gives a sampling of the best the chef has to offer, and on a recent visit I was particularly taken with these stuffed artichoke hearts.

There is something about the taste of artichoke, shrimp, ham, and hollandaise sauce that creates an extraordinary blend of flavors. This tapa is great for large parties, since it can be eaten without a fork (the artichoke heart is firm enough to pick up) and needs only a last-minute baking. Hollandaise sauce can be made in advance and refrigerated. SERVES 8 (MAKES 8)

> 8 medium artichokes
> Fresh lemon juice
> Hollandaise Sauce (p. 127)
> 4 teaspoons butter
> 2 teaspoons minced shallot
> ¼ pound raw shrimp,
>   shelled and coarsely chopped
> 3 tablespoons minced cured ham
> 1 tablespoon minced parsley
> 2 teaspoons dry (fino) Spanish sherry

Cut off the stems and remove all leaves and the fuzzy "choke" from the artichokes, leaving only the hearts. Sprinkle with lemon juice to prevent discoloration. Place in a pan with salted water that does not quite cover the hearts. Bring to a boil, cover, and simmer for about 20 minutes, until tender but still firm. Drain with the hollowed side down. While the artichokes are cooking, make the hollandaise sauce.

Melt the butter in a skillet and sauté the shallot for a few seconds. Add the shrimp and ham and cook for less than a minute, just until the shrimp turn pink. Stir in the parsley and sherry and cook quickly until most of the liquid has evaporated.

Fill the artichoke hearts with the shrimp mixture and cover each with 1 tablespoon of the hollandaise sauce. Allow to sit for a few minutes so that the sauce mixes a bit with the filling. [May be prepared ahead] When ready to bake, cover each of the filled hearts with another teaspoon of hollandaise sauce and bake at 400°F for 10 minutes, or until golden.

VARIATION

A filling of pork and mushrooms is also excellent for these artichokes. To prepare, heat 2 tablespoons olive oil in a skillet and sauté 3 tablespoons minced onion with 2 cloves garlic, minced, until the onion is wilted. Add 6 ounces ground pork, salt, and pepper and cook until the meat is no longer pink. Stir in ½ cup minced mushroom and 1 tablespoon minced parsley, cook for a minute, then add 2 tablespoons dry white wine and cook until the liquid has evaporated. Fill the artichokes and cover with hollandaise sauce as directed.

Asparagus Wrapped in Fresh Salmon
(ESPÁRRAGOS CON SALMÓN)

This tapa is simple and eye-catching and an excellent vegetable addition to a tapas menu. SERVES 6

> 12 thin asparagus spears, tips only
>   (about 3 inches)
> Salt
> Chicken broth (optional)
> 12 very thin strips (about ¼ pound)
>   fresh boneless salmon, cut in
>   4 × 1-inch rectangles
> Hollandaise Sauce (p. 127)

Place the asparagus in a small skillet and barely cover with salted water, or preferably with a mixture of water and chicken broth. Bring to a boil, cover, and simmer until barely tender, about 5 minutes. Drain and cool. Arrange the asparagus spears in pairs and wrap a strip of salmon close to both ends of each pair (two strips salmon around every two spears). Place in a buttered baking dish.

Make the hollandaise sauce according to directions. [May be prepared ahead] Spoon it over the asparagus and run under a broiler until golden, about 1 minute or less (watch carefully).

Egg-Coated Fried Pimiento
(PIMIENTO REBOZADO)

The bars on Madrid's Victoria Street are always a hub of activity on afternoons before a bullfight. It is here that aficionados gather to purchase tickets and to discuss the merits of this or the other bullfighter over a drink and, of course, a tapa. At the Vista Alegre bar the color red predominates in accordance with this bullfight ambience—enormous red wine vats, red brick arched doorways, red tiled walls, red wine, and the house specialty, red peppers, which are prepared on a grill facing the street.

Only home-prepared pimientos will do for this tapa. SERVES 6

> 2 pimientos, home prepared
>   (see p. 204) and cut
>   in 1-inch-wide strips
> Flour for dusting
> Salt
> Freshly ground pepper
> 2 tablespoons olive oil
> 1 egg, lightly beaten with
>   1 teaspoon water

Coat the pimiento strips with flour that has been seasoned well with salt and pepper.

Heat the oil in a medium skillet. Dip the pimiento strips into the beaten egg, then immediately into the skillet. Cook till golden on both sides. Drain.

Cherry Tomatoes Filled with Tuna

(TOMATES RELLENOS DE ATÚN)

SERVES 8

24 medium ripe but firm
    cherry tomatoes
Salt
1½ tablespoons butter
1 tablespoon minced onion
A 7-ounce can light meat tuna, drained
1 tablespoon minced parsley
Dash of nutmeg
1 teaspoon Worcestershire sauce
1 teaspoon Dijon-style mustard
1 teaspoon grated Parmesan cheese
½ teaspoon crushed red pepper or a
    few drops Tabasco sauce
Freshly ground pepper
4 tablespoons mayonnaise, preferably
    homemade (p. 47)
Parmesan cheese and minced parsley
    for garnish

WHITE SAUCE
3 tablespoons butter
3 tablespoons flour
1 cup milk
Salt
Freshly ground pepper
2 teaspoons dry (fino) Spanish sherry

Slice off the tops of the tomatoes and, with the aid of a knife, loosen the pulp and seeds. Scoop out with a small spoon. Sprinkle the tomatoes inside with salt and turn upside down to drain on a cooling rack or other meshed surface for about 10 minutes.

Heat 1 tablespoon of the butter in a small saucepan and sauté the onion until it is tender but not brown.

To make the white sauce, melt the butter in the saucepan in which the onion has cooked, stir in the flour, and cook for a minute. Add the milk gradually and stir constantly until thickened and smooth. Season with salt and pepper and stir in the sherry.

In a bowl break up the tuna with a fork, then stir in the white sauce, parsley, nutmeg, Worcestershire sauce, mustard, grated cheese, chili pepper, salt, and pepper. Fill the tomatoes with this mixture. Using the cup side of a small spoon, coat the tomato tops with a smooth dome of mayonnaise. Sprinkle with grated cheese and minced parsley and dot with the remaining butter. [May be prepared ahead] Bake at 400°F until the tops are brown but the tomatoes still fairly firm, about 10 minutes.

Glazed Pearl Onions

(CEBOLLETAS GLASEADAS)

Glazed with caramelized sugar and placed in a white sauce, these lovely onions are an excellent vegetable addition to a tapas selection. If such small onions are unavailable, use slightly larger ones, decreasing the number, or peel off the outer layers to make the onions smaller. SERVES 4-6

1½ cups chicken broth
30 very small pearl onions, about the size of large grapes, unpeeled
2 teaspoons sugar
4 tablespoons butter
1 tablespoon flour
¼ cup milk
Salt
Freshly ground pepper

In a saucepan bring the chicken broth to a boil. Add the unpeeled onions, return to a boil, cover, and simmer until tender, about 20 minutes. Drain the onions, reserving ¼ cup plus 1 tablespoon of the cooking liquid. Slip off skins and trim stems.

Place the sugar in a shallow casserole large enough to hold the onions in one layer. Cook over medium heat, stirring constantly, until the sugar is lightly caramelized. Add 1 tablespoon of the cooking liquid and 3 tablespoons of the butter, stirring until smooth. Add the onions and transfer to the oven. Bake at 350°F for about 20 minutes, shaking the pan occasionally to prevent sticking, until the onions are well coated with the butter mixture and golden.

While the onions are baking, melt the remaining tablespoon of butter in a small saucepan. Stir in the flour and cook for a minute. Add gradually the remaining ¼ cup of cooking liquid, the milk, salt, and pepper and cook, stirring constantly, until the mixture is thickened and smooth. [May be prepared ahead] Pour the sauce over the bottom of a serving dish, arrange the onions on top (the sauce is not spooned over the onions), and serve.

Tuna-Stuffed Potatoes

(PATATAS RELLENAS)

In order for these tuna- and mushroom-filled potatoes to be tapas size, you will need very small potatoes, not more than 1½ inches in diameter. SERVES 6

6 very small potatoes, such as red waxy (about ½ pound)
1 small egg, separated
2 teaspoons butter, melted
¼ cup finely flaked light meat tuna
2 tablespoons minced fresh wild mushrooms or dried wild mushrooms, softened
Salt
Freshly ground pepper
Butter
Grated cheese

Slit the tops of the potatoes and bake at 350°F for about 45 minutes, or until tender. Slice off a cap on top and hollow out the potatoes with a small spoon.

In a bowl mash the potatoes with a fork and mix in the egg yolk, melted butter, tuna, mushrooms, salt, and pepper. Beat the white of the egg until stiff but not dry and fold into the potato mixture. Fill the potato shells, forming a smooth dome. Dot with butter, sprinkle with cheese [May be prepared ahead], and bake at 400°F for 10 minutes.

Zucchini, Peppers, and Tomato in Potato Nests

(PISTO MANCHEGO EN NIDOS DE PATATA)

It was at the Parador Marqués de Villena in Alarcón that I ate this version of Pisto Manchego, enclosed in small potato nests that looked like flower petals. This medieval castle is an awesome sight, perched in isolated splendor on a mountaintop and encircled by the snaking aquamarine Júcar River. The *parador's* impressive vaulted dining room is particularly popular at lunchtime with passing motorists, and you could easily make a meal of their Entremeses Variados, fifteen tapas presented on individual dishes.

SERVES 6

Pisto Manchego (p. 5)
1 medium potato, peeled and sliced
    paper thin, as for potato chips
Oil for frying
Minced parsley

Make the Pisto Manchego according to instructions.

To make the potato nests you will need a 3½-inch (inner measurement) nest fryer. Grease the fryer by dipping it into oil, then line with overlapping rows of potato to within ½ inch of the rim. Secure the nest with the smaller fryer that fits inside. Plunge the nest into hot oil (about 390°F), enough to cover the potatoes, and fry until the potatoes are golden. Remove the inner fryer, tap the outer fryer against a hard surface to loosen the potatoes, then turn out the potato nests and drain. Repeat for the other nests, keeping the fried nests warm in a 200°F oven (or make ahead and reheat at 350°F for about 1 minute). To serve, divide the vegetable filling into 6 portions, fill the nests, and sprinkle with parsley. Once the nests are filled, they should be served right away.

Potato and Spinach "Sandwiches"

(EMPAREDADOS DE PATATA Y ESPINACA)

Here's a nice little tapa in which potato slices take the place of bread to enclose a spinach filling.

SERVES 6 (MAKES 12)

¾ pound spinach leaves
Salt
2 cloves garlic, chopped
4 anchovies, finely chopped
Freshly ground pepper
1 medium potato
Flour for dusting
1 egg, lightly beaten with
    1 teaspoon water
Bread crumbs
Oil for frying

Wash the spinach and leave damp. Place in a pot, without additional water, sprinkle with salt, cover, and cook until just tender, about 5 minutes. In a processor or blender purée the spinach, garlic, anchovy, salt, and pepper.

Parboil the potato until soft but not quite done. Peel and cut in ⅛-inch slices (there should be about 24 slices). On half of the slices spread the spinach purée (about 2 teaspoons per slice), then cover with the remaining slices of potato. Press gently so the "sandwiches" hold together. Dust with flour, dip in the egg, then coat with bread crumbs. [May be prepared ahead] Fry in hot oil at least ½ inch deep until golden on both sides. Or, better, use a deep-fryer. Drain on paper towels. [May be kept warm in 200°F oven up to 30 minutes]

Potatoes with Piquant Tomato and Alioli

(PATATAS BRAVAS)

Although Patatas Bravas is a well-known tapa, it is difficult to find well prepared. This version is one of the best, adding a coating of garlic mayonnaise to the traditional spicy tomato sauce. You may choose to prepare the potatoes by other methods, such as sautéing or deep frying. (Note: The Tomato Sauce recipe below will make more than needed for this tapa. You can refrigerate or freeze it and use for other tapas.) SERVES 4

2 medium-large potatoes, peeled
    and cut into ¾-inch chunks
Olive oil
Salt
Alioli Sauce (p. 191), thinned to sauce
    consistency if necessary

TOMATO SAUCE
2 tablespoons olive oil
2 tablespoons minced onion
1 clove garlic, minced
3 medium tomatoes (about
    ¾ pound), chopped
1 tablespoon tomato paste
¼ cup dry white wine
2 tablespoons water
1 tablespoon minced parsley
½ dried red chili pepper,
    seeded and crumbled, or
    ¼ teaspoon crushed
    red pepper
Dash of Tabasco sauce
1 bay leaf
⅛ teaspoon sugar
Salt
Freshly ground pepper

Grease a roasting pan and arrange the potatoes in one layer. Brush with olive oil, sprinkle with salt, and bake at 375°F for about 45 minutes, or until golden and crisp.

Meanwhile, make the tomato sauce. Heat the oil in a skillet and sauté the onion and garlic until the onion is wilted. Add the tomatoes and sauté for another few minutes. Stir in the tomato paste, wine, water, parsley, chili pepper, Tabasco, bay leaf, sugar, salt, and pepper. Cover and simmer for 30 minutes. Strain. The sauce should not be too thick—thin with water if necessary.

To serve, arrange the potatoes in a bowl or on a dish. Spoon on several tablespoons of the tomato sauce, then 3 or 4 tablespoons of the Alioli. (Note: You may make this dish without the Alioli, if you prefer.)

Fried New Potatoes with Alioli

(PATATITAS FRITAS CON ALIOLI)

These tiny unpeeled potatoes, so good that I wanted to make a meal of them, began appearing at tapas bars as we arrived at the Alicante coast of Spain. I had never seen them before as tapas, nor have I seen them since. The best ones were at the Nou Manolín bar in the city of Alicante. SERVES 4

> Alioli Sauce (p. 191)
> 16 very small new or red waxy potatoes,
>   1¼–1½ inches, skin on
> Salt
> Oil for frying

Make the Alioli as directed and leave at room temperature until ready to use.

Place the potatoes in a pot with salted water to cover. Bring to a boil, cover, and boil rapidly for about 5 minutes. Remove from the heat and let sit, covered, for about 15 minutes, or until the potatoes are tender. Drain and dry completely on paper towels. (Do this in advance so the potatoes are well dried before frying.)

Heat the oil at least ½ inch deep in a skillet. Or, better, use a deep-fryer. When the oil is very hot (about 400°F), add the potatoes and fry rapidly, turning once, until golden and crisp. Drain on paper towels and serve on toothpicks with the Alioli on the side.

Cheese Puffs

(BUÑUELOS DE QUESO)

These fried cheese puffs are light and airy and will vary in taste according to the kind of cheese you wish to use. They should be eaten right after frying, accompanied by pickled cucumbers, which are the perfect counterpoint to the mild taste of the cheese. The cucumbers should be prepared at least several hours in advance. SERVES 4 (MAKES 8)

> 2 egg whites
> 1 cup grated Spanish cheese (see p. 203),
>   such as Tetilla or Manchego
>   (not too aged), or Swiss
>   or Gouda
> Dash of cayenne pepper
> 3 teaspoons flour
> Eight ½-inch cubes cured or
>   boiled ham (optional)
> Oil for frying
> Eight ¼-inch-thick pieces
>   Pickled Cucumber (p. 48)

Beat the egg whites until stiff but not dry. Stir in the cheese, cayenne, and flour. With floured hands shape into walnut-size balls and press a cube of ham into the center. Heat the oil at least ½ inch deep to about 390–400°F and fry until golden. Or, better, use a deep-fryer. [May be kept warm in 200°F oven up to 30 minutes] Spear a cucumber piece on top of each cheese puff with a toothpick.

Spinach and Cheese Puffs

(BUÑUELOS DE ESPINACA Y QUESO)

These tasty puffs are also excellent with Spanish *chorizo* sausage (see following recipe). SERVES 6-8 (MAKES ABOUT 24)

3/4 pound spinach,
    thick stems removed
Salt
2 teaspoons olive oil
1 small clove garlic, minced
3 tablespoons grated cheese, such
    as Manchego (see p. 203)
    or Parmesan
Oil for frying

BUÑUELO DOUGH
1 cup water
3 tablespoons butter
1/4 teaspoon freshly
    ground nutmeg
3/8 teaspoon salt
1 cup flour
2 eggs

Wash the spinach leaves and drain in a colander. Place in a pot with no additional water, sprinkle with salt, cover, and cook until barely tender, about 4~5 minutes. Drain well on paper towels and chop.

Heat the olive oil in a medium skillet. Sauté the garlic for a minute, then add the spinach and sauté lightly for a minute or so.

To make the dough, place in a saucepan over medium heat the water, butter, nutmeg, and salt. When the water comes to a boil and the butter has melted, add the flour all at once. Lower the heat and stir with a wooden spoon until the dough leaves the sides of the pan and forms a ball. Continue cooking and stirring for a minute or two. Turn off the heat and beat in the eggs one at a time. The dough will separate, then hold together again. (This step may be done effortlessly in a food processor: once the flour has been added and forms a ball, transfer the dough to the processor. Process for 15 seconds. Add both eggs and beat for 45 seconds.)

Stir in the spinach and cheese. (This can also be done in the processor.) [May be prepared ahead] In a skillet heat the oil at least 1/2 inch deep to about 380°F. Drop the dough by teaspoonfuls into the oil and fry over medium heat, turning occasionally, until puffed and golden. Drain on paper towels. [May be kept warm in 200°F oven up to 30 minutes]

Chorizo Puffs

(BUÑUELOS DE CHORIZO)

SERVES 6-8 (MAKES ABOUT 24)

1/4 pound chorizo sausage,
    skinned and finely chopped
Buñuelo Dough (see preceding
    recipe), omitting the nutmeg
Oil for frying

Sauté the *chorizo* in a skillet for a couple of minutes until it starts to give off its oil. (Drain off some oil if there is a lot.)

Make the buñuelo dough, combine with the *chorizo*, then fry according to the instructions in the preceding recipe.

Vegetable and Truffle Croquettes

(CROQUETAS DE LEGUMBRES Y TRUFA)

Although you could eliminate the truffles from these delicious croquettes, I don't recommend doing so—they add a haunting flavor that makes the croquettes quite out of the ordinary. SERVES 8 (MAKES ABOUT 24)

1/4 pound fresh or
   frozen peas
Salt
12 green beans
2 small carrots, scraped and
   cut in halves lengthwise
6 tablespoons olive oil
8 medium mushrooms,
   brushed clean
3 tablespoons butter
3/4 cup flour
1 1/2 cups milk
1/2 cup strong chicken broth
Freshly ground pepper
1-2 tablespoons drained and
   finely chopped truffles
2 eggs, lightly beaten with
   2 teaspoons water
Bread crumbs
Oil for frying

Place the peas in a small pot of salted water, bring to a boil, and simmer until tender. In another pot of salted water cook the green beans and carrots until tender. Drain very well on paper towels. Chop all the vegetables finely.

While the vegetables are cooking, heat 1 table-spoon of the oil in a small skillet until very hot and sauté the mushrooms quickly over high heat for about 1 minute. Chop finely.

In a saucepan melt the butter with the remaining 5 tablespoons of oil. Stir in the flour and cook for about 2 minutes, stirring constantly. Pour in the milk and broth gradually. Season well with salt and pepper. Stir constantly until the sauce is thickened and smooth and has reached a boil.

Mix the sauce with all the vegetables (including the chopped truffles). Cool, then chill for several hours until the mixture is firm enough to handle. (This may be speeded up by spreading the mixture in a thin layer on a large plate.) [May be prepared ahead]

Form the croquettes into walnut-size balls, dip in the egg, then coat with the bread crumbs. [Refrigerate] Heat the oil at least 1/2 inch deep to about 390°F and fry the croquettes quickly, turning once, until they are golden. Or, better, use a deep-fryer. [May be kept warm in 200°F oven up to 30 minutes]

Egg Croquettes
(CROQUETAS DE HUEVO)

These croquettes, which conceal a wedge of hard-boiled egg, are a favorite in Spain and always a hit in my household. SERVES 4 (MAKES 12)

> 2 tablespoons butter
> 3½ tablespoons olive oil
> ½ cup plus 1 tablespoon flour
> ¾ cup milk
> ¾ cup chicken broth
> Salt
> Freshly ground pepper
> Dash of nutmeg
> 6 tablespoons (about 2 ounces) finely
>   minced cured ham
> 3 hard-boiled eggs, quartered
> 1 egg, lightly beaten with 1 teaspoon water
> Bread crumbs
> Oil for frying

Heat the butter and oil in a saucepan until the butter melts. Add the flour and cook for 2 minutes, stirring constantly. Pour in gradually the milk, broth, salt (not too much—the ham may be salty), pepper, and nutmeg and cook over medium heat, stirring constantly, until thickened and smooth. Add the ham and cook over low heat about 5 minutes more. Check the seasoning.

Spread the sauce on a dinner-size plate and with a rubber spatula coat each egg quarter with sauce and place on a lightly greased dish. Refrigerate until firm, at least 1 hour. [May be prepared ahead]

Coat the croquettes with the beaten egg, then roll in the bread crumbs. [Refrigerate] Fry quickly in hot oil (about 380°F) at least ½ inch deep until golden. Or, better, use a deep-fryer. [May be kept warm in 200°F oven up to 30 minutes]

Batter-Dipped Pimiento Croquettes
(FRITOS DE PIMIENTO PICANTE)

A center of puréed pimientos with a crunchy batter coating, instead of the standard bread crumbs, makes these croquettes unusual. SERVES 4-6 (MAKES 12)

> 3 medium red peppers
> 2 tablespoons olive oil
> Salt
> Freshly ground pepper
> ¼ teaspoon cayenne pepper
> 4 tablespoons butter
> 6 tablespoons flour
> ¾ cup milk
> Batter (p. 180)
> Oil for frying

Roast the red peppers according to the directions for pimiento on page 204. Peel, core, and seed, then chop coarsely. Heat 1 tablespoon of the oil in a skillet and sauté the peppers for 2 minutes, seasoning with salt, pepper, and cayenne. Transfer to a processor or blender and purée.

To make the croquettes, heat the butter and the remaining tablespoon of oil in a saucepan until the butter melts. Add the flour and cook for 3 minutes, stirring constantly. Pour in the milk gradually and cook over medium heat, stirring constantly, until the sauce is thickened and smooth. Add the puréed pimientos, season with salt and pepper if necessary, and continue cooking and stirring 10 minutes more, until the mixture begins to bubble. Cool, then refrigerate for several hours, until cold and firm. (Cut down the time by spreading the mixture in a thin layer on a flat dish.) [May be prepared ahead]

Prepare the batter according to directions (it too

can be made in advance). In a skillet heat the oil at least ½ inch deep until hot (about 390°F). Or, better, use a deep-fryer. Shape the croquettes into walnut-size balls, coat with the batter, and fry until golden. Drain on paper towels. [May be kept warm in 200°F oven up to 30 minutes]

Shrimp and Cheese Croquettes
(CROQUETAS DE GAMBAS Y QUESO)

The taste of the great Spanish cheese, Manchego (available in cheese stores and food specialty shops), gives these croquettes a special flavor, although you may substitute the cheese of your choice. SERVES 4 (MAKES 12)

4 tablespoons sweet butter
1 tablespoon salad oil
1 teaspoon minced shallots
6 tablespoons flour
¾ cup milk
3 medium (2 ounces) shrimp, shelled and finely chopped
5 tablespoons (about 2 ounces) grated Manchego cheese (see p. 203), or similar cheese, such as Italian or French sheep's-milk cheese
Salt
White pepper, preferably freshly ground
A grating of nutmeg
1 egg yolk
½ cup bread crumbs
Oil for frying

Melt the butter and oil in a saucepan, then sauté the shallots for a minute or two. Stir in the flour and cook, stirring, for another minute or so. Pour in the milk gradually and stir constantly until the mixture is thickened and smooth and has reached the boiling point. Add the shrimp, cook for another minute, then remove from the heat. Stir in 3 tablespoons of the cheese, salt, pepper, and nutmeg (the mixture should be well seasoned). Cool, then chill for several hours. (The chilling process may be speeded up by spreading the mixture in a thin layer on a flat dish.) [May be prepared ahead]

With floured hands, shape the dough into walnut-size balls. Cover with egg yolk, then roll in the bread crumbs, which have been mixed with the remaining 2 tablespoons of cheese. [Refrigerate] Fry in hot oil (about 390°F) at least ½ inch deep until golden, turning once. Or, better, use a deep-fryer. Drain. [May be kept warm in 200°F oven up to 30 minutes]

Mussel Croquettes

(CROQUETAS DE MEJILLÓN)

SERVES 4-6 (MAKES 12-15)

1½ dozen medium mussels
  (see p. 204)
1 slice lemon
1 bay leaf
1 tablespoon olive oil
4 tablespoons sweet butter
6 tablespoons flour
¾ cup milk
A generous grating of nutmeg
Freshly ground pepper
2 tablespoons minced cured ham
Salt
1 egg, lightly beaten with
   1 teaspoon water
Bread crumbs
Oil for frying

mixture in a thin layer on a flat dish.) [May be prepared ahead]

With floured hands, shape the mixture into walnut-size balls. Coat with the beaten egg and roll in the bread crumbs. [Refrigerate] Fry in hot oil (about 390°F) at least ½ inch deep, turning once, until golden. Or, better, use a deep-fryer. Drain on paper towels. [May be kept warm in 200°F oven up to 30 minutes]

Place the mussels in a skillet with ¾ cup water, the lemon slice, and the bay leaf. Bring to a boil and remove the mussels as they open. Reserve ¼ cup of the cooking liquid (boil down if there is more). Discard the mussel shells and chop the meat finely.

Heat the oil and butter in a saucepan until the butter melts. Add the flour and cook, stirring, for 3 minutes. Pour in gradually the milk and reserved cooking liquid, seasoning with nutmeg and pepper. Cook, stirring constantly, until the mixture is thickened and smooth. Add the ham and mussel meat and continue cooking and stirring 10 minutes more, or until the mixture begins to bubble. Taste for salt. Cool, then refrigerate for about 2 hours, until cold and firm. (Speed cooling time by spreading the

Monkfish and Lettuce Croquettes

(CROQUETAS DE RAPE)

Monkfish, mild flavored and firmly textured, is an ideal ingredient for croquettes, especially when paired with chopped lettuce leaves.

SERVES 4 (MAKES 12)

1/4 pound skinned and boned monkfish
(see p. 86) or other firm-bodied,
mild fish
4 tablespoons butter
1 tablespoon olive oil
1 tablespoon minced onion
4 tablespoons minced romaine lettuce
6 tablespoons flour
1/2 cup milk
Salt
Freshly ground pepper
Dash of nutmeg
1 egg, lightly beaten with
1 teaspoon water
Bread crumbs
Oil for frying

COOKING LIQUID
1 sprig parsley
1 slice onion
Salt
4 peppercorns
1 small bay leaf
1/4 teaspoon thyme
Water

Place the monkfish in a pan and add the cooking liquid ingredients, with enough water to barely cover the fish. Bring to a boil, cover, and simmer for 10 minutes. Remove the fish, flake, and reserve. Boil the liquid down, strain, and reserve 1/4 cup.

Heat the butter and oil in a saucepan until the butter is melted. Add the onion and lettuce and sauté briefly until the onion is wilted. Add the flour and cook for 3 minutes, stirring constantly. Stir in the milk, the 1/4 cup reserved cooking liquid, the fish, salt, pepper, and nutmeg. Cook slowly, stirring frequently, until the mixture begins to bubble, about 10 minutes. Cool, then refrigerate for several hours, until firm. (You can speed this up by spreading the mixture in a thin layer on a flat dish.) [May be prepared ahead]

Shape the chilled fish mixture into 1-inch balls, dip in the egg, then roll in the bread crumbs. [Refrigerate] Heat oil until hot (about 390°F) at least 1/2 inch deep and fry the croquettes quickly until golden. Or, better, use a deep-fryer. Drain. [May be kept warm in 200°F oven up to 30 minutes]

Fish and Cheese Croquettes

(CROQUETAS DE MERLUZA Y QUESO)

We sampled these delicious croquettes at the poolside of the delightful Hotel Atlántico in Cádiz. The hotel is set in a choice spot overlooking the Atlantic Ocean, where the sunsets are dazzling. SERVES 8-12 (MAKES ABOUT 25)

4 tablespoons butter
1½ pounds fresh cod steaks
1 cup water
4 slices onion
1 carrot, cut in 4 pieces
2 sprigs parsley
1 bay leaf
¼ teaspoon thyme
Salt
Freshly ground pepper
5 tablespoons olive oil
¾ cup flour
1 cup milk
Dash of nutmeg
2 teaspoons dry (fino)
   Spanish sherry
2 tablespoons minced parsley
¼ pound mild cheese, such as
   Spanish Tetilla (see p. 204), Fontina,
   or Jarlsberg, finely chopped
2 tablespoons grated Parmesan cheese
2 eggs, lightly beaten with
   2 teaspoons water
Bread crumbs
Oil for frying

Heat 1 tablespoon of the butter in a skillet and sauté the fish quickly (about 1 minute to a side).

Add the water, onion slices, carrot, parsley sprigs, bay leaf, thyme, salt, and pepper. Bring to a boil, cover, and simmer for 15 minutes.

Discard the skin and bones from the fish and flake the fish with your fingers. There should be about 1 cup. Set aside. Strain the cooking liquid and reserve. (You will need 1 cup—if you have more, boil down; if less, add water.)

Heat the remaining 3 tablespoons of butter and the oil in a saucepan until the butter melts. Add the flour and cook for 3 minutes, stirring constantly. Add gradually the milk, the reserved fish broth, salt (if necessary), pepper, and nutmeg and cook over medium heat, stirring constantly, until the sauce is thickened and smooth. Add the sherry, parsley, the flaked fish, and the chopped and grated cheeses and continue cooking and stirring 10 minutes more, until the mixture reaches the boiling point. Cool, then refrigerate until cold, at least 3 hours. (Cut down the cooling time by spreading the mixture in a thin layer on a flat dish.) [May be prepared ahead]

With floured hands, form the mixture into 1-inch balls. Coat the croquettes with the beaten egg and roll in the bread crumbs. [Refrigerate] Fry quickly in hot oil (about 390°F) at least ½ inch deep, turning once, until golden. Or, better, use a deep-fryer. Drain. [May be kept warm in 200°F oven up to 30 minutes]

Chicken and Cured Ham Croquettes

(CROQUETAS DE LHARDY)

I love croquettes in all their many varieties, but I am especially partial to these delicious croquettes from the delightful and elegant turn-of-the-century Madrid restaurant, tapas bar, and pastry shop called Lhardy. SERVES 12-15 (MAKES ABOUT 35)

1 whole chicken breast,
   split in half
1 sprig parsley
1 bay leaf
1/4 teaspoon thyme
1 slice onion
Salt
4 peppercorns
3 tablespoons butter
5 tablespoons olive oil
3/4 cup flour
1 1/2 cups milk
Freshly ground pepper
A generous grating of nutmeg
1/2 cup very finely
   hand-minced cured ham
2 eggs, lightly beaten with
   2 teaspoons water
Bread crumbs
Oil for frying

Place the chicken breast in a saucepan with the parsley, bay leaf, thyme, onion, salt, peppercorns, and water to cover. Bring to a boil, cover, and simmer for 15 minutes. Remove the chicken from the broth, cool, bone, and skin. Return the skin and bones to the broth and continue cooking until the broth is strongly flavored. Reserve 1/2 cup. Mince the chicken breast. (This can be done easily in a processor.)

Heat the butter and olive oil in a saucepan until the butter melts. Add the flour and cook for 3 minutes, stirring constantly. Add gradually the milk and the reserved broth, a little salt, the ground pepper, and nutmeg and cook over medium heat, stirring constantly, until the sauce is thickened and smooth. Add the chicken and ham and continue cooking and stirring about 10 minutes more, until the sauce reaches the boiling point. Check the seasoning, then cool. Refrigerate until cold, at least 3 hours. (Less time is necessary if the mixture is spread out in a thin layer on a flat dish.) [May be prepared ahead]

With floured hands, divide the mixture into 1-inch balls. Dip the croquettes in the beaten egg and coat with the crumbs. [Refrigerate] Fry quickly in hot oil (about 390°F) at least 1/2 inch deep, turning several times, until golden. Or, better, use a deep-fryer. Drain. [May be kept warm in 200°F oven up to 30 minutes]

Little Tuna Pies

(BUÑUELOS DE ATÚN)

These doughnutlike turnovers, made with a yeast dough, were served to me, compliments of the house, at the elegant bar of one of Europe's great hotels, El Hostal de Los Reyes Católicos, in the magnificent city of Santiago de Compostela. They are a specialty in that city, offered with either a tuna filling or a delicious pork filling (see following recipe). The dough is easy to prepare and can be kept in the refrigerator for a day or two (in which case you should eliminate the rising time because that will take place in the refrigerator). SERVES 6-8 (MAKES 18 LITTLE PIES)

START PREPARATION AN HOUR AND A HALF IN ADVANCE

Oil for frying

DOUGH
1 teaspoon dry yeast
2 tablespoons warm water
1¾ cups flour
¼ teaspoon salt
1 egg, lightly beaten
½ cup warm milk
1 tablespoon butter, melted

FILLING
1½ tablespoons fruity olive oil
1 cup finely chopped onion
2 large cloves garlic, minced
Half a 7-ounce can light meat tuna,
   drained and flaked
Salt
¼ teaspoon paprika,
   preferably Spanish style
2 teaspoons chicken broth

To make the dough, dissolve the yeast in the warm water. Mix together in a bowl the flour and salt. Add the egg, then stir in the warm milk, butter, and the yeast mixture. Turn onto a working surface and knead for a minute or two, just until the dough is smooth and no longer sticky, adding more flour as necessary. Place the dough in a bowl greased with oil, turning to coat with the oil. Cover with a towel and leave in a warm spot until doubled in bulk, about 1½ hours.

Meanwhile, prepare the filling. Heat the olive oil in a skillet and sauté the onion and garlic slowly until the onion is wilted. Stir in the tuna, cook for a minute, then sprinkle with salt and paprika. Stir in the chicken broth and turn off the heat. [May be prepared ahead]

Punch down the dough and divide into 1-inch balls. Roll each into a 2-inch circle. Place 2 teaspoons of filling in the center of each circle, pull up the sides, and pinch to seal.

Heat the frying oil at least 1 inch deep in a skillet. Lower the heat to medium and fry the meat pies slowly, turning frequently, until they are puffed and golden. Or, better, use a deep-fryer. Drain.

Little Pork Pies
(BUÑUELOS DE CERDO)

SERVES 6-8 (MAKES 18 LITTLE PIES)

Dough (see preceding recipe)
1½ tablespoons fruity olive oil
1 cup finely chopped onion
2 large cloves garlic, minced
¼ pound lean pork, very finely
**   chopped (not ground)**
¼ cup minced skinned tomato
½ teaspoon paprika, preferably
**   Spanish style**
Salt
Oil for frying

Make the dough and leave in a warm spot to rise.

Meanwhile, prepare the filling. Heat the olive oil in a skillet and sauté the onion and garlic slowly until the onion is wilted. Add the meat, turn up the heat, and cook, stirring, until the meat loses its color. Stir in the tomato, paprika, and salt. Cook for a minute, then turn off the heat. [May be prepared ahead]

To fill and fry the dough, see the instructions in the preceding recipe.

Grilled Shrimp
(GAMBAS A LA PLANCHA)

Grilling is one of the two favorite ways to prepare shrimp in Spain (the other is plain boiling, ideal when the shrimp are fresh and flavorful). And if your shrimp are not the tastiest, which they often are not in America, grilling somehow seems to bring back some of the sea taste that has been lost. The shrimp are cooked in their shells—each guest is expected to peel his own.

I particularly remember grilled shrimp at the Bar Fitero in Pamplona, right on Estafeta Street, where the bulls run for eight mornings in July. During that week of madness, known as the fiesta of San Fermín, this bar and all other establishments on the street are boarded up carefully for the morning runs, but by afternoon hungry crowds once again fill the bars. At Bar Fitero beautiful fresh shrimp are constantly on the grill. SERVES 4

Olive oil
Coarse salt
¾ pound large or jumbo
**   shrimp, unshelled**
**   (if possible, heads on also)**

Brush a large skillet or stove-top grill very lightly with olive oil. Heat until very hot and sprinkle with coarse salt. Add the shrimp and cook over high heat for about 5 minutes, turning once. Serve right away.

Prawns Grilled with Garlic Mayonnaise

(LLAGOSTINO A L'ALLIOLI)

As the spelling of this recipe's title suggests, this dish is Catalán, served at the charming Agut D'Avignón restaurant in the Old Quarter of Barcelona. SERVES 4

> 1/4 cup mayonnaise,
>   preferably homemade
>   (p. 47)
> 2 cloves garlic, mashed to
>   a paste or put through a
>   garlic press
> 1/2 pound large or
>   jumbo shrimp, shelled
> Salt
> Bread crumbs
> Butter

Combine the mayonnaise with the garlic and set aside.

Grease a broiler dish, preferably one in which the shrimp can be served. Arrange the shrimp in close rows, fitting one shrimp against another. Sprinkle with salt.

Place under the broiler, about 4–5 inches from the heat, for about 2–3 minutes, depending on the size of the shrimp. Turn the shrimp, keeping them in rows. Spoon a strip of mayonnaise down the centers of the shrimp. Sprinkle bread crumbs over the mayonnaise and dot the crumbs with butter. Broil about 2 minutes more, until the mayonnaise topping is golden and the shrimp done.

Pasta with Shrimp in Garlic Sauce

(FIDEOS CON GAMBAS)

This and the following recipe are two versions of a tapa that was unheard of several years ago (Spain still uses very little pasta) but has recently come into vogue. These garlicky shrimp mixed with pasta come from the talented hands of Luis Bejarano at Enrique Becerra in Sevilla (see p. 71). SERVES 4

> 3 tablespoons olive oil
> Salt
> 1/4 pound imported spaghetti, broken
>   into three lengths
> 1 large clove garlic, in thin slices
> 1/4 pound smallest available shrimp
> 2 teaspoons fresh lemon juice
> 2 teaspoons veal broth, or a mixture
>   of chicken and beef broth
> 1/4 teaspoon crushed dried red chili pepper
> 2 tablespoons minced parsley

Bring a pot of water to a boil with 1 tablespoon of the oil and salt. Add the spaghetti and cook, stirring occasionally with a fork, until tender but still firm. Drain, return to the cooking pot, mix with another tablespoon of the oil, and keep warm.

Heat the remaining tablespoon of oil in a skillet and add the garlic. Just as it begins to color slightly, add the shrimp and stir for about 2 minutes, until they turn pink. Add the lemon juice, broth, red pepper, salt, and parsley and cook for another minute. Mix into the spaghetti, reheating if necessary, and serve in individual casserole dishes, preferably Spanish earthenware.

Clams with Pasta

(FIDEOS CON ALMEJAS)

This pasta and clam combination acquires its Spanish flavor from the chopped red pepper and a trace of saffron. SERVES 8

2 tablespoons olive oil
1 large onion, finely chopped
1 clove garlic, minced
1 red pepper, finely chopped
1 medium tomato, skinned, seeded, and finely chopped
1 tablespoon minced parsley
1 bay leaf
Few strands saffron
Salt
Freshly ground pepper
1/2 pound spaghetti, broken into three lengths
3/4 cup veal broth, or a mixture of chicken and beef broth
2 dozen very small clams (see p. 203)
3 tablespoons fresh or frozen peas

Heat 1 tablespoon of the oil in a skillet, sauté the onion, garlic, and red pepper for a minute, then cover and cook slowly until the vegetables are tender but not brown, about 20 minutes. Add the tomato, parsley, bay leaf, saffron, salt, and pepper to the onion mixture and cook for 5 minutes, uncovered.

Meanwhile, bring a large pot of salted water to a boil with the remaining tablespoon of oil. Add the spaghetti and cook, stirring occasionally with a fork, until almost tender, but still quite firm. Drain and return to the cooking pot. Combine the onion and tomato mixture in the pot with the spaghetti, add

1/2 cup of the broth, the clams, and the peas. Mix well. Cover and continue cooking until the clams have opened, about 10 minutes.

To serve, add the remaining 1/4 cup broth (the mixture should be a little soupy) and taste for salt and pepper—it should be well seasoned. Serve in small individual casserole dishes, preferably Spanish earthenware. Although best prepared at the last minute, this dish can be made in advance and reheated.

Baked Clams

(ALMEJAS AL HORNO)

SERVES 4

1 dozen medium clams (see p. 203)
4 tablespoons butter
2 large cloves garlic, minced
2 tablespoons minced onion
2 tablespoons minced parsley
1/4 teaspoon paprika, preferably Spanish style
1/4 teaspoon thyme
Salt
Freshly ground pepper
3 teaspoons bread crumbs
1/4 teaspoon olive oil

Shuck the clams and drain the juices. Remove one shell and loosen the meat from the remaining shell. Melt the butter in a skillet and sauté the garlic, onion, parsley, paprika, thyme, salt, and pepper for 2 minutes, stirring. Cover the clams with this mixture.

In a cup mix the bread crumbs with the oil. Sprinkle over the clams [May be prepared ahead] and run under the broiler until browned.

Stir-Fried Mushrooms, Shrimp, Ham, and Peppers
(TÍO DIEGO)

Tapas can sometimes have the oddest names. This one is called literally "Uncle Jimmy" and is a specialty at an excellent tapas bar in Sevilla, Bar Modesto, where it is served in huge portions. Since this is a quick-frying dish, assemble and chop all ingredients in advance. Cooking time will be only about 5 minutes. SERVES 4–5

3 tablespoons olive oil
½ green pepper, cut in ½-inch-wide strips
½ pound medium shrimp, shelled
½ pound mushrooms, in ¼-inch-thick
  lengthwise slices with stems
3 cloves garlic, minced
A ¼-pound piece cured ham,
  in ½-inch cubes
⅛–¼ teaspoon crushed red pepper
Salt
Freshly ground pepper
3 tablespoons dry (fino) Spanish sherry
3 tablespoons chicken broth

Heat 2 tablespoons of the oil in a large skillet, preferably nonstick. Stir fry the green pepper over medium-high heat for a minute, then add the shrimp and stir fry 1 minute more. Add the mushrooms, garlic, ham, crushed red pepper, salt, pepper, and the remaining tablespoon of oil. Cook, stirring, until the mushrooms are softened. Add the sherry and broth, stir to deglaze the pan, and serve right away.

Lemon- and Garlic-Flavored Steamed Mussels
(MEJILLONES AL VAPOR)

These mussels are a favorite tapa or first course before a typical Valencian *paella* at the famous beachside La Pepica restaurant in Valencia and are easily eaten by the dozens. Take this into consideration when determining the quantity to prepare. Make sure your mussels are absolutely fresh—black and shiny and closed tight as clams. SERVES ABOUT 4

2 dozen small–medium mussels
  (see p. 204)
3 tablespoons olive oil
2 tablespoons fresh lemon juice
2 cloves garlic, minced

Place the mussels in a skillet without water. Cover and cook over medium heat, removing the mussels to a warm platter as they open. Discard any that do not open.

Reduce the liquid in the skillet to about 2 or 3 tablespoons, then return the mussels to the skillet. Sprinkle with oil, lemon juice, and garlic and heat for a minute. Serve immediately, with plenty of good bread for dunking.

Béchamel-Coated Mussels with Cured Ham

(MEJILLONES VILLEROY)

Cured ham and mussels are a great taste combination. In this tapa the mussels are wrapped in the ham, then dipped in a white sauce, breaded, and fried. Delicious! And they can be prepared a day in advance up to the final frying.

So good are these mussels that our 100-pound black Tibetan Mastiff, Osito, managed to slip out to my terrace (which serves as an extension of my refrigerator for our Christmas tapas party) and consume three platters of them (triple this recipe) in the blink of an eye. He slept contentedly all night and on into the next day. SERVES 6

18 fresh medium mussels (see p. 204)
1/4 cup water
1/4 cup dry white wine
1 bay leaf
3 ounces cured ham, in very thin slices
1/2 cup bread crumbs
1 tablespoon grated cheese, such
   as Manchego (see p. 203) or Parmesan
2 eggs, lightly beaten with 2 teaspoons water
Oil for frying

WHITE SAUCE
5 tablespoons sweet butter
6 tablespoons flour
3/4 cup milk
Salt
Freshly ground pepper
Dash of nutmeg

Place the mussels in a skillet with the water, wine, and bay leaf. Bring to a boil, lower the heat to medium, cover, and cook, removing the mussels as they open. Transfer the cooking liquid to a bowl, remove the mussel shells, and place the mussels in the liquid until ready to use. Drain the liquid from the mussels, reserving 3/4 cup (if there is less, add a little water).

To make the white sauce, melt the butter in a saucepan. Add the flour and cook, stirring, for a minute or two. Stir in gradually the reserved mussel broth, the milk, salt, pepper, and nutmeg and cook, stirring constantly, until the sauce reaches the boiling point. Turn off the heat and stir the sauce occasionally until ready to use.

Dry the mussels well on paper towels. Wrap a piece of ham of about the same width around each mussel. Coat with the white sauce and place on a dish. Refrigerate for at least 1 hour, or until the sauce becomes firm. [May be prepared ahead]

Combine the bread crumbs with the grated cheese. Coat the mussels with the beaten egg, then cover with bread crumbs. [Refrigerate] In a skillet heat the oil at least 1/2 inch deep to about 380°F and fry the mussels quickly until golden. Or, better, use a deep-fryer. Drain.

Tuna-Stuffed Mussels

(MEJILLONES RELLENOS DE ATÚN)

These are not stuffed mussel shells, as might be supposed—it is the mussels themselves (the shells discarded) that are filled with the tuna, fried, then bathed in vinegar, parsley, and shallots. They are extremely simple to prepare, but most unusual and delicious. SERVES 6

> ¼ cup flaked light meat tuna
>   in oil (save the oil)
> 2 teaspoons red wine vinegar
> 4 teaspoons minced shallots
> 2 teaspoons minced parsley
> 18 large mussels (see p. 204)
> 1 slice lemon
> 2 hard-boiled egg yolks
> Flour for dusting
> 1 egg, lightly beaten
> Bread crumbs
> Oil for frying

In a cup combine 2 tablespoons of the tuna oil, the vinegar, shallots, and parsley.

Place the mussels in a skillet with ½ cup water and the lemon slice. Bring to a boil and remove the mussels as they open. Discard any that do not open. Remove the mussel meat and discard the shells.

In a small bowl mash together the egg yolks and the tuna. Fill each mussel with about 1 teaspoon of this mixture (the mussels have an opening into which you will place the filling). Dust with flour, cover with the beaten egg, and coat with the bread crumbs. [May be prepared ahead] In a skillet heat the oil at least ½ inch deep to about 380°F. Or, better, use a deep-fryer. Fry the mussels quickly until golden on both sides. Drain.

Drizzle the oil and vinegar mixture over the mussels and serve warm.

Stuffed Mussels

(MEJILLONES GAYANGO)

Ever since I discovered these incredibly good stuffed mussels some years ago at the Bar Gayango in Madrid (which has, unfortunately, since closed its doors), they have been a favorite at my tapas parties and among my cooking students. You can prepare them the day before, except for the final frying. SERVES 6

> 18 medium mussels (see p. 204)
> 1 slice lemon
> 1 tablespoon olive oil
> 4 tablespoons minced onion
> 2 tablespoons minced cured ham
> 1 clove garlic, minced
> 1 teaspoon tomato sauce
> 1 tablespoon minced parsley
> Salt
> Freshly ground pepper
> 1 cup bread crumbs
> 1 tablespoon grated cheese
> 2 eggs, lightly beaten with 1 teaspoon water
> Oil for frying

> WHITE SAUCE
> 3 tablespoons butter
> 4 tablespoons flour
> ½ cup milk
> Salt
> Freshly ground pepper

Scrub the mussels well and remove the beards. Place them in a pan with ¾ cup water and the lemon slice. Bring to a boil and remove the mussels as they open. Do not overcook. Reserve ½ cup of the mussel broth.

Mince the mussel meat. Separate the shells and discard half of them. Heat the olive oil in a small skillet. Add the onion and sauté until it is wilted. Add the ham and garlic and sauté 1 minute more. Stir in the tomato sauce, the minced mussel meat, parsley, salt, and pepper. Cook for 5 minutes. Half fill the mussel shells with this mixture.

To make the white sauce, melt the butter in a saucepan over moderate heat. Add the flour and stir for a minute or two. Pour in gradually the reserved mussel broth and the milk. Cook, stirring constantly, until the sauce is smooth and thick. Season with salt and pepper. Remove the pan from the heat and cool slightly, stirring occasionally.

Using a teaspoon, cover the filled mussel shells with the white sauce, sealing the edges by smoothing with the cupped side of a spoon. Refrigerate for 1 hour or more, until the sauce hardens. [May be prepared ahead]

Mix together the bread crumbs and the cheese. Dip the mussels into the beaten egg, then into the crumb mixture. Heat the oil at least ½ inch deep in a skillet. Or, better, use a deep-fryer. Fry the mussels filled side down until they are well browned. Drain.

Scallops Baked with Onion and Cured Ham

(VIEIRAS AL ESTILO DE SANTIAGO)

The magnificent city of Santiago de Compostela, site of one of the world's great cathedrals and a place of pilgrimage since the ninth century, is famed for its scallops, served with their pink roe and attached to their shells. The scallop is the very symbol of the city, and pilgrims returning to their homelands from Santiago would sew scallop shells to their capes as sure proof that they had indeed reached this city of miracles.

Since the scallops in Santiago are so fresh, the preparations tend to be simple, designed to allow the delicate flavor to shine through. Served in shells, these scallops are cooked in white wine, mixed with onion and cured ham, and topped with crumbs.

SERVES 6

> 1 cup dry white wine
> 1 pound bay scallops or halved
>   sea scallops
> 2 tablespoons olive oil
> 1 medium onion, very finely chopped
> ¼ cup minced cured ham
> Salt
> Bread crumbs
> Butter

In a large saucepan bring the wine to a boil, add the scallops, return to a boil, then remove from the heat and drain.

In a skillet heat the oil, then sauté the onion and ham until the onion is wilted. Mix in the scallops and remove from the heat. Place the scallop mixture in 6 scallop shells. Sprinkle with salt [May be prepared ahead] and bake at 400°F for 10 minutes. Sprinkle with bread crumbs (about 2 teaspoons for each shell), dot with butter, and run under the broiler until golden.

VARIATION

A similar recipe, but simpler because the ingredients are not cooked first, calls for ½ cup finely diced cured ham, ½ cup very finely chopped onion, a few drops white wine vinegar, 5 tablespoons olive oil, salt, 2 tablespoons minced parsley, and 1 cup fresh bread crumbs. Place the scallops and ham in buttered shells. Sprinkle on some onion, a little vinegar, and 1 teaspoon of the oil over each. Season with salt and sprinkle with the parsley. In a small bowl mix the crumbs with the remaining 3 tablespoons of oil, divide among the shells, and bake at 400°F for 15 minutes.

Stuffed Crab

(TXANGURRO)

Txangurro is made from the meat of a large, incredibly sweet spider crab called *centollo*, which is found along Spain's northern coast. One of my most memorable meals in Spain centered around a two-pound freshly boiled *centollo* at La Nansa restaurant in Tazones, a tiny fishing village tightly enclosed by mountains. The crab meat was cut into large chunks and the shell, filled with its strongly flavored broth, served with a spoon.

To make Txangurro, flaked crab meat is mixed with a very well seasoned and spiced sauce. As a substitute for *centollo*, use crab meat from any kind of local crab (this is often sold already shelled, but fresh, by the pound) or use Alaska king crab (less desirable because it is usually frozen and often watery).

Txangurro is particularly well prepared at the Café San Martín (see p. 95) in New York. SERVES 6~8

3 tablespoons olive oil
1 medium onion, finely chopped
2 small shallots, minced
1 medium carrot, scraped and
   finely chopped
1 scallion, finely chopped
1 medium tomato, skinned and chopped
1/4 cup brandy, preferably
   Spanish brandy or Cognac
2 tablespoons dry (fino) Spanish sherry
1/2 cup fish broth (p. 27),
   well seasoned and made,
   if possible, from shellfish
1/4 teaspoon tarragon
4 tablespoons minced parsley
Salt

Freshly ground pepper
1/2 dried red chili pepper, seeded,
   or 1/4 teaspoon crushed red pepper
1 pound crab meat
Bread crumbs
Butter

Heat the oil in a skillet and sauté the onion, shallots, carrot, and scallion until the onion is wilted. Add the tomato and continue cooking until it is softened. Pour in the brandy and, keeping well away, ignite. When the flames die, add the sherry, fish broth, tarragon, 2 tablespoons of the parsley, salt, pepper, and chili pepper. Cover and simmer for 10 minutes. Add the crab meat and cook 5 minutes more, uncovered. Remove the chili pepper.

Divide the crab mixture into 6~8 scallop shells (if you have crab shells, all the better). [May be prepared ahead] Sprinkle with bread crumbs and the remaining 2 tablespoons of parsley. Dot with butter and bake at 400°F for 10 minutes, running under the broiler, if necessary, to brown.

VARIATION
In "nouvelle" Spanish cooking, this same mixture is used as a filling for crêpes (see p. 191), which are then covered with a white sauce (about 3 cups) made with milk and meat broth (veal, or beef and chicken combined), sprinkled with crumbs, dotted with butter, and baked at 350°F for 5~10 minutes.

Grilled Baby Squid

(CHIPIRONES A LA PLANCHA)

I know of no simpler or tastier way to prepare squid. This recipe will not take more than 5 minutes, but note two things: only very small squid can be used (it is rare to find a fish market with a large supply of squid of just this size; I usually rummage through the available squid to pick out the tiniest) and the squid will toughen if overcooked.

I always remember the squid we had, prepared in this manner, at an unpretentious bar/restaurant, Bellamar, on the beautiful beach at Foz in the green unspoiled lands of Galicia. They were succulent, tender, and as garlicky as could be. SERVES 4

Olive oil
1½ teaspoons coarse salt
16 baby squid (the body must not
    be more than 3 inches long),
    cleaned (see p. 204)
1½ tablespoons minced parsley
2 cloves garlic, minced

Coat a large skillet or stove-top grill very lightly with olive oil and heat until very hot. Sprinkle with the coarse salt. Add the squid quickly and cook over high heat for about 2 minutes. Turn and continue cooking for another 2 minutes. Do not overcook. Sprinkle with parsley and garlic and serve right away.

Fried Squid, Spanish Style

(CALAMARES FRITOS A LA ROMANA)

Fried squid are a classic on the tapas circuit, and you are likely to find them almost anywhere in Spain. When frying squid at home, be very careful, for they are tough and rubbery when overcooked, but tender and moist when cooked very briefly. SERVES 4-6

½ pound smallest available cleaned
    squid (see p. 204), or about
    1 pound uncleaned
Flour for dusting
Oil for frying
2 eggs, lightly beaten
Salt
Lemon wedges

Cut the squid bodies into ½-inch-wide rings and leave the tentacles in one piece. Dry well between paper towels; otherwise, the squid will spatter when fried. Dust the pieces with flour.

In a large skillet heat the oil at least 1 inch deep to about 380°F. Or, better, use a deep-fryer. Coat the squid rings and tentacles completely with the beaten egg. Remove them one at a time and place directly in the hot oil. Cook until they are golden, not more than 2 or 3 minutes. Drain, sprinkle with salt, and serve immediately, garnished with lemon wedges.

VARIATION
Instead of covering the squid with flour and egg you could use a batter, either the one on page 190 or the Beer Batter (p. 191). They will produce a crunchier coating.

Spicy Boiled Octopus

(PULPO A FEIRA)

Octopus is a strange spineless creature that turns beautifully pink and firm once it hits hot water. When properly cooked, it is very tender and not at all chewy.

This simple yet delicious octopus dish is called *a feira* (fiesta style) because it is boiled outdoors in water-filled metal drums during local festivals in Galicia. The classic way to serve this *pulpo* is on wooden dishes—a most attractive presentation. SERVES 4

1 pound octopus, preferably small
1 medium potato
4 teaspoons fruity olive oil
Coarse salt
1/2 teaspoon paprika, preferably
  Spanish style
Dash of cayenne pepper

COOKING LIQUID
12 cups water
2 tablespoons oil
1 bay leaf
1/2 onion, peeled
4 peppercorns
2 sprigs parsley
Salt

Tenderize the octopus by throwing it forcefully about ten times into your kitchen sink.

To make the cooking liquid, combine the water with the oil, bay leaf, onion, peppercorns, parsley, and salt in a large pot. Bring to a boil. Dip the octopus in and out of the liquid three times quickly (this also helps to tenderize or to "scare" it, as they say in Galicia), return to the liquid, cover, and simmer for about 1 hour. (The cooking time can vary greatly depending on whether the octopus has been frozen. After an hour, taste a small piece; if it is not tender, continue cooking.) Turn off the heat and leave the octopus in the cooking liquid until ready to use. [May be prepared ahead]

Place the potato in salted water to cover and boil until just tender. Turn off the heat and leave the potato in the water until ready to use.

Reheat the octopus and remove all loose skin (you may remove all the skin if you prefer) and cut the tentacles with scissors into 1-inch pieces.

Peel and slice the potatoes 1/8 inch thick. Arrange on a serving dish, preferably wooden, and place the octopus on top. Drizzle with the olive oil, sprinkle with the coarse salt, paprika, and cayenne and serve immediately.

Baby Eels in Garlic Sauce

(ANGULAS A LA BILBAÍNA)

Here is the classic recipe for baby eels (see p. 127). Although there are several other ways to cook this delicacy (such as in an omelet, p. 197, or on toast, p. 127), this is still the way you are most likely to find them prepared in Spain or in the few Spanish restaurants in the United States that serve them. (In New York the Café San Martín always has them on hand.) They are always prepared in individual portions in earthenware ramekins and eaten with small wooden forks, which prevent transmission of heat and to which the tiny eels cling more easily than to metal forks. SERVES 1

> 3 ounces (about ¾ cup) baby eels
> 3 tablespoons olive oil
> 1 large clove garlic, peeled and sliced
> ½ dried red chili pepper, seeded,
>   cut in 3 pieces

Drain and dry the baby eels very well on paper towels. Heat the oil in an individual heatproof ramekin, preferably earthenware (about 5 inches in diameter), until very hot. Add the garlic and chili pepper and cook over high heat until the garlic begins to sizzle and just turns golden. Add the baby eels all at once and remove immediately from the heat. Cover with a dish and take to the table, then uncover, give the eels a quick stir, and eat right away.

Whiting, Red Pepper, and Onion Kabobs

(BANDERILLAS FRITAS DE PESCADILLA)

These mini-kabobs are skewered on toothpicks for easy eating and combine a tasty variety of flavors. SERVES 6-8 (MAKES 16)

> A ¾ pound whiting, in 1-inch
>   crosswise slices, skinned and boned
>   and cut in 1-inch chunks
> 1 red pepper, cored and seeded,
>   in ¾-inch pieces
> 4 small pearl onions, peeled and
>   cut in quarters
> Salt
> Freshly ground pepper
> Oil for frying
> Flour for dusting
> 1 egg, lightly beaten with 1 teaspoon water
> Alioli Sauce (optional; p. 191)

On toothpicks skewer a piece of fish, a piece of red pepper, an onion quarter, and another piece of fish. Repeat to make 16 skewers. Sprinkle well with salt and pepper. [May be prepared ahead]

Heat the oil at least ½ inch deep in a skillet. Or, better, use a deep-fryer. Dust the skewers with flour, coat with the beaten egg, and transfer immediately to the hot oil. Lower the heat and fry slowly, allowing the red pepper and onion to cook a bit. Drain. Serve, if you wish, with Alioli sauce.

Fried Whiting with Ham

(MONTADITO DE JAMÓN Y PESCADILLA)

A slice of cured ham topped with a piece of whiting, egg coated, then fried, is a winning harmony of tastes. You may serve this tapa with mayonnaise or Alioli sauce (p. 191) on the side. SERVES 6-8 (MAKES 18)

A ¼-pound piece (about ⅛ inch thick) cured ham, cut in 1 × 1½-inch rectangles
¾ pound whiting, skinned and boned and cut in 1 × 1½-inch rectangles about ½ inch thick
Flour for dusting
Oil for frying
2 eggs, lightly beaten with 1 teaspoon water

Cover each ham rectangle with a piece of the fish and dust with flour. In a skillet heat the oil at least ½ inch deep to about 380°F. Or, better, use a deep-fryer. Coat the ham and fish combination with the beaten egg, then place directly in the hot oil, frying until golden on both sides. Drain.

Rounds of Whiting with Mushrooms and Olives

(PESCADILLA AL HORNO)

This is a delicious tapa, simple to make and to serve, since each small round of whiting is "wrapped" in its own skin. The topping of mushroom, olive, egg, parsley, and onion is, I think, ideal. SERVES 6-8

Two ½-pound whitings, cleaned, skin on, cut crosswise in ½–¾-inch-thick slices
Coarse salt
2 tablespoons minced green Spanish olives
1 hard-boiled egg, minced
2 tablespoons minced parsley
6 tablespoons minced mushroom (about 6 medium mushrooms)
½ small onion, peeled and slivered
4 teaspoons fresh lemon juice
2 tablespoons bread crumbs
3 tablespoons butter, melted

Sprinkle the fish slices on both sides with salt. In a small bowl mix together the minced olives, egg, parsley, and mushroom.

Grease a shallow casserole and cover with the slivered onion. Arrange the fish on top, sprinkle with the lemon juice, then cover each piece of fish with the mushroom mixture. Sprinkle with bread crumbs and drizzle with butter. [May be prepared ahead] Bake at 350°F until the fish is done, about 15 minutes.

Fish Wrapped in Swiss Chard Leaves

(MERLUZA EN HOJA DE GRELOS)

There is a stunning new restaurant in Madrid, Cenador del Prado, whose charming young chef, Tomás Herranz, worked for many years in New York at the Café San Martín. There he developed his style of cooking, exemplified by the number of exciting dishes he now serves in Madrid. On a recent tasting menu, this unusual fish wrapped in leaves made a successful appearance. SERVES 4

A 1-pound piece fresh cod or hake
4 Swiss chard leaves, stems trimmed
Salt
1 tablespoon olive oil
2 very thin slices cured ham
2 tablespoons butter
2 cups (about ¼ pound)
    sliced mushrooms

Skin and bone the fish. Cut into 4 thick chunks. Place the leaves in a pot with water to cover, the salt, and the oil. Bring to a boil and cook just until tender, about 7 minutes. Drain. Cut off and discard the thick white stems.

Wrap each piece of fish in half a slice of the ham, then wrap each piece in a leaf. Butter a piece of foil, arrange the wrapped fish, leaf seam down, on top, and close tightly. [May be prepared ahead] Place in a baking dish and bake at 350°F for 15 minutes.

When the fish is almost ready, heat the butter in a skillet until very hot and sauté the mushrooms, sprinkled with a little salt, just until tender, not more than a minute or two. Remove the foil from the fish and serve on a bed of the mushrooms.

Fish Roll with Pine Nuts and Cheese

(MERLUZA RELLENA DE PIÑONES Y QUESO)

You may prepare these fillets ahead and refrigerate until baking time. SERVES 4

Two ¼-pound fish fillets, preferably
    hake or fresh cod
2 tablespoons olive oil
Salt
2 tablespoons ground pine nuts
2 tablespoons grated sharp cheese,
    such as Spanish Manchego
    (see p. 204) or Parmesan
2 tablespoons bread crumbs
2 tablespoons minced parsley
Fresh lemon juice

Brush the fillets on both sides with the oil. Season with salt, then sprinkle each with ¾ tablespoon of the pine nuts, cheese, bread crumbs, and parsley. Roll and arrange seam side down in a baking dish that has been brushed with oil. [May be prepared ahead] Brush the tops of the fish rolls with a little more oil and sprinkle each with the remaining pine nuts, cheese, bread crumbs, and parsley. Bake at 350°F for 15 minutes.

Cut the fish rolls into 1-inch slices and turn the pieces on their sides. Sprinkle with lemon juice and serve right away.

Egg-Coated and Fried Fresh Cod
(MERLUZA REBOZADA A LA GADITANA)

Chunks of cod are soaked for at least an hour in beaten egg, dusted with flour, and fried, producing a succulent fish with a crunchy coating. This preparation can, of course, be used for almost any other kind of fish and comes to me from my favorite city of Cádiz and my good friend Paqui Delfín. SERVES 4

1 pound cod steak, 3/4–1 inch thick,
    cut in 1 1/2-inch pieces
2 eggs, lightly beaten with 2 teaspoons water
Flour for dusting
Salt
Freshly ground pepper
Oil for frying
Lemon wedges
Alioli Sauce (optional; p. 191), adding
    1 tablespoon chopped capers

Mix the fish pieces gently into the beaten egg. Let sit for 1 hour or more, stirring occasionally. Remove the fish from the egg and coat with the flour, which has been mixed with salt and pepper.

In a skillet heat the oil at least 1/2 inch deep to about 380°F and fry the fish pieces until golden, turning once. Or, better, use a deep-fryer. [May be kept warm in 200°F oven up to 30 minutes] Serve with lemon wedges.

If desired, accompany the fish with the Alioli sauce.

Hake and Zucchini Kabobs
(BANDERILLAS DE MERLUZA Y CALABACÍN)

SERVES 4 (MAKES 8)

2 tablespoons olive oil
2 tablespoons minced onion
Four 1/2-inch slices zucchini,
    each slice quartered
1/8 teaspoon thyme
Salt
Freshly ground pepper
Flour for dusting
1/4 pound skinned and
    boned hake or fresh cod,
    in 1-inch pieces

Heat 1 tablespoon of the oil in a skillet and sauté the onion until it is wilted. Add the zucchini, thyme, salt, and pepper (the mixture should be well seasoned) and sauté for another minute. Cover and continue cooking until the zucchini is tender, less than 5 minutes. [May be prepared ahead]

Flour the fish pieces and heat the remaining tablespoon of oil in a separate skillet. Sauté the fish until golden and cooked through. Skewer onto toothpicks a piece of zucchini, a piece of fish, then another piece of zucchini. Serve right away.

Fish, Green Pepper, and Bacon Brochette

(BROCHETA DE RAPE)

The flavors of these brochettes blend beautifully. The tapa is even tastier when barbecued. SERVES 4

3/4 pound boneless fish,
    preferably monkfish (see p. 86),
    fresh cod, or halibut, cut in
    1 1/2-inch cubes
Coarse salt
2 thick slices bacon,
    cut in twelve 1-inch
    pieces
1 large green pepper, cut in
    twelve 1-inch pieces
Olive oil
Freshly ground pepper
Paprika, preferably Spanish style

Sprinkle the fish pieces with coarse salt and let sit for 15 minutes (this helps to firm the flesh). On 7-8-inch skewers, spear a piece of fish, a piece of bacon, and a piece of green pepper. Repeat twice, ending with a piece of fish. [May be prepared ahead] Brush with oil and sprinkle with ground pepper.

Place on a preheated greased broiler tray very close to the heat for 2 minutes. Turn the skewers, brush with oil again, and sprinkle with paprika. Broil 2 minutes more. Serve with any juices poured over the brochettes.

Sole with Raisins, Pine Nuts, and Hazelnuts

(LLENGUADO A LA NYOCA)

As the ingredients would indicate, this excellent dish is a Catalán specialty, and it can be found at a Barcelona restaurant, Agut D'Avignón, that concentrates on Catalán cuisine. It is a quick-cooking dish that must be made at the last minute. SERVES 8

2/3 cup raisins
4 sole fillets, about 1-1 1/2 pounds
Flour for dusting
3 tablespoons olive oil
3 tablespoons butter
Salt
Freshly ground pepper
4 slices lemon
2 tablespoons chopped parsley
4 tablespoons pine nuts
30 hazelnuts (filberts), split

Soak the raisins for 20 minutes in 1 cup warm water. Drain.

Cut the fillets in half crosswise and dust with flour. Heat the oil and butter in a large skillet. When the butter just begins to color, sauté the fillets until golden on both sides. (Do in two stages if necessary, adding more oil and butter if needed.) Do not overcook. Remove the fillets to a warm serving platter. Sprinkle with salt and pepper and decorate with the lemon slices and parsley.

Cool the skillet slightly, then add the raisins, pine nuts, and hazelnuts. Sauté slowly until the pine nuts just begin to turn golden. Pour this nut mixture, along with any oil and butter remaining in the skillet, over the fish and serve right away.

Salmon Baked in Foil
(SALMÓN SAN MIGUEL)

Orense, in the interior of Galicia, is not a city on many touristic itineraries, yet the Bar/Restaurante San Miguel, which created this subtly flavored dish using Galicia's wonderful salmon, is one of the area's most highly regarded restaurants.

The recipe calls for individual portions, but you could also cook the fish in one piece and divide after cooking. SERVES 4-6

3/4 pound thick salmon fillets,
  cut in 4-6 tapas-size portions
1/2 teaspoon Dijon-style mustard
2 teaspoons dry (fino) Spanish sherry
Few drops Tabasco sauce
2 teaspoons veal broth, or a mixture
  of chicken and beef broth
4 teaspoons fresh orange juice
1/2 teaspoon brandy, preferably
  Spanish brandy or Cognac
Salt
2 medium mushrooms, coarsely chopped
2 very thin slices cured ham
Minced parsley

Arrange the salmon pieces on 4-6 pieces of foil that have been greased with butter. Spread the fish with the mustard and sprinkle with the sherry, Tabasco, broth, orange juice, brandy, salt, and then the mushrooms. Cut each ham slice into 2-3 pieces and place on top of the salmon. Close the foil tightly [May be prepared ahead] and place in a roasting pan that has been filled with 1/4 inch hot water. Bake at 350°F for about 20 minutes. Open the foil, chop the already cooked ham slices, sprinkle the ham over the fish, and garnish with parsley.

Trout with Cured Ham and Garlic
(TRUCHA "TRUCHANA")

La Trucha is currently one of Madrid's most popular tapas bars, and the well-dressed clientele are three and four deep just about any evening or afternoon. The tapas selection is casually painted in white on a yellow opaque glass that separates the bar from the kitchen and lists among more than forty possibilities three of the bar's namesakes: marinated trout, smoked trout, and this quickly sautéed trout. SERVES 4

3/4 pound trout fillets, skin on
Flour for dusting
4 tablespoons olive oil
Coarse salt
3 tablespoons minced cured ham
1 clove garlic, minced
1 tablespoon minced parsley

Dust the trout with flour and heat the oil in a skillet. Sauté the trout quickly on both sides until done. Remove to a warm serving platter, cut into tapas-size pieces, and sprinkle with salt. Cool down the oil remaining in the skillet and sauté the ham and garlic for a few seconds. Sprinkle the mixture over the trout, along with the parsley, and serve right away.

Marinated and Fried Shark

(CAZÓN EN ADOBO)

If shark is hard to get, more expensive swordfish is a perfectly acceptable substitute in this delicious recipe, a popular tapa in Andalucía. I especially liked this version, which I sampled at an excellent tapas bar, Bar Miami, in Sevilla. Some of the spices used, like oregano and cumin, are characteristic of this area of Spain, the result of centuries of Moorish domination. SERVES 4

START PREPARATION SEVERAL HOURS IN ADVANCE

1 tablespoon wine vinegar,
   preferably white
1/4 teaspoon paprika,
   preferably Spanish style
1/2 dried red chili pepper,
   seeded and crumbled, or
   1/4 teaspoon crushed
   red pepper
1/4 teaspoon oregano
1/2 teaspoon ground cumin,
   preferably freshly ground
1/4 teaspoon thyme
Coarse salt
2 cloves garlic, mashed to a paste
   or put through a garlic press
3/4 pound shark, monkfish, or
   swordfish, in 1-inch cubes
1 bay leaf
Flour for dusting, preferably
   semolina flour or a mixture
   of all-purpose and whole
   wheat flour
Oil for frying

In a small bowl combine the vinegar, paprika, chili pepper, oregano, cumin, thyme, salt, and garlic. Place the fish in a shallow bowl with the bay leaf and pour on the marinade. Stir to coat well. Cover and marinate for several hours at room temperature, stirring occasionally, or refrigerate overnight.

Drain the fish on paper towels, then dust with flour. Heat the oil at least 1/2 inch deep and fry until golden. Or, better, use a deep-fryer. Drain. [May be kept warm in 200°F oven up to 30 minutes]

Grilled Fresh Tuna on Dressed Tomatoes

(ATÚN FRESCO CON TOMATE ALIÑADO)

Fresh tuna is a delicious red-fleshed fish that, when grilled, tastes somewhat like steak. Our good friend Pepe Delfín in Cádiz, who is as fussy about his fish as anyone I know, will eat tuna only when prepared in this manner and on a bed of dressed tomato, which he feels complements the flavor of the fish beautifully. I could not agree with him more. SERVES 6

START PREPARATION 2-3 HOURS IN ADVANCE

5-6 tablespoons olive oil
1 large clove garlic, minced
1 tablespoon minced parsley
Salt
Freshly ground pepper
3/4 pound fresh tuna,
   cut in 3/8-inch slices
1 1/2 teaspoons
   white wine vinegar
1/2 pound ripe and flavorful
   tomatoes, in 1/4-inch slices,
   at room temperature
Parsley for garnish

In a shallow dish combine 3 tablespoons of the oil, the garlic, parsley, salt, and pepper. Add the tuna steaks and turn to coat. Marinate at room temperature for about 2 hours.

Meanwhile, in a small bowl combine 2 tablespoons of the oil, the vinegar, salt, and pepper. Arrange the tomatoes in one layer in a shallow dish and pour on this dressing. Marinate at room temperature for about 2 hours.

Heat the broiler and place the tuna on the grill close to the heat. Broil for about 2-3 minutes to a side, being very careful not to overcook. (If you prefer, you can sauté these steaks in a skillet in 1 tablespoon hot olive oil.) Cut the tuna into 12 tapas-size pieces.

Arrange the tomato slices on a serving plate (cut the slices in halves if they are much larger than the tuna pieces) and place a piece of tuna on top. Garnish with parsley and serve right away.

Marinated Fried Sardines

(SARDINAS FRITAS EN ADOBO)

My husband contends that if fresh sardines were not so inexpensive, they would be considered a great delicacy. Certainly these delicious fish have been underrated, and, given the extra special touch of marinating before frying in this recipe, perhaps sardines will gain some new fans.

Sardines never seem to be available on a regular basis in fish markets. Try special-ordering them, or save this recipe for a time when they are plentiful. SERVES 6

START PREPARATION SEVERAL HOURS IN ADVANCE

1 pound very small sardines
(5-6 inches long), cleaned, with
heads, tails, and fins removed
1/2 cup water
1/2 cup red wine vinegar
4 cloves garlic, minced
2 teaspoons oregano
2 bay leaves
Salt
Freshly ground pepper
Flour for dusting
Oil for frying
2 eggs, lightly beaten with
2 teaspoons water

Butterfly the sardines, leaving them joined at the back and pulling out the bone with your fingers.

In a shallow bowl large enough to hold the sardines, combine the water, vinegar, garlic, oregano, bay leaves, salt, and pepper. Place the sardines skin side up in this mixture and marinate for several hours.

Drain the sardines well on paper towels and fold them back together. Dust with flour. Heat the oil at least 1/2 inch deep to about 380°F. Or, better, use a deep-fryer. Coat the sardines with the beaten egg and place directly in the hot oil. Fry until golden, drain, and serve.

VARIATION

Sardines are also delicious without a marinade. Simply coat with flour (not necessary to remove bones) and fry, or eliminate the flour and grill them. Sprinkle with coarse salt.

Fried Cod Sticks

(SOLDADITOS DE PAVÍA)

This appetizer, "Little Soldiers of Pavia," refers to the Spanish troops that occupied the northern Italian town of Pavia in the nineteenth century. Why this codfish tapa is so named is a matter of controversy. Some say it is because the cod is cut in "sticks," resembling straight-backed soldiers; others claim that the golden color brings to mind the short yellow jackets of the soldiers' uniforms. In any case, these delicious tapas have been a favorite in Madrid bars and taverns for over a century. There are two versions, one in which the cod is simply sprinkled with lemon juice then batter fried, and another in which the cod is marinated in garlic, onion, and saffron before frying. It's hard to decide which I prefer. If you like the pure taste of cod, select the first method. If you are looking for a more unusual taste, marinate the cod using the second recipe.

VERSION I SERVES 4-6

START PREPARATION ONE DAY IN ADVANCE

A ¼-pound piece skinned
  and boned dried salt cod
  (see p. 203), cut from the thin end
  (no more than ½ inch thick)
Fresh lemon juice
Oil for frying

BATTER
¾ cup flour
1½ teaspoons baking powder
⅛ teaspoon salt
¼ cup water
¼ cup milk
3 tablespoons salad oil

Cover the cod with cold water and let sit at room temperature for 24~36 hours, changing the water occasionally. Drain well. Remove any membrane. Cut into strips about 2 inches long and ½~¾ inch wide. Sprinkle the cod pieces on both sides with lemon juice.

To make the batter, combine the flour, baking powder, and salt in a bowl. Stir in the water, milk, and oil and mix until smooth. [May be prepared ahead]

In a skillet heat the oil at least ½ inch deep to about 380°F. Or, better, use a deep-fryer. Dip the cod pieces in the batter and fry until golden on both sides. Drain.

VERSION II SERVES 4-6

START PREPARATION TWO DAYS IN ADVANCE

A ¼-pound piece skinned and boned
  dried salt cod (see p. 203), cut from the
  thin end (no more than ½ inch thick)
Batter (see Version I)
Oil for frying

MARINADE
Juice of ½ lemon
1 clove garlic, mashed to a paste
  or put through a garlic press
1 tablespoon minced parsley
2 thin slices onion
Few strands saffron

Soak the cod according to the instructions in Version I.

To make the marinade, combine in a shallow bowl the lemon juice, garlic, parsley, onion, and saffron. Add the cod and turn to coat well with this mixture. Marinate for a few hours or overnight in the refrigerator. Drain well on paper towels. Cut the cod into strips about 2 inches long and ½~¾ inch wide.

Prepare the batter and fry the cod as in Version I.

Dried Cod Perfumed with Garlic

(BACALAO AL PERFUME DE AJOS CONFITADOS)

Spanish cuisine does wonders with salt cod. It is a fish that lends itself to an enormous variety of preparations, usually quite "country" in character. But this exquisite dish, from one of Barcelona's most elegant restaurants, Reno, transports cod into the realm of haute cuisine. SERVES 4

START PREPARATION ONE DAY IN ADVANCE

¾ pound skinned and boned
   dried salt cod (see p. 203),
   cut from the thick end
4 cloves garlic, peeled
Mild olive oil to "boil" garlic
Flour for dusting
4 tablespoons olive oil
2 medium tomatoes, skinned, seeded,
   and coarsely chopped
Salt
White pepper, preferably
   freshly ground
Pinch sugar
4 tablespoons mayonnaise,
   preferably homemade (p. 47)
4 teaspoons fish broth (p. 27)
   or clam juice

Soak the cod in cold water to cover for 24~36 hours at room temperature, changing the water occasionally. Drain on paper towels and cut into tapas-size pieces, about 2½ × 2 inches and ½~¾ inch thick.

Place the garlic in a very small saucepan with oil to cover. Cook over low heat for 20~25 minutes, or until the garlic is softened but not brown. Remove the garlic and mash well. Save the oil for some other use.

Dust the pieces of cod with flour. In a skillet heat 2 tablespoons of the olive oil. Sauté the cod lightly until golden outside but still juicy within, about 5~10 minutes, depending on thickness. Remove to a warm platter. Wipe out the skillet.

Heat the remaining 2 tablespoons of oil and sauté the tomato for a couple of minutes, until its liquid evaporates. Season with salt, pepper, and sugar. Spread the tomato on the bottom of a shallow casserole, preferably earthenware, where the cod will just fit. Place the cod pieces on top. [May be prepared ahead]

In a small bowl combine the mayonnaise with the fish broth. It should have the consistency of a thick sauce. Mix in the mashed garlic and spread this over the cod. Run quickly under the broiler—about a minute or so—to brown lightly.

Baked Dried Cod with Garlic and Sherry

(BACALAO A LA LLAUNA)

Although salt cod is not to everyone's taste, this simple preparation presents cod in an altogether delicious manner, which I recommend even to those who think they do not care for cod. *La llauna* of the recipe title is a metal baking dish commonly used in Cataluña. This recipe comes from an outstanding Barcelona restaurant, Quo Vadis, which is carefully supervised by its charming and attentive owner, Martí Forcada. Also not to be missed at Quo Vadis is its large variety of wild mushrooms, simply prepared with garlic and parsley (see p. 143). SERVES 6-8

START PREPARATION ONE DAY IN ADVANCE

1³/4 pounds skinned and boned dried
   salt cod (see p. 203), preferably cut
   from the thick end
5 tablespoons olive oil
8 cloves garlic, minced
4 teaspoons paprika, preferably
   Spanish style
³/4 cup dry (fino) Spanish sherry
4 tablespoons minced parsley
Salt

Soak the cod for 24–36 hours in cold water to cover at room temperature, changing the water occasionally. Drain and dry the cod well, then divide into tapas-size portions.

Heat the oil in a large skillet and sauté the cod until lightly golden on both sides. Transfer to a metal baking dish in which the cod fits snugly. To the oil in the skillet add half the minced garlic, the paprika, and the sherry. Boil for a minute [May be prepared ahead], then pour over the cod. Sprinkle with the remaining minced garlic, the parsley, and the salt. Bake at 350°F for 10–15 minutes.

Orange-Flavored Sautéed Chicken Pieces

(POLLO AL SABOR DE NARANJA)

Orange juice and sherry make a wonderful marinade for chicken. And the orange and walnut dipping sauce enhances the chicken's faint scent of orange. SERVES 6 (MAKES 12)

START PREPARATION ONE DAY IN ADVANCE

2 tablespoons semisweet (oloroso) Spanish
   sherry
¹/4 cup freshly squeezed orange juice
Rind of ¹/2 orange (orange part only),
   in julienne strips
4 tablespoons olive oil
Salt
Freshly ground pepper
1 whole chicken breast, boned,
   skin on, in 1-inch pieces
Orange and Walnut Sauce (p. 98)

In a bowl combine the sherry, orange juice, orange rind, 2 tablespoons of the oil, salt, and pepper. Add the chicken pieces and marinate overnight.

Remove the chicken from the marinade and dry on paper towels. Reserve the orange rind. Heat the remaining 2 tablespoons of oil in a skillet and sauté the chicken until just done but still juicy, adding the orange rind for the last minute of cooking. Serve with the Orange and Walnut Sauce.

Béchamel-Coated Fried Chicken Strips

(POLLO VILLEROY)

Chicken bathed in béchamel, then breaded and fried, is a great favorite in Spain. In this version the chicken breast is cut in strips for easier tapas presentation. SERVES 8 (MAKES ABOUT 16)

2 whole chicken breasts, skinned,
    boned (reserve bones), halved,
    and cut into 1½ × 1-inch strips
1 onion, halved
1 small bay leaf
¼ teaspoon thyme
1 sprig parsley
Chicken broth
Salt
Freshly ground pepper
1 egg, lightly beaten with
    1 teaspoon water
Bread crumbs
Oil for frying

BÉCHAMEL SAUCE
5 tablespoons sweet butter
6 tablespoons flour
¾ cup milk
Salt
Freshly ground pepper
A grating of nutmeg

Combine the chicken, bones, onion, bay leaf, thyme, and parsley in a saucepan. Add enough chicken broth to cover and season with salt and pepper. Bring to a boil, cover, and simmer until the chicken is just barely cooked, about 10–15 minutes. Do not overcook. Remove the chicken from the broth, drain and let cool, reserving ¾ cup of the broth.

To make the béchamel, melt the butter in a saucepan, stir in the flour, and cook for a minute. Add gradually the reserved broth and the milk, season with salt, pepper, and nutmeg, and continue cooking, stirring constantly, until thickened and smooth. Cool the sauce, stirring occasionally.

Dip the chicken pieces into the sauce, coating each piece completely. Arrange on a platter and chill until the sauce is firm, at least 1 hour. [May be prepared ahead]

Dip the chicken pieces in the beaten egg and coat well with the bread crumbs. Fry in hot oil (about 385°F) at least ½ inch deep until golden on all sides. Or, better, use a deep-fryer. Drain on paper towels. [May be kept warm in 200°F oven up to 30 minutes]

Chicken in Beer
(POLLO EN CERVEZA)

This chicken has a subtle lemony flavor, and although I have chosen to use the wing portion for easy handling, you might also use small drumsticks or any other part of the chicken (skin on), cut in small pieces. SERVES 6

START PREPARATION SEVERAL HOURS IN ADVANCE

> 12 chicken wings
> A 12-ounce bottle of beer
> Salt
> Freshly ground pepper
> 1 teaspoon thyme
> 1 bay leaf
>
> SAUCE
> 1/4 teaspoon thyme
> 2 tablespoons olive oil
> Salt
> Freshly ground pepper

Chop the wings into three parts and discard the tip portion (or save for broth). In a shallow bowl where the chicken will fit in one layer, mix the beer (except 1 tablespoon, which should be reserved for the sauce), salt, pepper, thyme, and bay leaf. Arrange the wings in the marinade, turn to coat, and let sit for several hours at room temperature, turning occasionally.

Combine the reserved beer and the sauce ingredients in a small bowl. Drain the wings well on paper towels. Arrange on a broiling tray and brush with the sauce. Sprinkle with salt and pepper. Broil (or charcoal grill) the wings for about 5 minutes, turn, baste with the remaining sauce, sprinkle with salt and pepper, and continue broiling until they are golden but still juicy, about 5 or 6 minutes more.

Marinated Broiled Quail
(CODORNICES A LA PLANCHA)

These quail are simple and delicately flavored and lots of fun to eat (with your fingers). The quail must not be overcooked, so please follow the broiling time closely. Choose either an onion and garlic marinade or a marinade of coriander and cumin, created by Ruperto Blanco in Sevilla (see p. 34). SERVES 4

START PREPARATION ONE DAY IN ADVANCE

> 4 quail, split in halves
>
> ONION AND GARLIC MARINADE
> 10 cloves garlic, peeled
> 1/2 small onion,
>   peeled and cut in pieces
> 2 tablespoons beef broth
> 2 tablespoons dry white wine
> 3 tablespoons olive oil
> 1 teaspoon red wine vinegar
> Salt
>
> CORIANDER AND CUMIN MARINADE
> 3 tablespoons olive oil
> 1 large clove garlic, minced
> 1/2 teaspoon freshly crushed
>   coriander seed
> 1/2 teaspoon freshly crushed
>   cumin seed
> 1/2 teaspoon paprika,
>   preferably Spanish style
> 1/2 dried red chili pepper,
>   seeded and crumbled,
>   or 1/4 teaspoon
>   crushed red pepper
> Salt

To make the onion and garlic marinade, beat the garlic in a processor until minced. Add the onion, broth, wine, oil, vinegar, and salt and process until the mixture is smooth and thickened. Pour into a shallow bowl in which the quail will just fit. Turn the quail in the marinade to coat and leave skin side down.

To make the coriander and cumin marinade, mix all the marinade ingredients in a shallow bowl large enough to hold the quail in one layer. Add the quail and turn to coat with the marinade. Leave skin side down.

Cover the quail and refrigerate overnight.

Heat the broiler (the quail could be grilled instead), arrange the quail skin side down on a broiler tray about 4–5 inches from the heat, and broil for 3 minutes. Turn, brush with the marinade, and broil for 1 minute. Turn and brush again, broiling for another minute, then place skin side up, coat well with the marinade, and broil for another 1–2 minutes, until golden, placing the broiler tray closer to the heat if necessary.

Sautéed Frogs' Legs

(ANCAS DE RANA SALTEADAS)

Frogs' legs, in this tasty version, make excellent tapas because of their easy-to-handle size. SERVES 6-8

1½ pounds small-medium
    frogs' legs (about 10–12 pairs),
    separated if the pairs are joined
Salt
Flour for dusting
4 tablespoons olive oil
¼ cup minced cured ham
12 cloves garlic, minced
1 dried red chili pepper, seeded
    and crumbled, or ½ teaspoon
    crushed red pepper
1 medium tomato, skinned and
    finely chopped
1 tablespoon minced parsley

Dry the frogs' legs well on paper towels, sprinkle with salt, and dust with flour. Heat the oil in a skillet and lightly brown the legs quickly (add more oil if necessary). Add the ham, garlic, and chili pepper and sauté for another minute or two. Stir in the tomato and more salt if necessary, cook 3 minutes more, sprinkle with the parsley, and serve. (Or wrap in foil and reheat at 350°F for 5 minutes, sprinkling with the parsley when ready to serve.)

Breaded Snails with Alioli
(CARACOLES EMPANADOS CON ALIOLI)

Snails are most often prepared in a sauce, but when they are a nice large size, I also like them poached in a seasoned broth, breaded, fried, and served with a garlicky mayonnaise. SERVES 6-8 (MAKES 24)

> 2 tablespoons dry white wine
> 2 tablespoons clam juice
> 1 clove garlic, coarsely chopped
> 1/8 teaspoon thyme
> 1 small bay leaf
> 1 sprig parsley
> Salt
> Freshly ground pepper
> 2 dozen large canned snails
> Flour for dusting
> 1 egg, lightly beaten with
>   1 teaspoon water
> Bread crumbs
> Oil for frying
> Alioli Sauce (p. 191)

Combine in a small saucepan the wine, clam juice, garlic, thyme, bay leaf, parsley, salt, and pepper. Bring to a boil and simmer, uncovered, for 5 minutes. Add the snails with their liquid, bring to a boil again, and simmer 3 minutes more. Cool the snails in the liquid [May be prepared ahead], then drain well on paper towels.

Dust the snails with the flour, cover with beaten egg, and roll in the bread crumbs. In a skillet heat the oil at least 1/2 inch deep until hot (about 390°F) and fry the snails quickly until golden on all sides. Or, better, use a deep-fryer. Drain [May be kept warm in 200°F oven up to 30 minutes] and serve with the Alioli on the side.

VARIATION
The snails can be coated with white sauce, breaded, and fried, as in Béchamel-Coated Mussels with Cured Ham (p. 165).

Grilled Marinated Pork
(PRUEBA DE CERDO)

This very spicy tapa is a specialty in the lovely town of Trujillo, home of the Conquistador Francisco Pizarro, who began his life as a desperately poor shepherd and ended it as a wealthy man, married to an Inca princess and living in a magnificent palace. His palace still stands in Trujillo's fascinating main plaza, one of the most beautiful in Spain.

This tapa is called "Moraja" in a small bar in Trujillo, Casa La Pata, which likes to call its tapas by odd names, and "Prueba de Cerdo" at other bars, like the very busy Cafetería Imperio on the main plaza. Prueba de Cerdo means "testing the pork," and in the fall when *chorizo* sausage is made in many small villages in central Spain, the pork is marinated (the marinade has similar ingredients to those that will go into the sausage) and grilled for a preview of that year's sausage. SERVES 6

> 1 tablespoon olive oil
> 2 tablespoons dry white wine
> 2 cloves garlic, mashed to a paste
>   or put through a garlic press
> 1/4 teaspoon oregano
> 1 1/2 teaspoons paprika,
>   preferably Spanish style

¼ teaspoon crushed red pepper
Salt
Freshly ground pepper
½ pound pork loin, cut in strips
  2½ × 1 inch and ⅛ inch thick
Lettuce leaves, at room temperature,
  for garnish

Combine in a bowl the oil, wine, garlic, oregano, paprika, red pepper, salt, and pepper. Add the meat and stir to coat well with this mixture. You can cook the meat right away, but it gains in flavor when left to marinate for a while or even overnight.

Heat a lightly greased skillet or grill until very hot. Add the pork strips and quickly stir fry—don't overcook. Sprinkle with salt and serve on a bed of lettuce.

Stuffed Pork Rolls
(ROLLITOS DE CERDO RELLENOS)

SERVES 4-6

½ pound pork cutlets,
  very thinly sliced, trimmed
  into about 5 × 3-inch pieces
1 tablespoon minced parsley
Salt
Freshly ground pepper
2 ounces Swiss cheese, in julienne
  strips (about ¼ cup)
½ pimiento, home prepared
  (see p. 204) or imported,
  in julienne strips
1 ounce cured ham, in
  julienne strips (about ¼ cup)
1 egg, lightly beaten
1 teaspoon fresh lemon juice
Flour for dusting
Bread crumbs
3 tablespoons olive oil

Sprinkle each cutlet on one side with the parsley, salt, and pepper. Divide the julienne strips of cheese, pimiento, and ham into little bundles, as many as there are cutlets. Place a bundle crosswise at one end of each cutlet and roll. Secure with a toothpick.

Beat together lightly the egg and lemon juice. Dust the pork rolls with flour, dip in the egg, then coat with bread crumbs. Let dry for a few minutes. [May be prepared ahead]

Heat the oil in a large skillet. Sauté the rolls over medium heat until golden, turning once. Remove the toothpicks and brown the remaining areas, until the cheese is melted and the meat cooked through. [May be kept warm in 200°F oven up to 30 minutes] To serve, cut each roll in half.

Cheese-Filled Pork Cutlets

(EMPAREDADOS DE LOMO Y QUESO)

SERVES 5-6

¾ pound boneless pork loin, in ⅛-inch
　slices, then pounded thinner
About 3 ounces mild melting cheese, like
　Spanish Tetilla (see p. 203), Gouda,
　Fontina, or Jarlsberg, in ⅛-inch slices
Flour for dusting
2 eggs, lightly beaten with
　1 teaspoon water
Bread crumbs, seasoned with salt
　and pepper
5 tablespoons olive oil
2 green peppers, cut in strips
1 tablespoon chicken broth
Salt
Freshly ground pepper

Divide the pork slices into groups of two that have more or less the same shape and size. Cover one of the pork slices from each group with the cheese slices, then cover with the remaining pork pieces. Cut each "sandwich" into two or more pieces to make tapas-size portions, about 2 × 1½ inches. Pound the edges lightly, dust with flour, dip in the egg, and coat with the bread crumbs. [May be prepared ahead]

To prepare the peppers, heat 1 tablespoon of the oil in a skillet. Stir fry the peppers for a minute or two, then add the chicken broth, salt, and pepper. Cover and cook over medium heat until tender.

Heat the remaining 4 tablespoons of oil in a large skillet and sauté the filled pork on each side until golden. Top with a piece of fried green pepper.

Chorizo with Pimientos

(CHORIZO CAFÉ SAN MARTÍN)

I have prepared this *chorizo* in the manner of the Café San Martín restaurant in New York (see p. 95) for countless cooking classes and home parties, and it is always a great favorite. I especially value this tapa for its simple make-ahead preparation, especially when other more involved tapas are on the menu. And by the way, if you are not yet acquainted with *chorizo*, you are missing a wonderful sausage, fragrant with garlic and paprika, that is unlike any other sausage found on the American market. SERVES 6-8

1 pound chorizo sausage,
　in ¼-inch slices
4 tablespoons dry red wine
2 pimientos, preferably home prepared
　(see p. 204) or imported, cut in strips
2 tablespoons chopped parsley
2 cloves garlic, minced

Place the *chorizo* slices in a large skillet (no greasing necessary) and sauté until lightly browned. Pour off the fat, if any, deglaze the pan with the wine, and add the pimiento, parsley, and garlic. Line a shallow casserole, preferably Spanish earthenware, with a large piece of foil that extends over the sides. Add the *chorizo* mixture and close the foil tightly, leaving a large air pocket above the *chorizo*. [May be prepared ahead] Bake at 350°F for 15 minutes. Present in the foil, then open the foil to serve.

Skewered Chorizo and Onion

(PINCHO DE CHORIZO Y CEBOLLA)

This is a nice way to serve *chorizo*, complemented by onion that has been boiled to reduce its sharpness.
SERVES 4

> 1 medium onion, peeled and
>   cut in quarters lengthwise
> 3 tablespoons olive oil
> 1 sprig parsley
> 1/8 teaspoon thyme
> 1 bay leaf
> 1/2 teaspoon paprika,
>   preferably Spanish style
> 1 teaspoon sugar
> Salt
> 1/4 pound chorizo sausage

Separate the onion into layers. Place in a saucepan with water to cover and add the oil, parsley, thyme, bay leaf, paprika, sugar, and salt. Bring to a boil, lower the heat to medium-high, and cook until the water has evaporated, about 20 minutes.

Slice the *chorizo* into 1/2-inch slices and with a toothpick spear 2 or 3 pieces of the onion on top of each slice. Place on the middle rack of a broiler, the toothpick sideways, and broil for about 1 minute.

Chorizo Marinated and Cooked in Wine

(CHORIZO AL VINO)

Marinating and cooking *chorizo* with liquor, as in this recipe and in the brandy variation below, gives extra flavor to the *chorizo*. This tapa comes from El Corrillo, one of Madrid's best-known tapas bars.
SERVES 4

START PREPARATION ONE DAY IN ADVANCE

> 1/4 pound chorizo sausage
> 1/2 cup dry white wine

Prick the sausage in several places with a fork and place in a small skillet with 1/4 cup of the wine. Bring to a boil, cover, and simmer for 20 minutes. Cool and keep at room temperature overnight.

To serve, cut the *chorizo* into 1/4-inch slices and place in a small skillet or casserole, preferably earthenware. Add the remaining 1/4 cup of wine and cook over high heat until the wine is almost completely evaporated. Serve in the same dish.

VARIATION

To make Chorizo al Coñac you will not need the marinating time or the second cooking. Simply place the whole *chorizos* in a small skillet and add 2 tablespoons brandy. Warm the brandy and, standing well away, ignite. When the flames die, continue cooking and turning the *chorizo* until it is browned outside and juicy within. Slice and serve.

Batter-Fried Pig's Feet

(MANOS DE CERDO REBOZADAS)

The city of Albacete, in a typical setting on the Castilian plains, has two things to recommend it: a lovely whitewashed *parador* in the architectural style of a local farmhouse…and the excellent tapas found around town. Nuestro Bar (see p. 144) has the most exceptional selection, but the busy Mesón El Cocinero has a wonderful variety as well, including delicious batter-fried lamb's feet. I have been unable to purchase lamb's feet, but pig's feet work beautifully. I consider this tapa a great delicacy.

Pig's feet have to cook a long time, but will keep for many days. The batter can also be made days ahead and refrigerated. SERVES 4-6

2 small pig's feet, cut in half lengthwise
   and crosswise (8 pieces)
2 cubes slab bacon, each about
   1 inch thick
1/2 carrot, scraped and cut in
   thick slices
1 small onion, peeled
1 sprig parsley
1/4 teaspoon thyme
1 bay leaf
1 cup dry red wine
3 cups chicken broth
4 peppercorns
Salt
Oil for frying

BATTER
1 cup plus 2 tablespoons flour
2 1/4 teaspoons baking powder
1/4 teaspoon salt

6 tablespoons water
6 tablespoons milk
4 1/2 tablespoons salad oil

Place the pig's feet in a deep pot with the bacon, carrot, onion, parsley, thyme, bay leaf, red wine, broth, peppercorns, and salt. Bring to a boil, then cover and simmer for 3 1/2 hours, or until the pig's feet are just tender.

Drain the pig's feet and dry well on paper towels. (If making in advance, keep the pig's feet in their cooking liquid until ready to use.) If some pieces seem a bit larger than tapas size, cut in half again.

To make the batter, combine the flour, baking powder, and salt in a bowl. Stir in the water, milk, and oil and mix until smooth.

Heat the frying oil at least 1/2 inch deep until hot (about 390°F). Or, better, use a deep-fryer. Dip the pig's feet in the batter, coating well, then fry until golden. Drain. [May be kept warm in 200°F oven up to 30 minutes]

This tapa is excellent accompanied by an Alioli sauce (see following recipe).

Pig's Foot Crêpe, Broiled or Fried

(CANELONES DE PIE DE CERDO)

Sensational prepared either of these ways—brushed with butter on a bed of Alioli and browned quickly under the broiler, or crisply and delicately fried in a beer batter. Although several steps are involved in making these crêpes, keep in mind that the pig's feet can be cooked days, even weeks, in advance and refrigerated or frozen. (You might want to cook extra and serve them for dinner.) The crêpes can also be frozen and kept for other tapas recipes in this book. SERVES 6-8 (MAKES 12)

2 pig's feet, split in halves
Two 1-inch cubes slab bacon
1/2 carrot, scraped and
 cut in thick slices
1 small onion, peeled and studded
 with 4 cloves
1 sprig parsley
1/4 teaspoon thyme
1 bay leaf
1 cup dry red wine
3 cups chicken broth
4 peppercorns
Salt
5 tablespoons butter
1/4 cup minced onion
2 cloves garlic, minced
1/2 pound mushrooms, brushed
 clean, finely chopped
1 1/2 tablespoons minced parsley
3 tablespoons bread crumbs
4 teaspoons dry white wine
Freshly ground pepper

Melted butter for brushing
 (broiled crêpes)
Oil for frying (fried crêpes)

CRÊPES
1 egg
1/2 cup milk
1/2 cup water
1 cup flour
1/8 teaspoon salt
3 tablespoons butter

ALIOLI SAUCE
1 cup mayonnaise, preferably
 homemade (p. 47)
4 or more cloves garlic, mashed to a
 paste or put through a garlic press

BEER BATTER
1 cup flour
2 teaspoons baking powder
1/4 teaspoon salt
2 tablespoons salad oil
1 cup beer

In a deep casserole place the pig's feet, bacon, carrot, peeled onion, parsley sprig, thyme, bay leaf, red wine, broth, peppercorns, and salt. Bring to a boil, cover, and simmer for about 6 hours, or until very tender.

Bone the pig's feet (there are many small bones— be sure to remove all of them) and discard the cooking liquid (or keep for stock). Chop the meat finely. (This may be done in a processor; just be sure not to overprocess—there should be some texture.) [The pig's feet may be made up to this point and refrigerated or frozen]

Melt the butter in a medium skillet and sauté the minced onion until it is wilted. Add the garlic, mushrooms, and parsley and cook for about 3 minutes. Stir in the chopped pig's feet and continue

Pig's Foot Crêpe, Broiled or Fried (continued)

cooking 5 minutes more. Turn off the heat and mix in the bread crumbs, white wine, salt, and ground pepper. The mixture should be well seasoned. [May be prepared ahead]

To make the crêpes, combine the egg, milk, water, flour, and salt in a processor or blender. Mix until smooth. Grease lightly a small skillet or crêpe pan (preferably 4 inches in diameter, but not more than 5 inches) and heat. Swirl in just enough batter to coat the pan, about 1 tablespoon. When the crêpe has set, turn and cook the other side. Do not brown — the entire process will not take more than a minute. If you have made 5-inch crêpes, you may wish to trim them to 4 inches for a more manageable tapas-size appetizer. The crêpes may be cooked in advance and kept between pieces of wax paper, either refrigerated or frozen, until ready to use.

To make the Alioli, combine the mayonnaise and garlic. Let sit at room temperature until ready to use.

To fill the crêpes, place about 1 tablespoon of filling in the center of each crêpe and roll. The crêpes can be kept unrefrigerated for several hours before completing.

You may now either broil or fry the crêpes. To broil, spread the Alioli over the bottom of an ovenproof dish. Arrange the crêpes over the sauce seam side down and brush with melted butter. Place under the broiler for a minute or two until golden. You may leave the crêpes whole or cut in halves to serve.

To fry the crêpes, prepare the beer batter by mixing the flour, baking powder, and salt in a bowl. Add the 2 tablespoons oil and the beer and stir well. Let sit in a warm spot for 20 minutes. Transfer the batter to a flat dish.

In a skillet heat the oil at least ½ inch deep until hot (about 390°F). Or, better, use a deep-fryer. Coat each crêpe with the batter and fry until golden, turning once. Drain. [May be kept warm in 200°F oven up to 30 minutes] Leave whole or cut in halves and serve with the Alioli as a dip.

Spicy Lamb Brochettes
(PINCHO MORUNO)

These brochettes are commonly found as tapas all over Spain. The Arab overtones in the seasonings are obvious, and although they are usually made in Spain with a very un-Arab ingredient — pork — occasionally they are found as they should be prepared, with lamb.

Since the meat for these brochettes is cut in small cubes, you must be extra-careful not to overcook. Broil or grill close to the source of heat so that the meat will brown outside and still be juicy and tender within. SERVES 6

START PREPARATION ONE DAY IN ADVANCE

1 pound boned leg of lamb, in 1-inch cubes

MARINADE
3 tablespoons olive oil
1 small onion, slivered
2 cloves garlic, minced
1 tablespoon minced parsley
1 teaspoon paprika, preferably
 Spanish style
½ dried red chili pepper,
 seeded and crumbled, or
 ¼ teaspoon crushed red pepper
Few strands saffron, crushed
¼ teaspoon oregano
¼ teaspoon freshly ground cumin
Salt
Freshly ground pepper

In a bowl combine the marinade ingredients. Add the lamb, stirring to coat well. Marinate in the refrigerator overnight.

Arrange the meat cubes on six 7-inch brochettes. Grill on the upper rack of the broiler not more than 3 minutes to a side, basting with the marinade. Serve immediately.

Chicken Liver Timbale with Sherry Sauce

(FLAN DE HÍGADO CON SALSA DE JEREZ)

The combination of chicken liver with caramelized sugar and semisweet sherry may be unexpected, but it is nothing short of sensational. For a larger group, make this in a ring mold. It will then serve about 6~8. SERVES 4

½ pound chicken livers
1 tablespoon butter
2 tablespoons minced onion
2 eggs, lightly beaten
¾ cup heavy cream
2 tablespoons plus 1 teaspoon semisweet
    (oloroso) Spanish sherry
1 teaspoon salt
Freshly ground pepper
Dash of cayenne pepper
¼ teaspoon paprika,
    preferably Spanish style
A generous grating of nutmeg
1 tablespoon minced parsley
4 tablespoons sugar
4 teaspoons water

Pick over the livers and cut in halves. Heat the butter in a skillet and sauté the liver and onion over high heat until the liver is brown outside and just slightly pink within. Do not overcook. Transfer the liver and onion to a processor or blender and blend until medium-fine.

In a bowl beat together lightly the eggs, cream, 1 tablespoon of the sherry, the salt, pepper, cayenne, paprika, and nutmeg. Stir in the parsley and chopped onion and liver. Divide this mixture into 6 lightly greased custard cups. Place in a pan of hot water (bain-marie) and bake at 325°F for 35 minutes, or until a knife inserted into the custard comes out clean.

While the custard is baking, make the sauce. In a small skillet combine the sugar with 2 teaspoons of the water. Cook over low heat, stirring constantly. The sugar will crystallize, then liquefy and begin to caramelize. As soon as the sugar is a light golden color, add 2 teaspoons of the sherry, stir until smooth, and remove from the heat. Stir in the remaining 2 teaspoons of sherry and another 2 teaspoons of water.

To serve, unmold the timbales onto a serving dish or dishes and coat each one with some of the sugar sauce. You can make the custard and sauce in advance, but don't combine until serving time. To reheat the custard, cover with foil and return to the bain-marie for 10 minutes. Reheat the sauce slowly, adding a little more water if it has become too thick.

Skewered Kidney, Mushroom, Bacon, and Potato
(PINCHO DE RIÑÓN)

A great way to prepare kidneys for a party. Be careful not to overcook them—the kidneys should be slightly pink inside. SERVES 6-8 (MAKES 14)

1 veal kidney
Juice of 2 lemons
1 potato
Fourteen 1-inch pieces sliced bacon
4 medium mushroom caps,
   brushed clean, quartered
Flour for dusting
2 eggs, lightly beaten with
   1 teaspoon water
Bread crumbs
Oil for frying
Alioli Sauce (optional; p. 191)

Soak the whole kidney in the lemon juice for 10 minutes. Cut in ¾-inch cubes, discarding fat and gristle. Rinse in hot water and dry on paper towels.

Peel the potato and cut into very thin slices lengthwise with a potato peeler. Cut the slices into 1-inch pieces. Arrange on a toothpick a piece of kidney; a piece of potato, folded in half; a piece of bacon, folded in half; a piece of mushroom; and end with another kidney piece. Repeat for the rest. Dust with flour, dip in the egg, and coat with the bread crumbs. [May be prepared ahead] In a skillet heat the oil at least ½ inch deep to about 370°F and fry the brochettes until golden on both sides. Or, better, use a deep-fryer. Drain and serve, if you wish, with Alioli sauce.

Batter-Fried Brains
(SESOS REBOZADOS)

Batter-fried brains are a great delicacy in Spain, and although brains meet some resistance in this country, they are delicious and well worth trying. SERVES 6

START PREPARATION ONE DAY IN ADVANCE

½ pound calf, lamb,
   pork, or beef brains
¼ cup water
¼ cup vinegar
1 small bay leaf
1 clove
2 peppercorns
1 sprig parsley
2 slices onion
¼ teaspoon thyme
1 slice lemon
Batter (p. 190), or flour for dusting
   and 1 egg, lightly beaten
Oil for frying

Wash the brains and place in a saucepan with the water and vinegar. Let sit for 15 minutes. Drain and remove all membrane and veins. Barely cover the brains with water and add the bay leaf, clove, peppercorns, parsley, onion slices, thyme, and lemon slice. Bring to a boil, cover, and simmer for 7 minutes. Cool in the cooking liquid, then marinate in this liquid overnight in the refrigerator.

Drain the brains and cut into small pieces, about 1½ × 1 inch and sliced to about ½ inch thick. Either coat with batter or dust with flour and dip in egg; fry in hot oil (about 380°F) at least ½ inch deep. Or, better, use a deep-fryer.

TORTILLAS

Spanish *tortillas* have no connection with Mexican *tortillas* except the word, which comes from the Latin *torte,* meaning a round cake. In Spain *tortillas* are omelets, often potato omelets, and are standard tapas just about anywhere in Spain. They are usually served at room temperature and may be made in two- and three-egg sizes when the filling is soft or as large, thick omelets when the ingredients are more solid. If you need more portions than the recipe allows, make another omelet rather than increasing the size.

Onion Omelet

(TORTILLA DE CEBOLLA)

Along the road from Valencia to Madrid there is an altogether charming inn called Venta L'Home. Its long curving bar is crammed with interesting tapas, and the restaurant overflows with country antiques and fresh fruit and vegetable displays. This omelet was my favorite tapa, and although its ingredients are quite basic, the large amount of onion makes it, I think, one of the best *tortillas* ever.

SERVES 2–3

4 tablespoons olive oil
2 medium onions,
   finely chopped
Salt

3 eggs
1 teaspoon milk
Freshly ground pepper

Heat 3 tablespoons of the oil in a medium skillet and sauté the onion for a minute or two. Sprinkle with salt, cover, and continue cooking for about 20 minutes, until the onion is tender but not colored. Beat the eggs lightly in a bowl with the milk, salt, and pepper. [May be prepared ahead] Mix the onion into the eggs.

Heat the remaining tablespoon of oil in a small skillet (better if it has straight sides) and add the egg mixture. Lower the heat and cook quite slowly until golden and firm enough to turn. Turn and cook until done—it should still be juicy inside. This can be eaten hot or at room temperature.

VARIATION

This *tortilla* can be made instead with scallions, to produce a very different omelet. Use 7 very thin scallions (removing any papery outer skin), chopped, and reduce the oil to 2 tablespoons (1 tablespoon to sauté the scallions and the other to cook the omelet). Use a smaller skillet to sauté the scallions and reduce the cooking time to 10 minutes.

Another delicious variation is with tomato and tuna. When the onion is cooked, turn up the heat and add 1 small tomato, skinned and chopped, and 3 tablespoons flaked light or white meat tuna. Cook for a couple of minutes, then proceed with the recipe as directed.

Swiss Chard Omelet

(TORTILLA DE GRELOS)

The slight tartness of Swiss chard lends a wonderful flavor to this simple *tortilla*. SERVES 4

½ pound Swiss chard,
  or other greens like
  collards, thick stems removed
  (weight after trimming)
Salt
3 tablespoons olive oil
1 tablespoon finely chopped onion
1 clove garlic, minced
4 eggs

Place the greens in a pot with salt, 1 tablespoon of the oil, and water to cover. Bring to a boil, cover, and simmer for 15 minutes. Drain well, using paper towels to absorb some of the excess liquid. Chop coarsely.

Heat another tablespoon of the oil in a small skillet. Sauté the onion and garlic until the onion is wilted. Add the greens and salt and stir fry for a minute or so. Beat the eggs in a bowl with a fork and season with salt. [May be prepared ahead] Stir the skillet mixture into the eggs and wipe the skillet clean.

Heat the remaining tablespoon of oil until quite hot. Pour in the egg mixture quickly, spreading it evenly with a pancake turner. Lower the heat slightly and cook until very lightly browned, shaking the pan constantly. Flip the omelet to the other side, adding a drop more oil if necessary, and continue cooking until the omelet is set but still juicy within. To serve, cut into wedges.

Green Pepper Omelet

(TORTILLA DE PIMIENTOS VERDES)

The green peppers in this *tortilla*, which I discovered in Logroño (see p. 55), are only slightly cooked, giving an appealing, fresh flavor to the omelet. SERVES 4

4 eggs
Salt
3 tablespoons olive oil
1 very small potato
  (about 2 ounces), in
  ⅛-inch slices, then
  cut into 1-inch pieces
1 green pepper, in ¼-inch
  strips, each cut in half

Beat the eggs lightly in a bowl with the salt. Heat 2 tablespoons of the oil in a small skillet. Add the potato, sprinkle with salt, and fry slowly until tender. Transfer the potato to the beaten eggs and let soak for 10 minutes. In the remaining oil in the skillet sauté the green pepper until just slightly softened, about 5 minutes. Add to the egg mixture.

Wipe out the pan and heat the remaining tablespoon of oil. Proceed as in the preceding recipe.

Baby Eel Omelet

(TORTILLA DE ANGULAS)

Angulas (see pp. 127 and 171) combined with eggs produce an extraordinarily delicate and delicious omelet. SERVES 4

2 ounces (about ½ cup) angulas
2 eggs, lightly beaten
1 teaspoon milk
Salt
Freshly ground pepper
1 tablespoon olive oil

Dry the *angulas* well on paper towels. Beat the eggs lightly in a bowl with the milk, salt, and pepper. Stir in the *angulas*.

Heat the oil in a small skillet and cook the omelet as on page 196.

Cheese and Truffle Omelet

(TORTILLA DE QUESO Y TRUFA)

What could be more luxurious than an omelet heady with the aroma of truffle. Most people, by the way, are unaware that truffles grow in large quantities in Spain, as well as in France and Italy, and that Spain is today one of the world's largest truffle producers.

If a tablespoon of chopped truffles is beyond your budget, you may reduce the amount, or eliminate it entirely to make a simple cheese omelet. SERVES 2

2 eggs
1 teaspoon milk
Salt
Freshly ground pepper
2 tablespoons diced
   mild melting cheese,
   such as Spanish Tetilla
   (see p. 203), or Fontina
1 tablespoon finely
   chopped truffle
¼ teaspoon truffle juice
1 tablespoon olive oil

In a bowl beat the eggs lightly with the milk. Season with salt and pepper and stir in the cheese, truffle, and truffle juice.

Cook the omelet in the oil as on page 196.

Spanish Potato Omelet

(TORTILLA A LA ESPAÑOLA)

Potato omelet is the all-time tapas classic, and I doubt there is any tapas bar in Spain that does not serve it. Although its ingredients are about as basic as can be—eggs and potatoes—it is a tapa that everyone falls in love with and no one ever tires of. And not only can it be made in advance, it tastes better and can be cut more easily when left awhile at room temperature. SERVES 8-10

1 cup olive oil, or a mixture
   of olive and other vegetable oil
4 large potatoes, peeled and
   cut in 1/8-inch slices
1 large onion, thinly sliced
Coarse salt
4 large eggs

Heat the oil in an 8- or 9-inch skillet and add the potato slices one at a time so they don't stick together. Alternate layers of potato with the onion slices and salt the layers lightly. Cook slowly over medium heat (the potatoes will really "boil" in the oil rather than fry), lifting and turning the potatoes occasionally, until they are tender but not brown. The potatoes should remain separated, not in a "cake." Drain the potatoes in a colander, reserving about 3 tablespoons of the oil. (The onion and potato give the oil a wonderful flavor, so save the rest for some other use.) Wipe out the skillet, scraping off any stuck particles. (If this is difficult to do, wash the skillet. It will be used again to set the omelet and must be completely clean to avoid sticking.)

Meanwhile, in a large bowl beat the eggs with a fork until they are slightly foamy. Salt to taste. Add the potatoes to the beaten egg, pressing the potatoes down with a pancake turner so that they are completely covered by the egg. Let the mixture sit for 15 minutes.

Heat 2 tablespoons of the reserved oil in the skillet until it reaches the smoking point. (It must be very hot or the eggs will stick.) Add the potato and egg mixture, spreading it out rapidly in the skillet with the aid of a pancake turner. Lower the heat to medium-high and shake the pan often to prevent sticking. When the eggs begin to brown underneath, invert a plate of the same size over the skillet and flip the omelet onto the plate. Add about 1 tablespoon more oil to the pan, then slide the omelet back into the skillet to brown on the other side.

Lower the heat to medium and flip the omelet two or three more times (this helps to give the omelet a good shape while it continues to cook), cooking briefly on each side. It should be juicy within. Transfer to a platter and cool, then cut in thin wedges or into 1–1 1/2-inch squares that can be picked up with toothpicks. [May be prepared ahead]

VARIATION

This *tortilla* is occasionally served in a sauce. To make the sauce, heat 1 tablespoon olive oil in a skillet and sauté 1 small onion, finely chopped, and 1 clove garlic, minced, until the onion is wilted. Add 1 small tomato, chopped, turn up the heat, and cook for a couple of minutes. Stir in 3/4 cup chicken broth and a few strands saffron. Cover and simmer for 15 minutes, then strain, pressing with the back of a wooden spoon to extract as much liquid as possible. Stir in pimiento strips, cut from half a pimiento (see p. 204). Cut the *tortilla* in 1 1/2-inch squares. Place in the sauce, cover, and simmer for 2 or 3 minutes. Cool to room temperature and serve.

Potato, Chorizo, and Vegetable Omelet

(TORTILLA TORCAL)

This is a wonderfully tasty *tortilla* that comes from the spectacular *parador* in Jaén (see p. 90) and is sure to be a hit at any tapas party. It can be made several hours ahead and served at room temperature.

SERVES 8-12

½ cup olive oil, or a mixture
   of olive and other vegetable oil
2 medium potatoes,
   in small cubes
6 eggs
Salt
1 small onion, chopped
¼ pound chorizo sausage,
   skinned and diced
¼ cup (about 2 ounces)
   diced cured ham
½ cup cooked peas
½ cup cooked baby limas

Heat the oil in a skillet and fry the potatoes slowly until they are tender—they should not color. (This could also be done in a deep-fryer.) Meanwhile, beat the eggs lightly with the salt. When the potatoes are done, drain, reserving about 4 tablespoons of oil, and add the potatoes to the eggs.

Heat 1 tablespoon of the reserved oil in the skillet and sauté the onion until it is wilted. Add the *chorizo* and ham and cook for another couple of minutes, until the *chorizo* begins to give off its oil. Stir in the peas and limas and cook 2 minutes more. Add this mixture to the eggs and let sit for 5 minutes.

Heat another 2 tablespoons of reserved oil in a clean 10-inch skillet until very hot. Proceed as instructed in the preceding recipe. Transfer to a platter and cut into 8-12 wedges.

VARIATION
Other cooked vegetables, such as asparagus, green beans, green pepper, pimiento, or mushrooms, may be added to the omelet instead of or in addition to the peas and limas.

Three-Layer Omelet

(TORTILLA DE TRES PISOS)

Three-, four-, even five-layer omelets are popular in Cataluña and often found in its capital, Barcelona. The possibilities, of course, are as endless as the omelet variations you can create. Sometimes these omelets are served hot with a tomato sauce, but I prefer this eye-catching version that I discovered in a Barcelona gourmet shop. It blends beautifully the flavors of spinach, mushroom, and shrimp and is held together with a *salsa rosada* ("Russian" dressing). The recipe may seem long, but it moves along quickly if you have your ingredients assembled. And remember it can and should be made a couple of hours in advance. (Do *not* refrigerate.) SERVES 6-8

¼ pound shrimp, shelled
Coarse salt
¼ pound spinach,
  stems removed (weight
  after trimming)
6 tablespoons olive oil
2 cloves garlic, minced
9 eggs
3 teaspoons milk
Freshly ground pepper
¼ pound mushrooms,
  brushed clean, chopped or
  sliced, stems trimmed
1 tablespoon minced parsley
1 tablespoon minced cured ham
2 tablespoons minced hard-boiled egg
Parsley sprigs for garnish

SALSA ROSADA
3 tablespoons mayonnaise, preferably
  homemade (p. 47)

2 tablespoons ketchup
¼ teaspoon Worcestershire sauce
Salt
Freshly ground pepper

Sprinkle the shrimp with coarse salt and let sit until ready to use.

Combine the *salsa rosada* ingredients in a small bowl and set aside.

To make the spinach omelet, wash the spinach and leave damp. Place in a pot without additional water, sprinkle with salt, cover, and cook for 5 minutes, or until just barely tender. Drain on paper towels to absorb any excess moisture. Chop coarsely.

Heat 1 tablespoon of the oil in a skillet. Stir in the spinach, 1 clove of the minced garlic, and a little salt. Stir fry for a couple of minutes.

Beat lightly with a fork 3 of the eggs, 1 teaspoon of the milk, salt, and pepper. Add the skillet mixture and stir to distribute the spinach evenly. (Wipe out the skillet to use for the next omelet.)

Heat another tablespoon of the oil in a 6-inch skillet with straight sides. Pour in the egg mixture, lower the heat slightly, and cook until very lightly browned, shaking the pan constantly. Flip the omelet to the other side, adding a drop more oil if necessary, and continue cooking until the omelet is set but still juicy within. Slide the omelet onto a dish and reserve. Keep this skillet clean to make the next two omelets.

To make the mushroom omelet, heat 1 tablespoon of the oil in a skillet. Add the mushrooms, the remaining clove of minced garlic, the parsley, and ham. Cook over high heat for a minute or two until the mushrooms are softened but have not released any liquid. Proceed as with the spinach omelet, using the same amounts of eggs and milk, and add the mushroom mixture to the eggs. Cook the omelet in the oil as directed.

To make the shrimp omelet, chop the shrimp coarsely. Heat 1 tablespoon of the oil in a skillet and sauté the shrimp quickly, about 1 minute. Proceed as with the spinach and mushroom omelets, adding the shrimp to the eggs. Cook the omelet in the oil as directed.

To assemble the *tortilla*, place the spinach omelet on a serving dish. Spread with a thin coating of the sauce, then top with the shrimp omelet, spreading again with sauce, and ending with the mushroom omelet. Cover with the remaining sauce, sprinkle with the hard-boiled egg, and garnish with parsley sprigs. [May be prepared ahead]

VARIATION

You can create your own omelet combinations, choosing, if you wish, from the following: an Onion Omelet (p. 195); a small Spanish Potato Omelet (p. 198), reducing proportions to 1 egg, 1 potato, and a few slices onion; a Scallion Omelet (p. 195); a Cheese and Truffle Omelet (p. 197); and a tomato omelet, using 1 small tomato, skinned, chopped, and sautéed. All omelets, except for the potato omelet, should be a 3-egg size.

GLOSSARY

CHEESES, SPANISH, in more than a dozen varieties, are finally available in this country and are an exciting addition indeed, bearing little resemblance to the hundreds of other cheeses already sold here. Some of the best-known and most popular kinds are the following:

Queso Manchego, a sheep's-milk cheese from La Mancha in central Spain, can be semisoft when lightly cured or as hard as a Parmesan (but not as strong tasting) when left to age. It is the most popular cheese in Spain and a great favorite of mine.

Queso de Cabrales is a pungent yet smooth blue cheese, wrapped in leaves, from the mountainous northern area of Spain called Cabrales. Made from a mixture of cow, goat, and sheep milk, it is strictly an artisan cheese, produced in mountain caves and in rural kitchens in very small quantities. Cabrales cheese lends itself beautifully to a variety of tapas.

Queso del Roncal comes from the Spanish Pyrenees and is made from sheep and cow milk. It is usually well cured and a bit similar in taste to Queso Manchego.

Queso de Idiazábal is made in the Basque country in northern Spain. It is a semisoft cheese with a slightly smoky taste.

Queso Tetilla, shaped like a large chocolate kiss, comes from Galicia. It is mild and creamy but at the same time slightly pungent and works well in recipes calling for cheese that melts easily.

CHORIZO is Spain's favorite sausage, flavored with garlic and paprika. Eat it as is, like salami, or sauté, bake, or cook it in sauce to produce dozens of other tapas. It is widely available in this country, mostly in specialty food shops, but also in some supermarkets. To make your own, consult *The Foods and Wines of Spain*, page 54.

CLAMS, in Spanish cooking, are often prepared right in a sauce. To avoid the grittiness that could result when clams open and release sand, scrub the clams (preferably very small and hard-shelled clams, such as littlenecks), then soak at least several hours or overnight in salted water to cover, sprinkling about 1 tablespoon of cornmeal or bread crumbs over the surface. The clams will eat the cornmeal or crumbs and release any sandy material. They will also become quite plump from their meal. Rinse again, then use for the tapas recipes in this book. Mussels should be treated in a similar fashion.

CODFISH, DRIED SALTED (BACALAO), is excellent for tapas recipes because it has a firm flesh and an assertive flavor. It must be soaked from 24 to 36 hours in cold water before using. The amount of time depends on how salty the cod is and how strongly flavored you wish it to be. Taste a small piece after 24 hours of soaking, then decide whether it needs more time or not. Except when otherwise noted, use cod that is skinned and boned. When buying cod, look for pieces that are well dried and as white as possible.

EARTHENWARE DISHES (CAZUELAS) are usually glazed on the inside and unfinished outside and underneath. They are the most popular cooking dishes in Spain, and many tapas are displayed in the shallow, serving-size earthenware dishes and served in the smaller ones. They retain heat or cold beautifully and will keep your tapas at the right temperature longer than any other kind of dish. *Cazuelas* are often found in Spanish food markets and sometimes in kitchenware mail-order catalogs (such as Williams-Sonoma). In Spanish cooking they are often used directly over heat and should first be "cured" before using in this manner. To do so, rub the unglazed outer sides and bottom of the dish with oil. Fill with 1/4 inch of oil and place in a 300°F oven for about 20 minutes. The dish is now ready to use, but will not tolerate sudden changes in temperature—do not put hot liquid in a very cold dish or vice versa.

HAM, CURED (JAMÓN SERRANO), sliced or cut in small cubes, is by itself one of the most popular tapas in Spain. But because of the wonderful flavor it lends to so many other foods, you will find it a part of dozens of tapas recipes in this book. Look for cured ham that is not too salty and never smoked. (Italian-style prosciutto comes closest to the ham found in Spain.)

MORCILLA is blood sausage made in the Spanish style, sometimes with the addition of rice. When it is well made and properly seasoned, it is one of my favorites and excellent for tapas. Avoid vacuum-packed blood sausage. The best *morcilla* I have found is called "Colombian-style"; it comes closest to the kind I am so fond of in Spain.

MUSSELS should be scrubbed, debearded, and cleansed of sand (see CLAMS for instructions).

OLIVE OIL is called for in almost every tapas recipe in this book. I use only Spanish olive oil because it is of very high quality and has a wonderfully fruity taste that gives foods a characteristic Spanish flavor. Spanish olive oil is available in food specialty shops and in some supermarkets, sometimes disguised under an Italian brand name. But Spanish olive oil producers are determined to bring their superior product to the attention of the American public, and within the next few years Spanish olive oils should be as familiar as Italian and French brands now are.

When a tapas recipe calls for a fruity olive oil, use either a pure olive oil with an assertive flavor or one of the virgin oils that have recently become so popular.

PAPRIKA (PIMENTÓN) is ground from sweet red peppers and can vary in flavor according to the pepper varieties from which it comes. Paprika is used extensively in Spanish cooking, and for authentic flavor buy paprika imported from Spain.

PEPPERS, DRIED HOT RED, spice a number of Spain's most popular tapas. They may be left whole or crumbled, after the seeds have been removed. There are different degrees of hotness in red peppers—choose those that are only moderately hot. If unavailable, substitute crushed red pepper, which can be found in supermarkets.

PEPPERS, DRIED SWEET RED, used to make the Spanish *romesco* sauce, give an appealing, earthy taste to foods. They are a bit difficult to come by—the closest I have found are the "New Mexico" peppers, which are slightly spicy but become quite mild after cooking.

PIMIENTO, to the surprise of many cooks, is nothing more than the Spanish word for peppers, and in this country we use the word to mean red peppers that are cooked, peeled, and packaged in jars or cans. If you must use commercially prepared pimientos, buy them in jars so you can see that they are brightly colored and buy only those imported from Spain, which have better flavor and texture. As good as they may be, however, purchased pimientos do not even come close to the deliciously sweet flavor of a freshly prepared pimiento. To make your own, simply place red peppers in an ungreased roasting pan in a 375°F oven for 17 minutes. Turn the peppers and roast for another 17 minutes. Remove from the oven and allow to cool for a few minutes. Then peel, core, and seed. You may keep them wrapped in foil in the refrigerator for several days.

RICE, SHORT-GRAIN, sometimes called pearl rice, is the only kind of rice used in Spanish cooking. It has a nutty taste and chewy texture that are especially important for *paella* and for the cold rice tapas in this book. You can find it imported from Spain and Italy, but it is also grown in California. Short-grain rice turns mushy when overcooked, so recipe cooking times should be carefully observed.

SAFFRON (AZAFRÁN) is the dried stigmas of a purple crocus flower, and the Arab word for yellow. The most expensive spice in the world, selling for over $2,000 a pound, saffron is not merely a colorant, as some suppose, but gives a very distinctive yet subtle flavor to foods and sauces. Substitutes like turmeric and Mexican marigold petals are unacceptable: use only pure saffron, preferably from Spain, and buy in strands rather than in powdered form. (Good saffron, when dry, has a deep red color, and it is very difficult to determine quality after it has been pulverized.)

SALT, COARSE, often called kosher salt, is always used in Spanish cooking, and although not absolutely essential, it is better than fine salt for sautéing or for sprinkling on already cooked food (it does not penetrate the food as fine salt does). Some even say coarse salt has a different flavor. Its qualities are really quite difficult to define, but I have found that once a cook switches to coarse salt he or she will rarely, if ever, use fine salt again.

SQUID, in all its many varieties, is a favorite seafood in Spain. It is delicious when quickly fried as well as slowly stewed. Many fish markets sell squid already cleaned (at a higher price) or will clean it for you. To clean it yourself, hold the body of the squid in one hand and pull out the tentacles with the other. Reserve the tentacles if they are called for in a recipe, cutting off all waste material but leaving the tentacles in one piece. Remove the skin from the body of the squid and pull off the fins. Turn the squid inside out, remove the cartilage, and wash the body well under running water. Turn the squid to the outside again and dry well on paper towels.

TAPAS MENUS

TAPAS TO START A MEAL

Clams in Sherry Sauce
Marinated Rice-Filled Pimientos
Spicy Meat Turnovers
Onion, Tomato, and Tuna Omelet

Tiny Meatballs in Saffron Sauce
A selection of *Banderillas*
Creamed Blue Cheese with Brandy
Fried Squid, Spanish Style

Shrimp in Garlic Sauce
Potato, Vegetable, and Tuna Salad
Chorizo in Puff Pastry
Mushrooms Sautéed with Garlic and Parsley

Meatballs in Almond Sauce
Marinated Trout Fillets
Shrimp Tartlets
Egg Croquettes

Mushrooms in Garlic Sauce
Shrimp in Caper and Pickle Vinaigrette
Spinach Turnovers
Tuna-Stuffed Mussels

Stewed Zucchini, Peppers, and Tomatoes
Marinated Seafood
Mushrooms in Puff Pastry
Spicy Lamb Brochettes

Tuna Balls in Wine Sauce
Marinated Mushrooms
Chorizo Wrapped in Bread and Leaves
Fried Eggplant with Garlic and Egg

Mussels in Chervil Sauce
Salad of Julienned Carrots
Smoked Fish Salad on Garlic Toast
Batter-Fried Pig's Feet

TAPAS AS A MEAL

You may wish to add to these more substantial tapas menus a few lighter tapas from the "Tapas to Start a Meal" menus.

After-Theater Tapas Party
Fish Mousse, Santa Catalina Style
Pimientos in Vinaigrette
Scallop Pie
Chicken in Garlic Sauce

205

Tapas into the Wee Hours of the Morning
Artichoke Hearts with Shrimp and Cured Ham
Green Pepper Omelet
Duck and Cured Ham Pâté
Sautéed Frogs' Legs

A Celebration of Seafood Tapas
Clams in Pine Nut and Almond Sauce
Fish and Vegetable Salad
Grilled Shrimp
Monkfish Baked in Foil

An Out-of-Doors Summer Tapas Affair
Smoked Fish on Avocado Rounds
Olive Paste and Blue Cheese Canapé
Marinated Salmon
Rice Salad, Barcelona Style
Vegetable Salad in *Romesco* Sauce

An Andalucian Tapas Party
Shrimp in Spicy Tomato Sauce
Green Olive Turnovers
Oxtail Stew, Cádiz Style
Potato Salad with Tuna and Egg

A Galician Tapas Party
Scallops Baked with Onion and Cured Ham
Octopus in Spicy Paprika Sauce
Pork and Green Pepper Pie
Swiss Chard Omelet

Tapas to Take You Through Dinner
Grilled Baby Squid
Vegetable Crêpes
Stuffed Pork Loin
Eggplant Salad

An Exotic Tapas Party
Anise-Flavored Beet Salad
Frogs' Legs and Shrimp in Puff Pastry
Baby Eel Omelet
Dried Cod Perfumed with Garlic

An All-Out Tapas Gala
Mussels Vinaigrette
Clams in Green Sauce
Cumin-Flavored Mushroom Salad
Pâté with Turkey Breast
Squid Pie
Shrimp in Green Mayonnaise
Spanish Potato Omelet
Manchego Cheese with Quince Preserves
Sausages with Sweet-Sour Figs
Mushrooms Stuffed with Soft-Set Eggs
Chorizo-Filled Dates in Bacon
Trout and Monkfish Mousse
Marinated Stuffed Squid
Pork Ribs in Garlic Sauce
Chorizo or Blood Sausage in Puff Pastry
Tuna Tartlets
Chicken and Cured Ham Croquettes

RECOMMENDED TAPAS BARS IN SPAIN AND THE UNITED STATES

ALBACETE
Mesón El Cocinero
Nuestro Bar

BARCELONA
Bodega Sepúlveda
Casa Tejada
Paco Alcalde (Barceloneta)

BILBAO
Bar Or-Konpon
Taberna Zizipot

CÁDIZ
Bar Bahía
El Callejón
El Faro
Joselito
Mesón El Candil

GIJÓN
Bar Villa
El Tiburón
La Dársena

MADRID
Bar Cascabel
Bar Hevia
Bar Santander
Casa Portal
Casares

El Águila
El Corrillo
El Pulpito
José Luis
La Chuleta
La Trucha
Lhardy
Los Pepinillos
Mallorca
Mesón El Caserío
O'Grelo
15 de Cascorro
Vista Alegre

OVIEDO
Cabo Peñas
La Gran Taberna
La Marchica

PONTEVEDRA
O'Merlo

SALAMANCA
Casa Conchas
El Arco
Imbis
Plus Ultra Bar

SAN SEBASTIÁN
Bar Aralar
Bar Portaletas

SANTIAGO DE COMPOSTELA
Bar Coruña
Bar Suso
Victoria

SEVILLA
Bar Casa Ruperto
Bar Miami
Bar Modesto
Bar Puerto
Bodegón Torre de Oro
Enrique Becerra
Figón del Cabildo
La Dorada
Río Grande
Sol y Sombra

VALENCIA
Cervecería Pema
Los Toneles
Palacio de la Bellota

ZARAGOZA
Bodegas del Tío Faustino
La Rinconada de Lorenzo
Mesón de Carmen

UNITED STATES
The Ballroom, New York, NY
Café Ba-Ba-Reeba! Chicago, IL
El Bodegón, Washington, DC
Mesón Galicia, Norwalk, CT
Don Carlos Tapas Bar, Miami, FL
Tío Pepe, Miami, FL
Casa Juancho, Miami, FL

INDEX

A NOTE ABOUT THE AUTHOR

Penelope Casas was born in New York City, was graduated from Vassar College with a magna cum laude in Spanish literature, studied at the University of Madrid, and for some time taught Spanish literature and language in New York. She lived in Spain from 1965 to 1968 and since then she and her husband, Luis, a doctor who was born in Spain, return there frequently.

Penelope Casas has written about Spanish food and travel in Spain for *Travel & Leisure, Vogue, Food & Wine, Connoisseur,* and *The New York Times*. She teaches Spanish cooking at cooking schools around the country and is also an adjunct professor at New York University, lecturing on Spanish food and travel and conducting tours to Spain. Mrs. Casas was awarded the Spanish National Prize of Gastronomy in Madrid in 1983. She lives in New York with her husband and their daughter, Elisa.

A NOTE ON THE TYPE

The text of this book has been set in Goudy Old Style, one of the more than 100 type faces designed by Frederic William Goudy (1865~1947). Although Goudy began his career as a bookkeeper, he was so inspired by the appearance of several newly published books from the Kelmscott Press that he devoted the remainder of his life to typography in an attempt to bring a better understanding of the movement led by William Morris to the printers of the United States.

Produced in 1914, Goudy Old Style reflects the absorption of a generation of designers with things "ancient." Its smooth, even color, combined with its generous curves and ample cut, marks it as one of Goudy's finest achievements.
Composed by Superior Type, Champaign, Illinois
Printed and bound by Halliday Litho, Inc.,
West Hanover, Massachusetts
Designed by Iris Weinstein